An Idea in Practice

Using the human givens approach

An Idea in Practice

Using the human givens approach

edited by

Joe Griffin & Ivan Tyrrell

PUBLISHING

PUBLISHING

First published in Great Britain 2007
Reprinted 2008

The right of Joe Griffin and Ivan Tyrrell to be identified as the authors of Parts I and III
of this work has been asserted in accordance with sections 77 and 78 of the Copyright,
Designs and Patents Act 1988. The material in Parts II and III (some of which has
been updated and expanded) has previously appeared in various issues of
the *Human Givens* journal.

Published by HG Publishing, an imprint of Human Givens Publishing Ltd,
Chalvington, East Sussex, BN27 3TD, United Kingdom.
www.humangivens.com

A catalogue record for this book is available from the British Library.

ISBN 1-899398-96-1
ISBN-13 978-1-899398-96-6

Typeset in Sabon, Signa Condensed and Conduit Condensed.
Printed and bound in Great Britain by CPI Antony Rowe.
Index by Indexing Specialists (UK) Ltd.

*"The value of an idea lies
in the using of it."*

THOMAS EDISON

CONTENTS

Acknowledgements

We would like to thank (in alphabetical order)
Joanne Ashmore, Angela Austin, Jessica Bavinton, Mike Beard,
John Bell, Richard Brook, Iain Caldwell, Helen Card, Chris Dyas,
Fred Grist, Sue Gwinnell-Smith, Mike Hay, James Hooton,
Emily Lindsey-Clark, Farouk Okhai, Liz Potts, Jim Tapper, Ian Walton,
and Pamela Woodford for their fascinating articles which demonstrate so
clearly the human givens approach in practice – their hard work and
dedication continues to benefit many. We are also grateful to the many
clients* who have happily allowed their case histories to be used to
illustrate the approach further, to Jane Tyrrell for her help in editing this
volume, and to Denise Winn, who originally edited the articles for
the *Human Givens* journal. Our thanks are also due to
Alex McGlaughlin for his introduction.

The Editors

*All client names used throughout
the book have been changed.

*"The strongest arguments prove
nothing so long as the conclusions
are not verified by experience."*

ROGER BACON

Introduction

IT IS ten years since Joe Griffin and Ivan Tyrrell first published the 'human givens' organising idea.[1] Five years before that they had become puzzled by the confusion and lack of agreement between the hundreds of different models of psychotherapy and counselling. They were also conscious of the unintentional harm being done by some well-meaning but misguided therapists (prolonging their patients' depression and creating false memories of abuse etc) and aware of the rising rates of mental illness and addictive behaviour. Their response was a firm resolve to bring clarity to the situation. They felt that improvements would come about only when practitioners shared a common under-standing based upon a truer knowledge of psychology and brain science. Sound information was available but few therapists were taking it on board and incorporating it into their work. Although many models contained useful psychological insights and therapeutic techniques, none offered a holistic understanding of what it means to be human or a comp-rehensive methodology as to the best way to treat mental illness and promote mental health and wellbeing.

This was an absurd situation that was prolonging suffering, so they set about describing some common guiding principles – undeniable truths about mental wellbeing and how to nurture it – that could be agreed upon by all but the most obtuse. They also foresaw that, were such guiding principles to become widely held in society, it would bring about enormous benefits far beyond the field of psychotherapy. They recognised that to achieve this, it was first necessary to, in that timeworn phrase, 'get back to basics'.

Under the microscope went the most renowned therapists of the 20th century and the schools that followed them. They discarded any psycho-therapeutic approach that was practiced mechanically or that research showed was not helpful, whatever its practitioners believed. They also studied what they could glean from the therapeutic wisdom of other cultures and times. With what was left they stepped back and set about understanding how the psychotherapeutic skills that were clearly most effective matched up to the emerging findings of neuroscience and psychology, asking each time, *"why does this work?"*

The result was a new synthesis of what can reliably be said about what human beings need in order to develop and function well, along with a realistic understanding of the givens of human nature – our innate physical and emotional needs and the resources Nature gives us to help us meet them. All this information was gathered together, along with a range of psychological interventions, derived from many sources, that were proven to be effective for treating emotional distress. This provided the solid foundation of evidence-based, human givens psychology and psychotherapy.

Added to this mix, and enriching it still further, was original work of their own, such as Griffin's research into why we evolved to dream, the importance of the REM state and his resulting 'expectation fulfilment' theory of dreaming.[2] This has had a profound impact on our understanding of depression and its self-perpetuating nature, the practical applications of which greatly improve the effectiveness of psychological treatment. Having established what dreams did for us each night, they went on to produce a theory that explained psychotic symptoms. This, too, has significant implications for improving treatment. Much of this work, and a far more comprehensive presentation of the human givens than I am able to do justice to here, is published in their seminal book, *Human Givens: A new approach to emotional health and clear thinking.*[3]

In Part One of *An Idea in Practice,* Griffin and Tyrrell summarise how our innate needs seek their fulfilment through the way we interact with the environment using the resources Nature gave us. If our needs are met in balanced, healthy ways, they say, we don't have mental health problems. With this understanding, health and care professionals can quickly identify what's missing in a person's life and tailor appropriate treatment so that they can move on under their own steam as quickly as possible (as the diverse articles by numerous contributors in Part Two clearly show[4]).

The human givens approach continues to grow organically, is refined as it is being taught, and merges with other knowledge that comes to light.

Thus Griffin and Tyrrell get and respond to a great deal of feedback from the wide range of people they have taught; psychologists, teachers, counsellors, psychiatrists, psychotherapists, nurses, police officers, social workers and many others who have completed the MindFields College Human Givens Diploma. One of the refreshing principles of this approach is that it is dynamic; new knowledge, insights and skills, (when they are backed up with scientific understanding), are incorporated whenever possible to further increase its effectiveness.

In Part Three, we are introduced to the latest example of this. Joe Griffin's 'molar memories' theory seeks to explain the origin of some instances of repeated often compulsive and irrational behaviours, such as anorexia, sexual obsessions and disproportionate anger reactions. Remarkably, he presents cases where he has used this understanding to successfully treat such severe conditions in a single session of therapy. Now other human givens therapists are integrating this into their own work and confirming his findings, to the enormous benefit of their patients. This is an exciting time for psychotherapy. Indeed, the potential benefits alone of dissolving the molar memories that ruin so many lives could prove enormous.

Because it is in tune with human nature, the human givens organising idea is easily integrated into fields as diverse as education, special needs, management, policing and diplomacy. I have met numerous professionals who say that it has brought tremendous clarity to their work. For myself, this clear thinking has been long overdue and particularly helpful, not least with regards to how we might approach ethical issues. (See Tyrrell's lucid contribution on ethical considerations in Part Three.)

I have come to regard 'HG', as it is often referred to, as the best organising idea in the mental health field today, largely because it both accounts for *why* people become mentally ill and gives us a reliable way to go about doing something about it. I particularly like the clarity of the way Griffin and Tyrrell present this rich body of knowledge, without psychobabble or excessive technical jargon. They make it so easy to understand that it can be applied to almost any situation that is actually or potentially distressing, as the many examples in Part Two show.

So, as you will read, in the last ten years many dedicated people have achieved great things using these ideas. All over the UK and, increasingly, in Ireland – in schools, universities, clinics, hospitals, GP surgeries, outreach centres and in private practice – strong individuals inspired by the HG approach are using it to improve people's lives and humanise organisations. *An Idea in Practice* celebrates this work and I commend it to you. All the contributors believe that there are efficient ways to make life fairer, less wasteful, and more fulfilled, now and for future generations. They vividly demonstrate as much by the quality of their work. I believe this book shows that we are at a stage where, if realistic political commitment was given to it, a mentally healthier society is within reach, one fit enough to cope with the dramatic social and environmental changes that so many predict we face over the next hundred years. The only question is, will the opportunity be properly grasped?

Alex McGlaughlin, BA PhD CPsychol

Reader in Psychology and Acting Dean,
School of Social Sciences,
Nottingham Trent University

---

1. Griffin, J. and Tyrrell, I. (1997) *Psychotherapy and the human givens: Why psychotherapy always works best when it comes, not from an emotional or theoretical standpoint, but from a real understanding of what it is to be a human being.* ETSI Organising Ideas Monograph.

2. Griffin, J. and Tyrrell, I. (2004) *Dreaming Reality: How dreaming keeps us sane, or can drive us mad.* HG Publishing.

3. Griffin, J. and Tyrrell, I. (2003) *Human Givens: A new approach to emotional health and clear thinking.* HG Publishing.

4. The articles featured in Parts Two and Three of *An Idea in Practice* first appeared in various issues of the *Human Givens* journal. They have been revised and updated, where applicable, for this book.

Part One

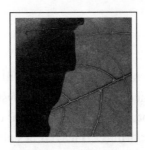

Learning from Nature

WHEN you watch a beautiful baby transforming into a child you are studying yourself. Although we've largely forgotten it, it's a process we all go through. From the day you were born, your eyes, ears and sense of smell began picking out details from a mass of confusing impressions and, guided by an inner knowledge that directed you to pay particular attention to your mother, on whom somehow you knew your life depended, you began life's journey.

As your astonishingly complex brain formed millions of new connections every day, you tuned these impacts into pulsations of meaning. As the weeks and months went by, with quickly developing precision your delicate little fingers and mouth explored the world around you. Much of the time, whatever captivated your attention kept you wide-eyed and intensely curious. You were dazzled by the sensory richness of every new experience.

Curious and driven to learn you connected up to the environment you found yourself in. With ridiculous ease you absorbed the language people were using around you and became part of the wider community. You communicated your feelings whether slight or extreme, happy or sad. You mimicked people, you laughed and cried and reacted to how others behaved. You asked question after question for as long as people gave you answers. You sought and exchanged attention. You learned, became more worldly and sophisticated, but still coexisted with primitive animal responses – a range of strong emotions, including appetites, that easily overpowered your ability to think and empathise.

For some people their early years were so vivid and full of wonder that they still hark back to them with an almost mystical sense of reverence, wishing they could recapture again that sense of immediacy that an acute awareness of being alive brings. "Heaven lies about us in our infancy!" said the poet, and for a child brought up in fortunate circumstances, whether rich or poor, as long as it makes friends, plays and explores the natural world, it can seem like that. But Wordsworth's next line betrays unease about what growing up in this world soon starts to feel like: "Shades of the prison-house begin to close upon the growing boy." As the years pass we all become constrained and conditioned by our families and the prevailing culture. We adopt patterns of belief and expectations about how things should be and are subjected to numerous minor and sometimes major traumatising events that leave psychological scars that affect our character and development. There is nothing so sad as seeing the openness and enthusiasm of a little child crushed in a school environment, which can so often be inimical to learning, and become subject to the conditioning of its new peers. But enter this restricted world we all must... because we have to learn to survive in it.

So what are we? With our left brain we classify ourselves as members of the species *Homo sapiens*, which is Latin for 'knowing man'. What we 'know' depends both on what we inherit through our genes and the quality of the feedback we get from the world, from our earliest days through, with luck, to a healthy old age. Feedback teaches us. As we are social creatures living in groups – families, communities and countries – that feedback comes, for the most part, from other people and is scanned by a part of the brain called the amygdala, which rates it for emotional salience and sends it elsewhere for pattern matching to past experiences and expectations. If the feedback is appropriate and teaches us how to accommodate our primitive responses, instead of being overwhelmed by them, all is well and good. If not, life can be hell, as it is for increasing numbers. Even in the currently most materially prosperous countries, rates of mental illness and addiction are rising fast and this means we have to ask, what is the quality of that feedback like and can it be improved?

For thousands of years a range of complex cultures and great civilisations arose on earth, mechanisms for passing on knowledge and creating rich environments in which to reproduce, meet our needs and, if we had any spare capacity, progress. Each evolutionary step forward took time, often many generations, but aided our survival in the long run. But this slow way of evolving is no longer working. It can't keep up with a rate of change that is clearly running too fast for many millions of us and making it increasingly difficult for us to obtain the emotional nutrition we need. So, instead of reaping the reward for thousands of years of struggle and awakening in a pleasant upland where most of us are healthily fulfilled in some way, we seem to be sleepwalking into bedlam.

What kind of world are we creating for our children and their billions of descendants? Is it as insane as many people claim? If, as it seems to be, one man's common sense is another's idiocy, one's right is another's wrong and the intelligence levels of all of us fluctuate minute by minute, hour by hour (as our emotions rise and fall), it would seem that it is.

To make progress as a culture we need to have shared perceptions. So what should we expect of sane behaviour?

Sanity is usually defined as being in possession of a healthy mental state – it means having, for at least some of the time, a degree of object-ivity together with sound reasoning abilities and judgement. It is the precursor of wisdom. Our actions and thinking, however, being largely the consequences of primitive emotionality and conditioning, mean that the majority may regard a sane action as an insane one and *vice versa* – which confuses things rather. A sane action is one carried out in a way the wider consequences demand rather than for narrow, selfish reasons or out of habit or approval.

The term 'sanity' has a long history going back via Middle English to ancient Latin (*sanite*, from Latin *sanitat-*, *sanitas* health, sanity, from *sanus* healthy, sane: the quality or state of being sane; especially sound-ness or health of mind). In law it denotes that an individual is of sound mind and therefore can bear legal responsibility for his or her actions. However, lawyers generally define it in terms of the absence of insanity, which is not particularly helpful. It is not a medical term, although the opinions of medical experts are often important in making a legal decision as to whether someone is sane or insane. Outside of legal defin-itions, Western scientists and psychologists have only recently begun investigating 'sanity'; until then the focus was mainly on illness. When psychologist Professor Martin Seligman suggested to his peers that they should change their focus and look at mental *health*, what he called 'positive psychology', it was rightly deemed a big step forward. And now measuring 'happiness' and spreading tips about how to cheer one another up has become an industry in itself. (According to Seligman it is possible to lift our biological set range of happiness, at least to some extent, if we work at it. "The best you can do with positive emotion is to get people to live at the top of their set range... I think you've got about 10 to 15% leverage but you can't take a grouch and make him giggle all the time.")

Happiness, however, is an abstract term, a nominalisation that means different things to different people. Feeling happy is a transient mood. Moreover, we don't appreciate it without a comparison with low moods. Seeking personal happiness, however, can make people more selfish. Therefore, feeling happy is better viewed as a by-product of living well rather than an aim in itself. Despite living in an entertaining, technologically advanced world, full of abundance and novelty for many of us, it is difficult for any but the most self-centred to ignore the amount of disappointment, misery, cruelty, starvation, sickness and madness large sections of humanity experience. The gap between rich and poor continues to widen. We greedily despoil and lay waste to the planet. Crime and corruption are rife on a scale never seen before. The rapidly rising rates of frustration, anxiety, anger, depression and addiction are powerful signals that something is seriously wrong. And the knowledge of how to stay sane in this rapidly worsening situation can seem hard to come by – as if it's hiding away from our crude, self-obsessed, materialistic culture. Consequently, many people live and die without ever knowing such wisdom exists, (though perhaps it was never withheld from those who sincerely sought it).

Another common refrain is that the particular pressures humanity faces today are fuelling the rise in selfishness and friction between people and this is causing, it is said, the rise in mental illness. But we know that individuals and communities have always endured great privations and difficulties and that, as a species, we are highly adaptable. With this in mind we think it is sensible to assume that there is still hope for the future.

The process of coming into possession of a healthy mental state is often referred to as being 'on a journey'. A journey implies a concrete destination, an in-depth understanding of what is required to travel there and an appreciation of the need for guidance from someone who has made the journey before us. First though, we must organise our thoughts about this journey. We cannot improve the way we educate children or help the mentally disturbed and seriously disadvantaged unless we go through this stage. There is no magic wand.

In order to understand anything at all, from the simplest fact to the most complex event, our minds must first contain ideas that can organise the information coming in. These ideas are the mental patterns to which we all refer when making sense of the world and what happens to us in it. Like maps, organising ideas define where we are and indicate where we could go and what might happen to us on the way. Without them we are lost. And unfortunately, like maps, our ideas vary in usefulness. They can be out of date, inaccurate or just surreal inventions, like the maps describing the imaginary worlds of science fiction and fantasy writers.

Many organising ideas are assumptions derived from cultural conditioning, for we are easily indoctrinated with foolish obsessions, beliefs and self-justifications that bolster our vanity and blind us: material possessions bring happiness, might is right, our family/group/country/belief system is the best, I have a 'right' to satisfy any appetite I want, my strongly held belief justifies the actions I take. We need to clear out useless or outmoded patterns of 'thinking' like these because the very urgency of our current predicament, living on a planet with finite resources, requires it. Clearly we have nothing to lose by examining the assumptions we hold about the times we live in and the way we were conditioned by the upbringing we had. And, if our cherished beliefs contradict the picture that emerges, we must be prepared to abandon them.

New ideas only form in the mind as a result of sincerely asking real questions, self-reflection and making the effort to think. That is how science progresses. In thinking we draw on previous ideas, experience and observation and make fresh connections between them. A really new idea not only explains more than earlier ones but also has the power to bring clarity of purpose to our actions so as to make us more effective.

To demonstrate this it is helpful to start with the elemental question: What is a living creature? By answering this we reveal the foundation for human givens psychology.

A human being is an *animate* life form. And what all life forms have in common, and what distinguishes them from *inanimate* forms such as a rock, is that they are complex orderings of matter that have to continuously rebuild themselves or they cease to exist. A lump of granite will pretty much stay a lump of granite for millions of years if you leave it alone, but a living thing will quickly degenerate, disintegrate and die unless it is continually rebuilt. So the first law of life is that a living thing, whether rose, maggot or rhinoceros, has to take in nourishment from its environment to maintain itself.

All humanity can agree on this; that every animate life form anywhere in the universe has to take in nourishment from its surroundings and thereby continually rebuild itself as it takes its allotted form. A human baby, like every other living thing, be it plant, fish or animal, must take in the nutriment that it needs in order to survive and grow. To do this it brings knowledge into the world – how to breathe, suckle, swallow, grasp, build rapport with its mother, swim, learn the language it hears etc. Because these patterns of knowledge about the physical and emotional nutriment we need are innate – what we come into the world with – they are called 'human givens', Nature's gift to each one of us. This is the most basic organising idea of all. It comes from what is given to us at conception: our core instincts and reflexes that have evolved from the collective experience of all mammalian species over millions of years, what scientists call 'the wisdom of the phylum'. This works continually to help us survive and maintain a healthy body and mind.

It is not difficult to appreciate this knowledge since we all have it. Take our *physical* needs, for example. Like all animals we know we need air to breathe, water to drink, nutritious food and sufficient sleep. These needs are paramount and obvious to us because, if they are not met, we quickly die – as people do wherever clean water is scarce and food in short supply. We also need the freedom to stimulate our senses and exercise our muscles. In addition, we instinctively seek sufficient and secure shelter where we can sleep safely and, as our sex drive rises, reproduce ourselves and bring up our young in safety.

Everyone can acknowledge these basic physical needs as 'givens'. But psychologists throughout the ages have also determined that there are *emotional* needs that are equally crucial for our survival and wellbeing. These are 'givens' too and include the needs for:

- Security – safe territory; an environment which enables us to live without experiencing excessive undue fear and allows us to develop fully.

- Volition: a sense of autonomy and control over what is happening around and to us – an essential form of feedback from the universe that we exist.

- Attention – receiving it from others, but also giving it; a form of essential nutrition that fuels the development of each individual, family and culture

- Emotional connection to other people – friendship, love, intimacy

- Connection to the wider community – we are a group animal – being part of something larger than ourselves

- Privacy – time and space enough to reflect on and consolidate our experiences

- A sense of status – being accepted and valued in the different social groups we belong to

- A sense of our own competence and achievements – which ensures we don't feel we are 'rubbish' (and develop what is often called 'low self-esteem')

- The need for meaning and purpose which comes from three main sources: being stretched mentally or physically (or both), serving and being responsible for other people (as, for example, in childrearing), having a belief framework or philosophy that helps us focus our fragmented consciousness on 'the bigger picture'.

By definition, an innate need is incomplete. It is a partial pattern that can only find completion by being matched up to something that it recognises as 'answering' its call in the world. How well that happens as we grow up determines many aspects of our personality: our character, how we develop physically and emotionally, interact with other people and whether we achieve our heart's desire in life or not. As we've said, if this matching up process goes well, life is good to us. If not, we soon get frustrated, stressed and angry and this can quickly lead us to develop one or more of a range of disturbing psychological states: anxiety disorders, depression, addictions or psychotic breakdown. As if that were not bad enough, the behaviour of psychologically and emotionally disturbed people impacts on those around them – family, friends, colleagues and the community. So-called 'anti-social behaviour', for example, clearly results from needs not being met or being met inappropriately (as when a young person's need to belong to a group leads him or her to join a dubious gang because nothing better is available).

Fortunately Nature leaves little to chance. She does not abandon us to helplessly thrash around in a random way. She provides us with the necessary tools and resources to guide us towards meeting each pattern of need in the environment.

Each and every living thing is provided with internal guidance systems that are appropriate to their form and help them get the nutriment they need. A plant, for instance, 'knows' how to direct its roots to grow deep underground and draw into itself whatever minerals and moisture it needs and it 'knows' how to get energy from the sun and convert it by photosynthesis into sugar, the 'fuel' used by all living things. This knowledge is what guides it to grow, maintain and reproduce itself.

A human baby has its own innate package of flexible innate guidance systems. These 'psychobiological abilities' drive the baby's development as it searches out matches to its innate needs with corresponding patterns for them from the environment. They steer it in the optimal direction towards whatever will sustain it in the environment, starting with its mother's flowing breast.

The wealth of abilities that nature gives us to help us meet our needs include:

- The ability to develop complex long-term memory, so we can add to our innate knowledge, learn new skills, improve our understanding and absorb language and pass on learnt knowledge via our culture.

- The ability to build rapport, empathise and connect with other people so knowledge can be shared and mutual need satisfaction can be enhanced.

- Imagination, which enables us to focus our attention away from our emotions and think about the past and future to problem solve more creatively and objectively.*

- A conscious, rational mind that can check out emotions, question, analyse, work things out and plan.

- The ability to 'know' – understand the world unconsciously through metaphorical pattern matching – hence our delight in discoveries, exceptions, resonances, harmony, music, biographies, stories and jokes.

- An observing self – that part of us which can step back and become aware of being a unique centre of awareness apart from our intellect, emotion and conditioning. (This is predominantly a frontal lobe facility.)

- A brain that dreams. Dreaming is nature's way of discharging accumulated stress and maintaining the integrity of our emotions. Every night we dream, even if we don't remember doing so, and any arousal of the autonomic nervous system during the day, that are not dearoused by taking the necessary action in the environment to do so, are metaphorically completed in dream stories during REM sleep, which dearouses the autonomic nervous system, leaving us refreshed and ready for the new day.†

---

* The sudden rapid development of imagination about 40,000 years ago made complex language possible. We know this because the archaeological evidence shows us that that was the time when humans began to show enormous creativity, and creativity requires imagination. Symbolic art and artefacts, drawings, paintings, carvings and a vast range of complex exquisite tools appeared for the first time. With imagination we began visualising possible different futures and could reflect on the past: complex language is not possible without a future, past and present tense. The added flexibility imagination gave modern humans was a huge advantage and soon all the other hominids with whom we had coexisted became extinct. (100,000 years ago, several species of hominids populated the Earth. *Homo sapiens* (us) lived in Africa, *Homo erectus* in Southeast Asia and China, and the Neanderthals in Europe. By about 28,000 years ago, we were the last ones left.)

† The 'expectation fulfilment theory of dreaming' is explained in detail in our book, *Dreaming Reality: How dreaming keeps us sane, or can drive us mad.*

So, inner resources – like our physical and emotional needs – are also 'givens'. They are the instinctive urges, our guidance systems for survival, a form of knowledge bequeathed to each new baby. All subsequently acquired skills and knowledge that we gain through consciously experiencing the world and remembering what we have learned is built on this foundation.

By really bringing into consciousness what Nature is constantly telling us to do, and working in tune with the human givens, more and more people are finding it easier to help people suffering from emotional and educational difficulties, as you will see in the second part of this book. But before we see how this process can move onto a bigger stage we need to look at what it is that is holding us back.

It's clear that when a family or social environment prevents a child from getting its innate physical and emotional needs met adequately, the child cannot flourish – it withers as surely as an unwatered plant. But with the right nourishment it grows healthily. This cannot be overstated. We are all subject to this universal law, which is as fundamental as the law of gravity and equally capable of being observed. If you drop a rock, it falls to the ground. When a living organism doesn't get nourishment, it dies. What is true about daffodils and oak trees, mosquitoes and moths, salmon and dolphins, bats, birds, cows, tigers, dogs, and all other living things, is true about us too: our innate needs have to be met in the environment for us to develop properly.

A baby will suckle happily on a finger for a short while but when no sustaining milk results, it quickly becomes fretful and anxious. The same happens to us throughout life with all our needs. We can tolerate things going awry for a short while, even enjoy it, but when we lose control over events, feel lonely, are starved of attention, lose status, or are not being stretched in life, we experience negative feelings and quickly become preoccupied by them. We first feel frustration, then anxiety, and maybe anger, and then, if the situation persists, depression can set in. If nothing is done, addictive behaviour can arise as we try to put pleasure back into our life by cheating nature and artificially reward ourselves with good feelings instead of making the appropriate effort that would reward us with good feelings naturally. Addiction is a form of greed. As the person focuses more and more on cheating their natural emotional processes instead of living, severe depression, anxiety disorders or bouts of mania can develop, and even complete psychotic breakdown.

In the last 30 years we have experienced an increasing acceleration of the rate of change such that most of us now have to re-equip and re-skill ourselves several times over within our working lifetime and adapt to changing social mores faster than ever before. Only those individuals and companies that are open and flexible enough to adapt to changing circumstances survive successfully. The rest get very stressed and contribute to the rapidly rising rates of mental dysfunction: according to many sources as much as one in five people in the UK and USA are mentally disturbed. The numbers suffering from anxiety disorders and clinical depression are increasing year on year; new forms of addiction are spreading through the community; every day we hear about drunken or drug-addicted children, collapsing families and relationship break-downs. The old family structures and institutions that held people together are breaking up. Schools reveal sections of society where five-year-old children are so emotionally damaged by the life they lead that normal school activities are beyond them. They arrive in class barely able to speak, unsocialised, unable to concentrate or delay gratification of their every whim. This has become so bad in some areas that, despite the best efforts of teachers, high proportions of children are leaving school functionally illiterate and innumerate, far worse off in this respect than children were a hundred years ago.

It really does seem that traditional social cohesion is melting away along with the collapse of trust in the institutions of religion, government and law.

Allied to all of this we know that the natural environment is also under great stress. Many resources like oil, on which we are so dependent, are running out fast. We have scientific confirmation that polluting the earth's atmosphere is causing a massive carbon dioxide imbalance contributing to rapid climate change. There isn't a spot on earth or in the deepest ocean that is not affected by our polluting ways. And on top of all of this we have huge populations in China, India, Indonesia and South America modernising so rapidly that whatever resources are left will be used up within a few decades. The extra pollution this is causing is adding to what is already too much, making the planet's ecological crisis even more serious.

In order not to become overwhelmed by such a bleak prospect we must take a step back and try to really think about the mess we're in. This is not just a job for the physical scientists and politicians; psychologists (which includes just about anybody who reflects on human behaviour seriously) must participate and we ought to do this before it's too late because, for every innate need – every human given – there are powerful negative cultural and political forces getting in the way of their realisation in the world.

Down the ages many children and adults travelled the road to insanity because they couldn't find appropriate physical and emotional nourishment in the environment to match their innate needs in healthily, balanced ways. It follows that the only answer there ever will be to mental illness must involve generating environments where it is possible for as many people as possible to do this on an ongoing basis.

All this gives rise to another fundamental question: What exactly stops someone from getting the necessary physical and emotional nourishment? From the human givens perspective, there are three possibilities.

ONE: The environment is sick and unable to provide proper nourishment at that time. Crops don't grow in a drought. Fish die when the water dries up, as do people when there is nothing to eat and drink. With people, once our physical requirements are taken care of, we must also consider our emotional needs, as we highlighted earlier: security, volition and control, attention, status, intimacy, connection to the wider community, feeling we have competence in some areas and are being stretched in what we do so that our life feels meaningful. Just as crops don't flourish in poor soil, even if they have the water they need, a society that prevents people from getting any one of these emotional needs met is ensuring we don't develop properly.

Furthermore, modern life presents several characteristics that disrupt our ability to use our internal guidance systems effectively. For example, the activities of large institutions can impact on the lives of individuals and families by imposing innumerable inappropriate rules and regulations on them in an attempt to legislate for every eventuality. The constant stress such autistic 'straight line thinking' causes the rest of us is palpable and affects huge swathes of the population.

Another is that we can no longer take it for granted, as past generations did, that our existing family, neighbourhood or political, religious and educational institutions will ensure social stability – those days are over. The only answer to that is to formally identify our emotional needs and create new, more flexible organisations that can keep up with the pace of change by constantly holding these needs in mind. Then we might be able to reduce the damage being done to people.

TWO: A person doesn't know how to operate his or her 'internal guidance systems' to help them get their needs met, as when they haven't learnt how to engage and disengage their attention at will, or they misuse their imagination by worrying, which leads them to become depressed. The more complex any animal organism is, the more learning input from the environment is needed to survive over and above what it inherits from its genes. Higher mammals that hunt, for example, learn how to do this from older members of the pack. But humans, whose capacity for learning is vast, need much more complex input from the surrounding culture than, say, a wolf, and the input has to be sufficient and of the right quality for healthy development.

THREE: An individual's internal guidance system is damaged. Now, obviously, when things go wrong in the transmission of genetic knowledge children can unfortunately be born damaged. And direct physical assaults on the brain due to attack, accident or poisoning by drug or alcohol use later in life, can also damage it. But these represent a comparatively small number of cases. Overwhelmingly the most frequent damage to human guidance systems arises from three sources: insufficient intake of nourishing food to rebuild the actual physical apparatus itself; psychological damage due to trauma; and unhelpful conditioning. Fortunately, enough is known about what food we should eat to be healthy and there is a wealth of easily available information available about nutrition. Fortunately too, many psychotherapists know how to decondition psychological trauma quickly (see page 59). But the way we are conditioned by the culture we live in and the harm it can cause is more problematic and less widely known; we don't often recognise our own conditioned behaviour and responses objectively and examine them consciously.

These three types of difficulty can, to varying degrees, be addressed. Take, for example, the quality of how we are conditioned. Conditioning is a kind of learning that grows out of how we develop automatic responses to familiar stimuli. The sneeze reflex, for example, is an uncontrolled reaction to the introduction of foreign particles in one's nose. Attempts to stifle a sneeze are often unsuccessful, as the involuntary reaction is already underway. When we are hungry and see food, we salivate. We do not need to learn how to do this, it is behaviour that passed through sensory consciousness into our genes millions of years ago in order to make swallowing easier. It is not conditioned into us during our own lifetime or even the lifetime of our species: other animals sneezed and salivated long before we appeared on earth.

The 'stimulus' is what produces emotional arousal in the autonomic nervous system and the 'response' is whatever ends the aroused state.

If we are regularly presented with a positive stimulus, food for example, when the clock chimes seven, after a while, at seven o'clock every evening, we will salivate in expectation of food. If one day the clock strikes seven and we start to salivate yet no food is presented, we can say we have been conditioned to salivate at seven o'clock. The chimes now elicit an innate response, salivation, rather than the sight of food. That, in essence, is classical conditioning, as first defined by the Russian scientist Ivan Pavlov when he did exactly that in his famous experiment with dogs at the end of the 19th century. Over repeated trials his dogs learned to associate the sound of a bell with food.

This is the essence of classical conditioning. It really is that simple. You start with two things that are already naturally connected with each other (food and salivation). Then you add a third thing (bell) on a number of occasions. Eventually, this third thing becomes so strongly associated that it has the power to produce the old innate reflex. Many unnecessary fears (phobias) are learned reflexes, conditioned into young children by negative example, as when an arachnophobic mother screams and pulls her child away from a harmless spider, reinforcing the gesture

NOTE: Of course, when a person experiences a real life-threatening event, they can become seriously traumatised: a form of conditioning called post-traumatic stress disorder (PTSD) that can interfere with how they live their everyday life. Fortunately this is usually easy for human givens therapists to treat within a few sessions of therapy.

by continued fearful behaviour.

More sophisticated examples of this type of conditioning influence are extremely common and always involve strong emotional arousal. Politicians use fear to convince us that their policies are for the common good, whilst their opponent's ideas would bring disaster, as when they use emotionally arousing abstract terms like 'terror', 'destruction' or 'serious situation' to blunt our ability to think straight about whatever actions they wish to take. It is clear that tyrants have always used emotional arousal in this way. But it is not only *negative* feelings of fear that are used to condition us. Advertisers work hard to get us to buy products and services by linking them with stimuli that arouse *positive* feelings and excite, such as attractive sexy people, humour, self-respect, success or security.

The type of life we lead also conditions us. Children not encouraged to strive and given too much material wealth when young, for example, can grow up deeply unsatisfied and prone to develop addictions. The reason for this is that, to be emotionally healthy, children have to be stretched which involves putting in an effort. Everyone has to overcome difficulties, solve real life problems and achieve competence *before* they are rewarded. If they are given too many material things too easily, it denies them the experience of being stretched and, indeed, devalues the stretching process. "Why struggle", they feel, "if I am being given everything on a plate anyway?" They won't see the very experience they need, which is the effort they must put in to life, as being worthwhile. This is why the sons and daughters of the wealthy so often slide into apathy and clinical depression when they grow up. Although they can afford therapy they are some of the hardest people to motivate because foolish or indulgent parents prematurely sprang their inner 'spring'.

So how we are conditioned is important to understand because unhelpful or harmful conditioning interferes with healthy development and our sanity.

As the many examples in this book show, people getting their innate needs met in balanced ways find life fulfilling and have no desire to harm themselves or others, except in cases of self-defence. Consequently they don't suffer mental illness; life is just far too engaging. The implications of this are far reaching but it's apparent to anyone who thinks about it that our society hasn't even begun the process of acting, constructing and running itself from a basis of working intelligently to meet our innate needs, primarily because of a general lack of awareness as to how important this is. For example, many organisations are ignorant of the stress levels they generate in their employees when they take away control of work processes from them, thwarting their need to have a degree of autonomy and discouraging people from taking real responsibility and stretching themselves.

Stress reactions are the first signs that a person is not getting their emotional or physical needs met adequately. Anxiety, anger and depression quickly follow if whatever is causing the stress is not dealt with. In their desperation to do something about the demands made upon them and the problems they face many managers unwittingly turn organisations into emotionally unhealthy environments, all because they have no overall insight into what is really needed. If the working environment is sick this has a negative effect on those enduring it. Which GP, police officer or teacher feels that they are being *stretched* as opposed to being *stressed* by the way they are expected to work?

The exponential rise in rates of mental illness over the last forty years is largely to do with the kind of society we have shaped – which is significantly influenced by what politicians allow and disallow through legislation. It is how we are governed that largely determines the ability of society and the environment to fulfil people's innate needs, enjoy life and serve the less fortunate. And how well a country is governed depends on the knowledge and skills of those individuals doing it: politicians, top bureaucrats and leaders of industry, commerce and the media. One excellent and simple measure of how well our leaders do their work is to ask; "is the burden of depression and mental illness *rising* or *falling* in our country?" If rates are rising and psychologically speaking life is getting worse for more people, we know that, however materially well off we are, we are badly governed. If they are falling, we are well governed.

So, if we are genuinely interested in reducing the rates of mental illness we cannot ignore politics unless we wish to be labelled 'idiots', in the original sense of the word. (The origin of the word idiot is the Greek word *idios*, meaning private or without public stature. It was used as a term of contempt in Greek cities, most notably the Athenian democracy, as it was considered the sensible duty of every citizen to participate in public life and vote on issues before the assembly. Citizens who didn't take an active part in public affairs because they were too selfishly focused on their own affairs to consider the bigger picture were held in low esteem – hence idiots.)

As adults we let many aspects of our own and our children's lives be governed by others. Of course complex societies need governing but the general lack of knowledge about human psychology is creating real problems that leave many feeling somehow cheated. Just as we often say, "children are nowadays robbed of their *childhood*," it's as if an inner voice is whispering louder and louder, "You are being robbed of your *adulthood*!"

For the most part we get along by forgetting about other people's problems. The majority of us live comfortably enough. We don't need to beg, go unshod or without a roof for shelter, nor are we reduced to eating grass as happens elsewhere. We're generally healthier and live for longer than a hundred years ago and, despite everything, four out of five of us don't have mental problems.

But to preserve what we have and put in corrections where all is not going well requires examining why it is that politics and bureaucracies so often inhibit progress while claiming to do the opposite. This phenomenon disturbs us and so it seems quite reasonable to ask the same question one would when dealing with a highly disturbed individual: is the modern type of government a danger to the community?

"If you are searching for a fundamental principle, observe Nature!" said Plato. He taught that answers to the practical and moral questions that arise in life are found by contemplating the nature of reality as displayed in the natural world – the aim being to find the archetypal forms behind temporal phenomena. He believed that the pattern that arises in the mind of anyone who sincerely does that will reveal what is necessary for discovering the laws of nature and how to live in tune with them. If this was right then, it follows that it is equally right now. By observing nature, which includes psychological and group behaviour, and contemplating the meaning behind what we see, we can generate the essential sustaining element of good government just as successfully as we can see what is needed in psychotherapy and education.

Plato was not talking about this process as an idle, navel-gazing exercise. He meant it as a day-to-day, bread and butter effort: *really* preparing our minds to see, *really* looking, *really* thinking. But nowadays those who we most need to be wise – who take our money and try to run the country with it – tend to ignore what nature constantly shows us is possible. We believe a marvellous and evolutionarily important transformation of private and public life could occur if more people took Plato's guidance to heart and learnt to think scientifically by analogy from Nature. Moreover it might be urgently necessary that we do so if we are to avoid a catastrophic collapse into an 'Age of Devastation', 'technoslavery' – or worse.

So, following what the ancients advised, let's now look at what Nature can tell us about how efficient and effective systems work.

As we all know from our biology lessons at school, the building blocks of life are cells. Since close observation of the marvel of cell structures is a comparatively modern achievement, following the construction of microscopes in the 18th century, let us start there.

When the earth formed over 4.5 billion years ago, it was a lifeless, inhospitable place. A billion years later it was teeming with living organisms resembling blue-green algae. These, the first living cells on the planet, were infinitely more complicated than a star or a lifeless planetary system. They each had to process incredible amounts of data efficiently enough to sustain themselves.

A cell is the simplest unit that can exist as an independent life form and cells are the basic constituents of all living things. Each one is actually an amalgamation of three independent entities that work together: the cell membrane, the nucleus, and between the two, the cytoplasm. They each bring an independent ability to the party to maintain the whole. Within the cytoplasm, for example, are intricate arrangements of fine fibres and hundreds and, in some types of cells, even thousands, of minuscule but distinct structures called organelles – small organs within cells that perform a huge range of dedicated functions. The principle of having specialised entities cooperating with others like this generated the evolution and increasing complexity of all living organisms, from unicellular creatures like bacteria, to animals like us; you contain about

100 trillion individual cells!

To make creatures that were more complicated than unicellular ones, Nature hit upon a plan – to follow the same pattern! That is to say, complex creatures should also be made up of separate organs, just like a cell is, each with a semi-autonomous function such as the skin, brain, heart, kidney or liver. All of the systems interact with one another just enough to keep an organism healthy; they are all interconnected and dependent on one another. The nervous system controls various organs of the body directly. The brain also receives information from many organs of the body and adjusts signals to these organs to keep them functioning well. A delicate but vital and strong balance is maintained.

Now what characterises all of the organs is that each one has its own field of expertise; an ability that no other part of the overall organism has. Because it has this specialised knowledge it is allowed to get on with its job. The heart doesn't tell the kidney what to do, the kidney doesn't tell the liver what to do, and the various organs that make up the brain have no idea what's going on unless something starts to go wrong. Each organ pursues its own special function. But they do all communicate with each other via various channels – and it is through *cooperation* that they maintain the integrity of the organism.

Of course, a kidney or a heart might become unsound. Nowadays when that happens we can bring in an outside expert to transplant a new one. But he would not then tell the patient to consciously control it. As soon as a new kidney or heart is in place you have to allow it to get on with its job. So the way Nature works is to delegate responsibility, to allow expertise to develop within an organ and not to interfere or inhibit that expertise from flourishing. The brain simply builds systems of cooperation and feedback into each organism.

Human groupings – brains coming together to cooperate – are living organisms yet we continually forget this. We are the result of natural laws and when we stray from what nature has proved works, we tend to create complexity and unnecessary problems for ourselves. We can illustrate this by considering a collection of individual brains gathered together in a building to provide medical services: a hospital. Like any organ of the body it serves – the body is the surrounding community – a hospital has a distinct function (as does a school, railway system, police force, a business, and any number of other groupings of people with specialist knowledge and skills). As such it should be allowed to carry out its function with *minimum* interference. Clearly this is not happening. The state, our government, exists to act as the brain and think strategically about how to keep the body politic safe. To do this well it needs to function in the way any natural system does: by *allowing* all of the organisations and individuals that make up the country to get on with their various jobs and roles without any unnatural interference. Whenever an individual area of expertise is functioning properly it is because it is left alone to use its specialist knowledge to do so, something no other organ, including central government, can do.

There are interesting parallels between the worlds of psychotherapy and politics. Each of the hundreds of different models of therapy have little bits of truth in them which they institutionalise and try to operate in isolation from, or opposition to, other models. The same thing happens in politics. It is clear in psychotherapy that all of the models cannot be right (hence the evolution of the human givens approach which, by making sense of what does work and pruning away the ideology and dogma, makes psychotherapy more effective). Likewise, the various different political approaches cannot be right.

Good government is there to keep us safe and secure in a changing world and to develop and refine (simplify) feedback between the various organisations in society so that we can continually inform each other of what our needs are. Now that's certainly not happening today. If it were, the way we govern ourselves would be getting simpler and easier, and the quality of civic life would be improving.

Whenever a government department steps outside its area of responsibility and tries to micromanage people, it causes chaotic effects because so many of its actions are irrelevant to what is needed. This has the effect of reducing great swathes of the population to a state of learned helplessness, unable to get on with real work. This way of running things is not natural: The brain cannot control how the kidney does its job.

Modern society needs to understand this concept: If the brain tries to control the organs of the body, the body will die. Government should not micromanage the country not because of any ideological objection but simply because it goes against the laws of Nature to let it do so.

Nature does not expect the higher intelligence system of a creature to be aware of how the kidney or liver functions moment by moment. On a day-to-day basis it ignores them, expecting them to function without intervention. It is only if there is a malfunction that conscious attention is addressed to the problem, and even then the higher intelligence doesn't directly control the kidney, it finds out what has gone wrong with it and creates the conditions for the kidney to function autonomously again. It doesn't destroy the kidney nor does it try to control it from the brain. It clearly doesn't have the expertise to be a kidney. The brain doesn't have a clue as to how the kidney performs its function. The relationship with the brain and the organs of the body closely parallels the relationship between the government and the various groups at work in society that help make it function.

Each step in the evolution of mammals involves a process of a creature mastering certain functions and then allowing them to operate unconsciously. Whenever we are thoroughly learning a new skill we do so consciously until we arrive at a point where the skill operates unconsciously and we don't need to think about it any more. This is so when we learn to drive a motor car or learn to ride a bicycle, in fact the more you consciously interfere, the more you disrupt the actual knowledge. The reason why we are such a relatively advanced organism, compared to an amoeba, is that our organism has, down the millennia, learned to master all kinds of skills that first required sensory consciousness, but then became controlled at an unconscious level and became part of our genetic knowledge.

The absence of organic thinking may be placing the survival of our species in jeopardy. And the suitability and quality of the organising ideas that we operate from is the reason. The trends people wrestling with social problems see getting worse every day – the increase in mental illness and drug addiction, rise in family breakdown, poor schooling, the alienation people feel towards the institutions of law and government, centralisation, and the harmful effects of using ever more sophisticated technology to stimulate greed in people for commercial gain – all relate to that. The materialistic achievements and success of the Western world were based upon straight-line thinking, on a model of reality that presumes that we can always have access to massive amounts of energy, minerals, and other sources of wealth such as pure air and water and fertile soil. It is clear to scientists around the world, however, that the planet's resources are finite – undeniably limited. It is also clear that the rate at which these resources are being used up is accelerating because other parts of the world are now copying the Western way of generating wealth which is based upon innate, and therefore natural, animal selfishness – that we can take (grab or steal) from the earth whatever we need, or want.

When we first evolved our situation was such that this didn't matter much; it is by such behaviour that all mammals find a niche in which to survive. But as we advanced, our impact on the landscape and the planet's resources did begin to matter, more and more, even though, for a while (since the most rapacious modern technologies took time to spread), the dangers weren't obvious, except to the most farsighted of individuals. But now, as populations have increased and technology has advanced exponentially, everything has changed. One doesn't have to be a pessimist to sense the problems piling up. The time in which second and third world countries can now develop and become advanced technological cultures is a fraction of the hundred years it took America; and this, inevitably, further depletes the planet's limited resources.

So it has never been more important that governments act wisely. But continual inappropriate top-down interference undermines the whole basis by which spare capacity and knowledge are accumulated. It creates chaos and is unnatural: a rot in society akin to something cancerous in the body. When enough politicians realise this they may be able to help tackle the huge problems we face – which, despite their best intentions, they now seem at a loss to deal with.

Psychotherapists deal with this kind of top-down thinking all the time. A large proportion of people with psychological distress also have physical problems – irritable bowel syndrome, for example, almost invariably becomes exacerbated when someone tries to regulate his or her bowels consciously. Therapists have to teach them how to forget about their bowels and get on with their life and use their conscious mind for what it is supposed to be used for, rather than using it to try and take over unconscious processes. The therapist has to explain; "There is another level of intelligence inside your body which can take care of these functions if you leave them alone and stop interfering!"

We believe that likewise there is a deeper level of intelligence in the community that is revealed when it's introduced to larger organising ideas that make sense of everyday phenomena. All over the UK and beyond hundreds of thousands of people have been inspired and helped by the human givens approach. When they hear or read about it people frequently say such things to us as, "it's as if a light's been switched on in my mind". Or else they say it resonates with a way they were instinctively working already. Many become intrigued that, as well as explaining the importance of innate needs and resources, human givens psychology is organically generating other findings that have major implications for making therapy and education more realistic and effective over the coming years. One psychiatrist remarked that it "advances psychology as much as the introduction of the Arabic numeric system with its zero digit advanced mathematics."

To stand any chance of reversing the rising rates of mental illness we must first deepen our collective knowledge of the science of human nature – the human givens – and learn how best to apply that knowledge to improve effectiveness and raise standards in healthcare, education and social care policy throughout the country. We, and thousands of others, believe the human givens approach offers the best way forward. The following chapters in Part Two illustrate why.

How alive and vital the underlying paradigm of any school of psychology or psychotherapy continues to be is indicated by the number of new insights and useful discoveries it generates. The following is a list of key insights and discoveries which have emanated from the human givens approach to psychology and psychotherapy to date:

- A new view of the unconscious mind – the APET model – which is compatible with neuroscience, clinical experience and experiment, and which describes how the brain works through pattern matching.

- New insight into sub-threshold traumas, including post-traumatic stress disorder (PTSD), and how best to treat them.

- The discovery of 'molar memories' which, when brought to consciousness have been shown to dissolve previously intractable problems and compulsive behaviour, such as anorexia and cross-dressing, in a single session of therapy. (See page 243.)

- An holistic understanding of the evolutionary origins and function of human dreaming which is to dearouse the autonomic nervous system from arousals that have accumulated during the day.

- The crucial link between thinking styles and fluctuations in emotional arousal.

- An holistic, integrated theory for why depression develops and is maintained which speeds up treatment.

- A new explanation for addiction and why withdrawal symptoms occur which offers real hope to addicts that they can overcome their addiction fairly easily.

- An understanding of why the use of metaphor is so powerful as a form of treatment.

- A comprehensive understanding of the placebo and 'nocebo' effect.

- A psychobiological explanation of clinical hypnosis, why it works and what mechanisms are common to *all* forms of hypnotic induction.

- A clearer understanding of the cause of childhood autism and Asperger's syndrome.

- A new insight into the nature of psychosis and the implications for prevention and treatment.

- A more comprehensive understanding of the importance of the REM (rapid eye movement) state in generating reality and accessing intuitive knowledge that brings better order to psychiatric classification and treatments.

- A new way of thinking about the nature of consciousness.

- Greater clarity when dealing with ethical dilemmas.

Everything begins with an idea. The human givens organising idea has grown into a healthy, knowledge-based, practical approach to educating people and helping those who are struggling. It has enriched our understanding and we hope it enriches yours.

* * * * *

Part Two

Part Two

Therapy that works

*Psychotherapist **Pamela Woodford** opens her casebook to show how working with the human givens approach has transformed her ability to help people in severe distress.*

TEN years ago, I was one of those nodding counsellors. I had undergone the extensive training and personal therapy deemed essential before I could work as a psychodynamic counsellor and start helping people in distress. I had always wanted to help people. But, after a few years in private practice, I found myself becoming increasingly frustrated. It seemed to me that, even after six months of intensive work with my clients, I was leaving them in pretty much the same depressed state as when we started. Some valiantly claimed to feel a little better, but I felt that we had spent our time simply stating the obvious (rehearsing the reasons for their misery over and over again) and not actually deciding what we could do about it.

I even found I was becoming somewhat depressed myself. After all, I had been taught to feel with my clients, to suffer with their suffering, and so I felt miserable too. At that point I decided that I, at least, had to do something different. I trained to become a social worker, so that I could take some practical action to help people. I went to work in child protection and, initially, was very happy in my job. I just happened, at this time, to hear of MindFields College and went to one of their seminars that was being held in Bristol. I can't even remember now what it was – perhaps *How to lift depression without drugs* or *Understanding anxiety and managing it without drugs* – because I have since attended so many, but what I vividly recall is that I found myself fascinated, excited and inspired to work differently. To me, the approach that I was hearing about represented *movement*: people were being given the tools to let go of unhelpful behaviours and beliefs and move on positively in their lives.

I started to apply my new knowledge to my social work, because many of the skills are everyday life skills and can be applied, to a degree, in any setting. A suggestion made here, an apposite anecdote told there, could help make the difference to the mood and attitude of someone needing social services' assistance for a practical problem. But, at the same time, I became more aware that clients who were depressed were being referred on to psychiatrists, psychologists or to community psychiatric nurses, yet nothing seemed to be happening to help them take their lives forward.

I again began to feel frustration in my work and so studied for and gained the diploma that would let me practise as a human givens therapist. It was liberating to learn how to focus attention on identifying individuals' unmet needs and helping them learn how to use, or stop misusing, their own innate resources in order to meet them. I learned that one does not slavishly have to follow any one 'model' of therapy but that skilled therapy is about using whatever tried and tested techniques are appropriate for achieving desired ends. Learning to deeply relax people, so that emotional over-arousal can be calmed, and helping the rational brain to take a wider perspective on concerns, are phenomenally important skills in the human givens repertoire.

Unsuitably qualified – or suitably unqualified!

The local authority I was working for as a social worker was, fortunately for me, quite visionary and allowed me to work as a therapist while still employed as a social worker. When they saw proof of the effectiveness of the method – particularly after it took me just two sessions to help back to normal life a seriously agoraphobic woman who, as a young girl, had been raped and subjected to hardcore pornography for many years – they recommended that I should be seconded to work with the local child and adolescent mental health services (CAMHS). CAMHS also were impressed by my track record. But, when they saw that the qualification I held for the type of work I planned to use was the Human Givens Diploma, they blocked the secondment, refusing to accept anything but psychodynamic or cognitive-behavioural therapy approaches. Exactly the same scenario played itself out when I applied to use my therapy and social work skills in another authority. (Fortunately, this head-in-the-sand attitude is starting to change at last.)

So I left social work and went back into private practice. One client was referred to me by the local Connexions service, which provides support and guidance, where necessary, for 14–19-year-olds. Because the work with this client was so successful so quickly, my Connexions contact was keen for me to see another of his clients, a young girl who attended Gordano Training, a training scheme for marginalised young people trying to develop skills to enable them to gain employment. He asked Christine Bates, the executive director, if the centre would pay for the therapy of this girl, who had gained the qualifications she needed to pursue work in her chosen area but suffered from such severe panic attacks and anxiety that she couldn't take the next step.

Christine agreed although, I learned later, she was expecting the therapy to be a long haul. She was stunned when, after one session, and one follow-up, the girl's life was completely back on track, and she found satisfying employment. Realising there was something different about the way I worked, Christine asked me to see an especially demanding boy, who was attending the centre. He, too, quickly moved on. So Christine invited me to offer sessions at the centre on one morning a week. Soon, this doubled and then extended to the five surgeries a week that I offer there now.

Moving people on

I see, each week, between 10 and 15 young people, who attend classes at one of the three Gordano sites in the Bristol area, in skills as diverse as art, computing, painting and decorating and sports. Many struggle with a range of difficulties, including alcoholism, drug-dependency, homelessness and a history of sexual abuse and other trauma. I am told that the learning environment is entirely different as a result of the human givens intervention: students are not carrying old baggage and displaying negative attitudes any more, and so classes are more focused and more stable. I am particularly encouraged in my work by the centre's open approach. If I say I feel I need a session with a young person and their mum and dad, all together, it is arranged immediately.

Sometimes it will emerge in a session that people don't like the course they have chosen but, because of a history of being controlled by or subservient to others in their lives, haven't dared to admit it. I say to Christine, "X isn't happy doing art/design/painting and decorating. Can they change?" And the answer is always an instant yes, regardless of any red-tape complications and nuisance.

The relationship has been so successful for all concerned that, two and a half years later, Christine and I established a partnership and together manage the Bristol Human Givens Centre, in a building shared with Gordano Training. With the aim of making therapy and family

CASE HISTORY:

Catching the rainbow

JENNY was only seven years old when her parents contacted me. I knew the family somewhat informally through friends of friends, who knew about the work I did from the human givens approach.

I visited the family at their home for an initial consultation, with view to putting them at ease. After all, the parents were desperately seeking help for their daughter, and were willing to put their trust in this (at the time) relatively new therapy approach.

Jenny was a very pretty and bright little girl, yet a highly troubled one. She had a violent temper and would go into wild rages, in which she would throw things and swear under her breath, and this was because of the voice she claimed to hear in her head. She banged her head repeatedly to try to get the voice to shut up, and had even resorted to cutting herself. She would steal things from her family and she felt the voice controlled her actions, making her do things she knew were wrong. She had swallowed loads of herbal supplements in an attempt to end her misery, which had left her parents distraught. Jenny's behaviour became so appalling and unpredictable that she had become pretty well ostracised by children at school and was never invited to parties.

This went on for 18 months, whilst the parents sought professional help. The family GP had referred her to a child psychiatrist with a year's work available for people of all ages, the centre is initially being marketed through social services, Connexions, the youth offending team, the local probation service and schools. It will be wonderful if people, who are normally faced with a long waiting list and no guarantee of effective help when they reach the top of it, can be quickly given the tools they need to enable them to move on.

I feel so very far from frustrated in my work now. It is just brilliant to see so many people able to turn their lives around, with just a little practical direction and creative thinking. After all, the human givens approach is about helping people take steps to meet their *own* needs

waiting list but also told her mother, in the presence of Jenny, that there was no way a child of that age could be hearing voices.

During my initial information gathering at the family home, I learned from the mother that she had given birth to identical twins girls when Jenny was two – one year after a miscarriage – and that Jenny's older brother had special needs. Mum recognised that, as a result of the pressures within the family, Jenny had missed out on the attention she needed, and so she had over-compensated by giving in to whatever Jenny wanted. Yet, Jenny had still remained unhappy and became increasingly aggressive.

I had two sessions with Jenny, who was looking forward to seeing me in my therapy room. To start building rapport, and because I knew that Jenny liked dogs, I suggested that we would take my dog for a short walk after the session, and she loved this idea. It was also a means to normalise things for her.

When I asked her about the voice and when she heard it, she said the voices (she called them voices, even though she said there was only ever one) were "dirty pieces of mud". This was a useful piece of information for me to store up, for later use in therapy. Could she 'see' the voices, when she closed her eyes? Yes, she could see lines and lines of words, telling her to kill babies. (There was a possible pattern match here to Jenny not getting her attention needs met at the time of her mum's loss of the baby and the subsequent birth of the twins.)

I asked if it might be possible for her to make friends with the ▶

and to understand and make best use of their *own* innate resources. I feel honoured to be asked to share, in this book, something of the way I work, and I hope the numbers of professionals in the caring and teaching professions who are learning these techniques continue swiftly to grow and grow.

Working quickly with depression

It never ceases to amaze and appal me how many people are left to struggle helplessly with depression, because of misunderstandings about what it is and how to lift it quickly. This is just one example. A

voices to get them to go away, but she was adamant that she could never make friends with them. I said, "But we'll still make the voices go away, shall we?" She eagerly replied, "Yes! Yes!" Now a goal had been set, her voices had been validated (in contrast with the GP's response) and she had the expectation that they would go away.

Before the session, I had asked for Jenny to bring a few favourite things to show me. (Remembering her need for security, I thought she would feel safer with her own special belongings around her.) She had brought two soft toys – a pink rabbit called Pinky and a purple giraffe called Purply. I have a lot of soft toys in my therapy room, so I asked if she wanted to pick one that she would like to introduce her own toys to. She chose a white cat. "White cat has a lot of different names. What would you like to call her?" I asked. When she chose the name Snowy, I suggested that Pinky and Purply and Snowy were all safe in the room together, and could help her as well. She loved that idea.

For a while, we played with the soft toys, making them say things to each other in put-on voices. Then, to encourage her into her imagination (an innate resource particularly strong in children), I asked Jenny her favourite food. She said, the chocolate bar she took to school. To get her to begin to use her senses, I asked, "If you think hard about that chocolate bar, can you smell it?" I sniffed the air myself and said, "I think I can!" She became excited and said she could smell it too.

Her mother had told me that she loved rainbows, and the story of Noah's ark, which ends with a rainbow. I asked her if, with her eyes distraught mother got in touch with me about her 31-year-old daughter, Bella. Thirteen years previously, Bella had been diagnosed by her GP as suffering from manic depression and had been on drugs for it ever since. She had dropped out of university and had returned to the family home, doing nothing with her life for all those years. Just recently, having been persuaded to go with her family to visit relatives abroad, she had felt so panicky that she couldn't get out of bed most mornings, and their stay had had to be cut short.

When I asked Bella what had happened all those years ago to make her depressed, she said that she was shy and unhappy and felt so terrible

closed, she could see any colours and she listed all the colours of the rainbow. "Wow!" I said. "That's a rainbow you've just seen!" She was so happy I had recognised it.

I hadn't known what I was going to do next but, in the moment, suggested that we catch a rainbow right there. I gently tapped the base of her spine and said in a whisper, "The rainbow starts here". I lifted my arm up over her head and down, to describe an arc that enveloped her. "Pinky, Purply and Snowy are all in your rainbow [they were lying beside her] and I'm coming in as well! ... Isn't it peaceful? Such lovely colours. I've never seen a rainbow like this before. Thank you for letting me in."

After a few moments, I said, "You know, I can see those bad words as water drops and rain, just flowing away, and instead all I can see are the good words from Pinky, Purply and Snowy. The bad words are going plop, plop, plop. How are the bad words going, Jenny?" And she laughed and said, "Plop, plop, plop".

Remembering that Jenny had told me that the voices were like dirty pieces of mud, I then suggested to her that there was so much rain that it was almost a flood and that, as she knew, when there was a lot of rain, it washed the mud away with it. Then, as she sat entranced, with her eyes closed, inside the rainbow, I told her the story of Noah's ark and how the rainbow was a sign that God would never flood the world again. "The voices can't bother you again, because we've got the rainbow right here." ▶

Jenny opened her eyes and smiled. "I'm going to close my eyes again and really imagine the rainbow and picking pretty flowers." She opened her eyes again. "I feel lovely," she said. "Now can we take your dog for a walk?" It was a natural, perfect end to the session.

When I saw her again three weeks later, she was much happier because half the words had gone. But she had forgotten to tell me about someone important, she said – Petula, her tooth fairy. She was worried because she hadn't told Petula she was coming to see me. "Is she a good fairy?" (Good human givens practice is never to make ungrounded assumptions. And I didn't question the existence of the fairy, just what type she was.) "She is? Then, she'll know you are here! Wait. Hang on. You'll never believe it, but Petula is here too!" Jenny was thrilled. "So," I asked her. "Would you like to get rid of the remaining words today or next time (creating the expectation that the words would definitely go, no matter when,)?"

"Today!" she cried. "Yippee!" I yelled, and we danced around the furniture – there is no place for dignity in my therapy room. We got down on the floor together and I produced a bowl of little coloured glass stones, which I keep in the room along with other potentially useful oddments. I encouraged her to use her creativity and make a river from the stones to wash away the rest of the words. It was a very pretty pink, blue and green river. I then found an empty pot, put it in the middle of the river and asked what we would put into it, as the remaining bad words. She looked around and chose pot pourri I had in a bowl. Some of the pieces were long and curling. "These are the tongues of the voice!" she proclaimed. "Brilliant!" I said, "Bring them here." She picked these pieces out and we put them in the pot. Then I asked her to close her eyes and imagine the sparkly pink, blue and green river washing them away, and to decide they would be gone forever.

While her eyes were closed, I thought quickly, removed the pot pourri pieces and hid them behind the couch. When she opened her eyes and saw they were gone, I told her that the river must have washed them further way. We searched and found them and decided to take them out into the garden to get rid of them once and for all. On the patio we that she had had to leave university. She had told her GP that sometimes she felt happy and sometimes she felt really sad, and he had decided, on that basis, that she suffered from manic depression and that she would need to take drugs for the rest of her life. She hated the idea and felt miserable on the drugs.

She said that, before she became depressed, she had been happy, outgoing, loved school and was good at exams. Even during her depression, she could often motivate herself for a day, then would collapse and spend two weeks in complete inertia. I quickly reframed her experience for her: "Clearly you are a determined young woman who wants to live life but some important needs are not being met, and that is what brings you down." This made much better sense to Bella than a diagnosis of manic depression.

broke them into tiny pieces. One very large piece was too hard to break. "This is the really bad one!" said Jenny. So, thinking fast, I told her to hold on to it while I fetched a small saw from the shed and I cut it up for her. Then I got a plastic bag and let her put the pieces in. "Would you like to forgive the voices?" I asked as, clearly, they had served a need for her once, although they no longer did now. She had just not known how to break that outmoded pattern of behaviour. Jenny looked in the bag and said, "I'm sorry I killed you but I've just about had enough of you." Then she tied up the bag; we put it in the dustbin and she banged down the lid. Jenny had now taken control over the voices with a cathartic experience – no anger, no anxiety, just all a part of her story.

Back in the therapy room, we made a rainbow to go over the stream, removed the pot and I gave her a greetings card I happened to have bought, which had a fairy like Petula on the front, and we wrote inside it to commemorate the day the voice and words went forever. Goal achieved. Then she said, "Can we take the dog for a walk now?" – which, of course, we did.

Jenny's mother told me later that people noticed a remarkable difference in Jenny instantaneously. She no longer banged her head or performed aggressive, antisocial behaviours. Two years later, she is still fine. ∎

I learned that 13 years ago, at university, Bella had had an experience she interpreted as bullying. It then emerged that she had been seriously bullied by a group of girls at the age of 10, when she was a new girl at a school in the area her family had just moved to. It was a highly upsetting time but, because she was outgoing and clever, she had managed to cope. At university, she fell out with some girls she had thought were her friends. One afternoon she saw them laughing and, because they glanced at her, was convinced they were laughing at her. It seemed she had pattern matched to the earlier trauma of being bullied (ie unconsciously associated the new event with, and responded as if it were, the earlier trauma) but this time she had fallen to pieces. She didn't dare talk to other girls after that, fearing she would be made fun of. At this stage she received her diagnosis.

I explained to Bella how the cycle of depression works,[1] and how the imagination is a marvellous resource but we can sometimes unwittingly misuse it. Bella was very interested to learn about inappropriate pattern matching. She responded very well to the rewind technique,[2] in which, while she was in a state of deep relaxation, I guided her to rerun the memory of both the original bullying incident and the university episode, as if they were on a video, rewinding and fast-forwarding until neither had the ability to arouse her emotionally anymore.

With the aim of helping Bella to engage with the world again, I set her the task of taking up some hobbies. Bella had used to like walking, playing the piano and cooking, and said she would like to rediscover her pleasure in them. At the end of the session, she said, "I can't believe how I feel! I'm so relieved."

When she returned three weeks later, she had done some cooking and had signed up to join a cordon bleu cookery course. She had started playing the piano and walking again, and understood how exercise helped her to feel physically good. In deep relaxation, she visualised herself feeling comfortable around women and having women friends once more. I particularly directed her to 'see' on their faces not the feared mockery but pleasure in Bella's company. I gave Bella a metaphor for how easy change could be: "You can go to bed at night and the view from your window is as normal. Then you wake in the morning and the garden is covered in snow. You haven't had to do anything to make that happen, but can just enjoy it."

As Bella was keen to stop her medication, I suggested that she see her GP to tell him about the therapy and ask for his advice about tapering off.

Bella needed no more therapy after that. Five months later, she sent me a letter, in which she said: "I have started going out again and making friends and feel as though I have begun life afresh. I've made four women friends, who are great fun to be with. Two of them I met at work – I am a part-time receptionist at the moment. I'm doing this while I decide on a career, and I am enjoying deciding what I want to do next, rather than just jumping into whatever is offered to me. I can't remember the last time I was so happy. Thank you for giving me my life back!"

But, really, she *took* her life back. All those words – *decide, enjoying*, jobs expected to be *offered* her – that isn't a negative, depressed person talking!

Working with addiction

At the first Human Givens Conference, held in York in 2004, Joe Griffin introduced his expectation theory of addiction (which was subsequently written up in the *Human Givens* journal[3] and underpins the book *Freedom from Addiction: the secret behind successful addiction busting* by Joe Griffin and Ivan Tyrrell). Since first hearing Joe's talk, I have now used the approach based on this explanation successfully with countless clients struggling to deal with addictive behaviours.

Harry, at 18, was a heroin addict and an alcohol abuser. He came to see me at the centre because he wanted to change his life, as he was sick of feeling so low when he came off heroin highs and having no money. When I asked about his interests in life, he said he loved playing and mixing his decks and had been a DJ in a few clubs, but the drinks and drugs often got in the way.

I relaxed Harry deeply and asked him, with his eyes closed, to think about both sides of his life: Harry as the talented deck-mixer and Harry as the drug abuser. I asked him to see himself standing at the centre of a long horizontal pole and, in his imagination, to walk to one end, where his drug life was. "Really see it, smell it and touch it," I said. ("It was vile," he told me afterwards.) Then I asked him to walk back to the middle, and on to the other end of the pole and to see that aspect of his life for what it really meant to him – enjoyment, achievement, freedom, money.

I had Harry repeat this several times, still in his relaxed state, with the length of the pole gradually shortening and the ends coming in closer and closer to the middle. Finally, for one very brief moment, I asked him to bring both sides inside himself and urged, "Make your choice – *now*!"

"Life! I choose life!" cried Harry. He was strongly affected by this experience and, when he came back for another session, four weeks later, he told me he hadn't taken drugs at all. However, he still had a craving for heroin and he had also been drinking heavily. Now he wanted to be able to stop both. This motivation had been reinforced by the fact that he had experienced some brilliant nights when he had realised just how talented he was with his mixing.

I asked him what he expected from drugs and drinking. He said it was the excitement and adrenalin rush he was after, but he had also realised that he didn't actually get it. He *had*, however, got a high from mixing and 'being clean'. So, making use of the fact that the floor represented a comfort zone to Harry – he would always sort out his DVDs and discs on the floor – I suggested we get down on the floor to do a simple drawing of the brain. I sketched out blobs representing the rational part of the brain, the dorsolateral prefrontal cortex – or, as Joe termed it, 'the boss'; the anterior cingulate – 'the boss's secretary', and two smaller structures called the amygdala and the hippocampus.

I asked him, then, what he thought the boss's secretary would look like, and he said, "A girl of about 16". He saw himself as the boss. I then explained, in much simpler terms than I am going to use here, the expectation theory of addiction: how, when Harry decided not to take heroin, the boss sent a message around, saying so. Sooner rather than later, however, something would happen that would arouse an emotional desire to snort it – it could be being with people who took heroin or a place he associated with it or whatever. When this happened, the amygdala would make the association (pattern match), creating an urge to snort, and, knowing the boss had said no more heroin, relay it to the boss's secretary in the form of mild niggling discomfort, as a means of getting her to change his mind.

I explained that the secretary doesn't take what the amygdala says at face value, however. She sends a message to the hippocampus, the organ where memories and their emotional associations are kept, for further

CASE HISTORY:

"I can't feel my head!"

JASON contacted me in some distress. This 38-year-old man had suddenly developed the sensation that he couldn't see or feel certain parts of his body. In his anxiety to check that he was still whole, he would injure the affected part to induce some feeling in it. He would, for instance, thrust his leg through glass. He was frightened to go out, was becoming very depressed and had been off work for a month. We arranged an appointment for two days later.

The next evening, however, he rang me in a petrified state. He didn't feel he had a head, and one leg had completely disappeared. He was very tempted to stick it in the fire to see if it was there or not. Clearly he was in a panic and I had to act at once. Off the top of my head, I directed him to do some 7/11 breathing (breathing in to the count of 7 and out to the count of 11, to slow the breathing) to help him to calm down. Then I asked if he had a mirror in his room. He said he did, a full-length mirror. As he was speaking on a cordless phone, I asked him to go over to it. He did so, and then started crying and saying that he couldn't see his right leg, his head or his face.

I said, "Don't worry about what you can see. What can the mirror see? Can it see your room?"

"Yes."

Very slowly, to induce a trance state, I asked him what it could see. "The table." "What else can it see? What else can it see? Can it see as high as the ceiling? Can it see to the floor? What else can it see?" Eventually, I said, "Can it see you?" "Yes." "Can it see your feet?" "Yes." I worked gradually up through the parts of the body, finally including his arms, head and face. He agreed the mirror could see these.   ▶

information about whether taking heroin is a good idea or not. Back comes the information that taking heroin is wonderful, and not taking it brings pain and misery. So, horrified, she sends an urgent message to the boss and, to get his attention, laces it with dopamine (a natural stimulant that works like cocaine and creates an appetite to do something). This message tells him he should authorise the heroin taking at once! The resultant desire is overwhelming; the consequences of not authorising it seem dire, and so the boss gives in.

What was happening here, I explained to him, was that the brain was calling up only the memories of heroin taking that were associated with excitement. But they were false, dopamine-soaked memories. The

"The mirror can see your face. Now, do you believe the mirror saw the table and everything else in your room, or did it tell lies?"

"It didn't tell lies."

"Can you see in the mirror?"

"Yes."

"What can you see?"

"I can see me."

I told him that was really good and then asked him to put the mirror away. I knew he was now calm enough not to stick his head through the window, to check it was there. He was out of his highly emotionally aroused state. I then asked if he had any friends that he could see that night. I suggested it would be a good idea to go out dancing. (My idea was that he should do something physical with his body.) Though somewhat puzzled by the suggestion, he liked the idea and agreed to do so.

When Jason came for his session two days later, I learned that he had been a keen, amateur footballer but, after an accident a year before, had had a plate put in his leg and was no longer able to play. He told me that he had been depressed and unable to feel his leg for some time. Then the lack of feeling had spread. I realised that this was his way of not accepting that the plate was there and stopping him doing his beloved sport. The accident had changed a major part of his life expectation of great excitement was never really satisfied at all, and all Harry was doing by indulging the addiction was preventing the discomfort of not doing it – the dopamine-inflated withdrawal symptoms – meanwhile suffering the anxiety about what it was doing to his life.

If, however, we could change the expectations (the memories called up from the hippocampus) to ones that let Harry see the true picture – feeling really low afterwards, not being able to do the things he loved and did best, feeling ill, worrying about the future, having no money, etc – there would be an ever-diminishing desire to perform the act, and the withdrawal symptoms would dwindle to nothing. It was only his *expectation* of pleasure and *expectation* of discomfort if he abstained

– he had played football for a local pub team on Sundays and trained every Saturday.

I relaxed him deeply and encouraged him to have awareness of his little toe, the arches under his feet and his armpits. "Just to have an awareness of those parts of the body is enough to know they are there, because these are parts of the body we don't really feel." I then asked him to work up through each part of his body, acknowledging it and expressing thanks for it. I ended the relaxation session with a wonderful story about a little boy who wanted to find the secret of success, and who finally learns from a wise man that, to achieve his heart's desire, he must pay attention at all times to the priceless gift of his five senses, staying focused and in the present.

At the next session, a week later, I again relaxed him deeply and this time did the rewind technique[2] with him, to remove the emotion from his memories of the accident and the operation. We had discussed new interests he might enjoy to develop, and, while he was still deeply relaxed, I encouraged him to see himself enjoying new social experiences to replace the sport.

He contacted me a few weeks later to let me know that he was feeling much more optimistic about, and in control of, his life and that there had been no recurrences of the frightening loss of sensation he had been experiencing. ■

that made the withdrawal symptoms agonising. If no pleasure is expected, there is no withdrawal.

Suddenly Harry realised that he – the boss, as he viewed himself – was being controlled by a young girl (his secretary) and that he was even paying her all his money to let him do things that weren't in his best interest! It became clear that, in his world, he expected to look after girls, not have rings run round him by them. I then showed him the cunning way that the young secretary was sprinkling on her own dusting of dopamine to make him want to take drugs – and that it was *her* urge, not his. "You could get her to sprinkle on the dopamine while you are playing your decks, and not pay her anything at all!" I said. This was an extremely powerful image to Harry.

I then relaxed him deeply and reminded him of the negative aspects of his drug addiction and all his good experiences without it, and of how these were now set up in his hippocampus – which he chose to think of as a new stack of DVDs in his disc collection. I encouraged him to challenge every positive memory of drug taking that came into mind, to strengthen the new stack of DVDs.

When he came back six weeks later, he was able to report that he had been doing some deck mixing, smoking just the occasional cigarette and drinking Pepsi. He has now gone to college to take a music technician course. His parting words to me were, "Respect, man, innit".

* * ✳ * *

Pamela Woodford is a human givens psychotherapist who lives in Bradford on Avon, Wiltshire, where she runs her private practice. She is also the principal consultant practitioner at the Bristol Human Givens Centre, a trainer for MindFields College and Principal Human Givens Psychotherapist for Brunel and Gordano Training, a highly successful training provider for adolescents, based over numerous campus sites in Bristol and North Somerset. Pamela's extensive expertise includes working in Child Protection, and designing policies for many voluntary organisations.

From self-harm to self-belief

*Lead occupational therapist **Emily Lindsey-Clark** describes how the human givens approach has provided a practical focus for working with women struggling to cope with everyday life.*

WHEN, at a conference on recovery attended by nearly 200 mental health professionals, Angela Western stood up to speak, she was a little nervous, as any presenter always is. However, Angela is not a professional and had never addressed a professional audience before. But what she had to say held them spellbound. She told them about her experience of self-harm and the impact on her life of the unhelpful attitudes taken by mental health and other health professionals during the many long years she had spent in and out of hospital. Now in her 50s and long ago 'written off' as suffering from borderline personality disorder, she spoke of how she now felt, for the first time, more in control, more confident, a sense of status, a desire for meaningful achievement and an awareness, at last, that she is not defined by self-harm (see "I was Angela long before I became a self-harmer", on page 50).

It is no coincidence that she spoke in terms which represent powerful human givens ideas, for the human givens approach provides the framework for our work at a community-based, residential rehabilitation unit for women in Sussex with complex mental health needs, one of whom is Angela. (For the purpose of confidentiality, the unit will be referred to as 'the house' in this article.) Although we know it as a rehabilitation unit, to anyone else it is just an ordinary house in an ordinary street (designated for post office purposes by its number and the street name). However, we are able to house women (six at any one time) who might otherwise have been held in hospital under a section of the Mental Health Act, and offer 24-hour nursing care and a rehabilitation programme involving a multi-disciplinary team.

We work with women who have struggled with living independently and with managing relationships and their emotions. They often use self-harm as a way of coping; many have suffered severe trauma or abuse in the past and can be abusive or violent towards others. Currently, the age range is from 22 to 56. Although we don't work with diagnoses ourselves, the majority of the women have been labelled with border-line personality disorder and have experienced many, many years of institutional care.

Our service was set up two and a half years ago, in line with two key government guidance documents.[1,2] It is based on a non-medical approach of hope and recovery, with the emphasis on building good relationships with clients and encouraging self-responsibility, rather than relying on physical security and restriction. The recovery and empowerment approach challenges negative views, previously held by mental health staff and society at large, about the prospects of those affected by mental ill health[3] and personality disorder, and emphasises that such people can and do recover and live satisfying lives, by learn-ing to manage their difficulties. The individuals who recover, it has been shown, tend to be those who have people who support and believe in them, and the essential components of recovery are client empowerment, reintegration into the community and a normalised life environment.

So our service aspires to enable people to take back responsibility for their own lives, to make their own decisions and to develop self-efficacy. It draws on a variety of theories including attachment theory and trans-actional analysis, as well as the human givens. It is highly hands on. During the day, there are around five members of the multi-disciplinary team present – always a nurse and two support workers, plus two occupational therapy staff and an assistant psychologist. Others involved include a psychiatrist, consultant forensic psychologist and manage-ment team. At night, one nurse and one support worker are on duty.

We are all strongly committed to what we are trying to do. And yet, we all also found it difficult to explain what exactly we were about, when talking or presenting to staff in other services, or even to the women themselves. The notion of recovery, laudable as it is, doesn't explain what it is that we actually *do* or how we arrive at it. What is it that makes a person able to feel empowered and live a normal life in a normal setting? I was already studying the human givens approach and it was when I started thinking about how we could bring it into the service that everything clicked into place.

A helpful framework

I soon spoke to our service managers about framing (and explaining) what we do in terms of meeting needs. Unlike some other models, which are seen as the province of particular health disciplines, the human givens idea of innate needs and resources resonated across the board because it is simple and concrete. Everyone was keen to work with it. We realised, however, that we would need to use it therapeutically in some way other than one-to-one therapy. The women we work with have commonly spent so many years in institutions where they have not felt listened to or genuinely cared for by staff that they find it extremely hard to trust anyone. Most are highly sceptical of one-to-one therapy and are unwilling even to be helped to relax, as that itself takes trust. So we tried to be more creative in how we integrated the human givens ideas into our daily work.

In some teaching sessions, I discussed with my team colleagues the basics about essential emotional needs, such as those for security, control, emotional and social connection, attention, achievement, status, friendship and fun, and meaning and purpose, and then we brainstormed how we would work with these. We came up with the idea of explaining, in the welcome pack we give to professionals and clients, that our goals are to help women who join us to meet these needs. We also decided to adapt our recovery plans to incorporate them.

What we call the recovery plan is traditionally known as the care programming approach (CPA) plan, in which a detailed plan is created to ensure that all professionals and agencies involved know what is being done in any individual case. They review the programme regularly, so that people at high risk of self-harm or harming others don't slip through the net. The plan is based around a standard form, which has to be completed by the client and team involved in their care and covers areas such as housing needs, mental and physical health and social needs. However, these plans are often written by health professionals without consultation with the client.

We had already varied this by asking the women to imagine a preferred future and come up with their own goals, based on working towards this future. Once we had decided to incorporate the general principles of the human givens approach into our plans, we asked the women at the house to tell us what they considered basic human needs to be, and drew up a list together. (The idea was to put them in control of this new way of viewing things, rather than imposing yet another new theory or therapy model on to them). Their list, unsurprisingly, turned out to match very closely with the human givens list of emotional needs, outlined above: for instance, "having contact with my family and friends", "getting a job/going to college", "feeling like I matter", "feeling like *I'm* in control of my life, not the staff" and "doing fun stuff that makes me feel good".

We then explained basic emotional needs, as defined within human givens thinking, and presented each person with a laminated sheet, which had these needs listed vertically on the left. Next, we asked them to review their own recovery plans and decide which needs they thought were being addressed by their current goals, and also where the gaps were. We made this active, asking the women to snip out their goals from their recovery plans and stick each alongside the need they thought it would meet. The completed sheets made it instantly clear, for each person, which important needs were not even being addressed. For instance, the need for status was largely unaddressed (a few women felt that they counted in the house, but none felt that they mattered much to anyone outside of it).

We typed up new plans using this format (with needs running vertically and the corresponding goals running horizontally), ticked the needs that were already met and, at each six-weekly review meeting, we now routinely check progress towards the others. In effect, we have used the list of needs as a template to shape the recovery plans around, so that we can be sure we are working together to set goals to address them all and thus provide maximum opportunity for our clients to get them met. One woman had resisted looking for work, so this had not featured as one of her goals. When we reviewed her plan, it was immediately clear that her needs for 'achievement' and 'status' were unmet and she realised, for the first time, that she did need to do something to enable her to meet them. She chose to visit Workability, an organisation that helps people with emotional difficulties get back into work, because she could now see that an essential need would remain unmet until she took action. The effect on her has been highly positive: having a role as a student has boosted her self-esteem immeasurably.

Managing self-harm

Everything we do is geared around helping the women we work with to meet their needs. For instance, one way that their need for control over their own lives is addressed is by their being entrusted to manage their own self-harming behaviour. In previous units, if people self-harmed, anything sharp and therefore potentially dangerous was removed from them, which could be experienced by them as punitive and intrusive. They would be subjected to one-on-one observation by a staff member. So, effectively, a person in great distress might be left in a bare room, stripped of anything meaningful and being constantly observed by someone she might not know that well, who might not even converse with her. In terms of meeting needs, this is clearly counter-productive.

In the house, people are given back control. The whole multi-disciplinary team carries out a thorough risk assessment when someone first joins us, agrees a management plan, and reviews both regularly, so we are confident about giving the women a high degree of autonomy. Every woman has a locked box containing her medication (for which she has the key). Whether it contains one day's supply or one month's supply depends on how responsibly she uses that control. If someone expresses a wish to self-harm, we spend time with her, helping her to think about other ways of coping or distracting herself. However, if a resident ultimately chooses to go through with the self-harm, she has to take the responsibility for dressing her wound with the first aid kit, kept in each bedroom. If staff feel a visit to the accident and emergency department is advisable, the resident is encouraged to go and transport is provided. If the incident is judged serious or potentially life threatening, however, (for instance, very severe cutting or overdose), staff's duty of care means making the decision for appropriate medical intervention. On rare occasions, this may mean the police have to be called to take the person to hospital.

CASE HISTORY:

"I was Angela long before I became a self-harmer"

"TODAY I am going to talk about self-harm and how different methods of dealing with it by professionals have affected me. Self-harm is still a taboo subject, but I have tried to be very honest in what I am saying.

I can't remember when I first started self-harming; it is just one of those things in a long line of events that are muddled up in my mind with no time scale to go by, because everything seems to blend together. Why do I do it? People do it for many different reasons. For some, it is a way of making people pay attention to them, but I don't think this is my reason because I rarely tell anyone that I have done it. It's a secret between me and my razor.

It's a way of relieving the stress that has built up inside me. Sometimes I know why I am feeling stressed and sometimes, only sometimes, I am able to work through it without self-harming by keeping my hands busy by making cards or doing crosswords or reading. This also stops me thinking about self-harming because I am thinking about what I am doing and it can help relieve the pressure. But, sometimes, the feeling comes from nowhere and the feeling is so overwhelming that it will not go until I have self-harmed.

It is at these times that being prevented from self-harming can be very negative, as the need just builds up and up, until at the first opportunity you self-harm and usually end up self-harming a lot worse than if you had been allowed to do it at the beginning, when you were more in control of the situation. Sometimes you can even end up being suicidal, because you feel your life is out of your control and there seems little point in continuing living.

The reason for these feelings is not always evident and even afterwards I do not know where they came from. They are buried too deep inside me.

At first, it is really scary being given back that control, especially if you have spent long stretches of time in places that take all control away from you (such as hospital), but it is the only way forward if you are to cope with living in and being part of the community.

Balancing attention needs

Focusing on the need for attention has been very helpful. As we know, attention needs must be met in balance but, as one of our clients observed, "My need for attention is huge and it doesn't get met!" She has been able to learn, however, that attention received may be more satisfying if sought appropriately. For instance, women who feel starved of affection may yearn for simple physical contact, such as a hug, but in traditional institutional settings such contact is taboo. It is not so surprising, then, that, when the hug is not forthcoming, a woman may resort to acting violently in some way, to ensure the need for physical restraint – and, therefore, contact. We work in a different way. If a

Sometimes we have these feelings because we feel we no longer matter; we no longer have a place in the world of so-called normal people. The one thing that most self-harmers have in common is that they have very little or no self-esteem or confidence. Maybe we feel that our bodies, like our feelings, are worthless: that, by self-harming, we are somehow making our bodies equal with our minds because, to us, they are ugly. Our thoughts are bad and we feel that our bodies are as well. It is a way of telling people to beware of us because we don't fit in with society's views of how people should think and behave.

People are very quick to condemn and isolate things that don't comply to the 'norm'. Because they cannot see mental illness they put everyone in one pigeonhole, as if we are all going to be axe murderers and in the end we believe there is something wrong with us. I cannot hurt other people, so I hurt myself [but] thereby perpetuate that view in society that I am dangerous. After all, if I can pull a razor through my own skin, what's to stop me doing it to someone else?

But we also self-harm because, when we draw blood, it somehow removes all the pressure in our heads, sometimes just for hours, sometimes for days or weeks. People, including mental health professionals, put us into little boxes. I am a 'self-harmer' – but I am also Angela and I was Angela long before I ever became a self-harmer. Here, in the house, I am Angela first and I wish the philosophy of the house could ▶

woman who is upset asks in an appropriate way to be cuddled or have her hand held, the staff member, if comfortable, will comply. The result has been that the need for such attention lessens and is asked for much more sparingly.

There is a major emphasis on fulfilling the need for emotional and social contact, as our aim at the house is to help women settle back into the community and to be a part of it. We encourage attendance at courses and social groups, so that women don't need to depend upon our unit, once they have moved on, although they are always welcome to spend a night on the sofa if they have a crisis of confidence. Most of the women are excited to move on to supported housing (usually a

be bottled up and given to all professionals, and especially to all students who are starting with a blank slate, because this is the way forward in mental health – to give people back their status in life and then perhaps end that overwhelming need to mutilate ourselves because we end up feeling that what everyone else thinks of us is true. We can begin to feel that we are people again and not just second-class citizens.

In the house, we are people with a status and the staff look beyond the self-harm and the negative behaviour and try to find the individual you once were and help you achieve some of the things you used to do. You might never be able to do all the things you used to do, but they teach you new skills, new ways of coping with life and, most important of all, they try to help you like yourself again. It's a long bumpy road but, as you begin to like yourself a bit more, the incidents of self-harm do lessen. They might never go away completely but you are reminded that just because you took a step backwards today doesn't mean that tomorrow will be the same. You are reminded of the good days you have had and often all you need is that little reminder and you feel that maybe, just maybe, there is hope; there is a way out of this self-mutilation because you are being given back your life in a way you can cope with.

Taking the first few steps is the hardest but they do say that the longest journey starts with the first step – and I think I have made that step." ■

Angela Western

housing association flat, where they are visited by a staff team who check they are shopping, cleaning and managing their bills) but it can also be frightening suddenly to be alone. (We have just been granted funding to set up our own supported housing, consisting of six supported flats, and this is going to give us a great opportunity to base this new service around meeting human givens needs from the outset!)

Moving on

To help our residents manage when they move on, we created a skills-based course, designed around the human givens. We call it a community living skills course, rather than a group, so that the focus is firmly on learning rather than 'therapy' and reinforces skills for those already attending college courses, or planning to, thus helping to meet needs for meaning, wider community involvement and achievement. The course lasted a pre-set number of weeks (10), so that women knew exactly what they were letting themselves in for (helping meet needs for security and control). It was held in the local community centre in town, to which the women travelled independently (helping meet the need for autonomy and feeling part of the wider community).

Attendance was voluntary, as we wanted participants to take responsibility for their own learning and to be motivated to learn (meeting the needs for control and status). To that end, too, they were asked what they wanted to learn on the course. The participants were encouraged to undertake to organise a social event to celebrate completion of the course.

We sent each participant a formal, introductory letter and a special ring binder, dividers and lined pad and pen, so that the material learned could be clearly organised and easily accessed long term. Most of the material was developed through brainstorming and group discussions, rather than being presented as a *fait accompli* (again to increase sense of control and status). We covered a variety of topics – from filling out forms, making official phone calls and shopping and cooking for one, to more emotionally challenging areas, such as assertiveness, raising confidence and self-esteem, meeting new people and responding to difficult or invasive questions, structuring time alone and self-management plans for times of crisis.

Participants gained a lot, even if not everyone's personal aims were achieved in full. Comments included, "I have been able to use assertive-ness skills to arrange an important meeting with my daughter's social worker in regards to her care"; "With staff support, I was able to use my self-management plan during a time of crisis"; "I was able to explain the scars on my arms to a young girl at church when she asked me what they were. I was able to tell the truth in a way that didn't scare her" and "I thought it was like looking on the outside world and that helped a great deal for me, for when I leave here".

Colleagues at our sister service, a medium-secure unit for six women, have also begun to embrace the human givens approach themselves and plan to write it into their own philosophy. I am currently working with them to introduce the concepts, which they believe will help them develop a very different, more effective style of forensic service, within constraints we do not have at the community-based house. For instance, we try, in consultation with our highly supportive consultant psychiatrist, to get people off their Mental Health Act 'sections' as quickly as possible – all as part of giving them back self-control. But, because some of the women at the medium secure unit have committed crimes and are on what are known as 'Home Office sections', their movements are restricted and they do not have the opportunity to integrate into the community and meet their needs for achievement and connection so easily. However, just identifying essen-tial needs has given the team a clearer structure for successful work in their more restricting setting. For instance, the team are working hard to provide opportunities for the women to experience achievement through tasks, such as individually cooking a meal for the whole house. For some of the women there, it is the first time they have ever achieved anything that brings them both admiration and personal satisfaction. Residents are also being given control over their self-harming behaviour and, even though self-harm there is generally more severe, it is now reducing.

Overall, staff within the service have really appreciated the input from the human givens approach, as they feel it gives them clear guidelines about what they are aiming to achieve with clients, and how to get there, rather than feeling submerged in vague and amorphous ideas of 'recovery' and 'hope'. We are also using the human givens as a template for supervision of staff, using it as a focus for discussion. One manager suggested it could be a way of identifying when things are not working as well as they could. For instance, if, after three supervision sessions, someone is still not getting sufficient sense of achievement or status from their work, they might need extra support. New workers undergo a thorough induction when they start with us but those who have never previously worked in mental health may have limited knowledge about the type of challenges our clients face and how best to help them. If their sense of control is revealed to be low, it may be a signal that they need to learn more about handling difficult behaviours.

As a result of all this, we have all seen a huge difference in women who had felt themselves to be pretty much written off by other services. Comments from them include, "I can see I will move on from here"; "I get the attention I need, staff time and help with the things I need to do"; and "I'm starting to achieve new things all the time". Women who had continually been involved in fracas, ending up shouting and lashing out in police stations and psychiatric hospitals, are now involved in training courses, voluntary and paid work, forming good relationships and becoming more socially skilled. Two women who have been with us since we opened are now moving on. One had been in institutional care, including prison, for almost 20 years. Now she has her own flat, and she is loving it.

The women we work with have very many difficulties to overcome, and working in such a setting can be quite a rollercoaster. I've lost count of the times I have left work on a Friday afternoon, with everything operating peacefully and have returned on a Monday morning to chaos and mayhem because, over the weekend, someone has become extremely distressed and seriously self-harmed or threatened violence or run away. At such times, having the human givens needs as a template to refer back to, to check we are on the right track and to keep us focused, is a welcome stress-reliever!

* * * * *

Emily Lindsey-Clark is lead occupational therapist working in a community rehabilitation unit for women with complex mental health needs. Her background includes nine years of experience, predominantly in community mental health settings. She holds the Human Givens Diploma and practises privately as a human givens therapist.

"A mind, once stretched by a new idea, never regains its original dimensions."

ANON

Human givens in primary care

*Community psychiatric nurse **Liz Potts** describes her experience as one of the few primary care professionals in Coventry using the human givens approach.*

WHEN I was training to specialise as a mental health nurse, my fellow students and I assumed our role was very different from that of clinical psychologists. We did the caring and supporting. Psychologists, we believed, did 'something else', something mysterious. They had skills in their toolboxes that were superior to anything we could offer to people in distress. We felt somewhat the same about psychotherapists and counsellors.

Psychiatric nurses aren't fully trained in any particular psychotherapy. We learn a bit of this and a bit of that: some listening and counselling skills and some elements of cognitive-behavioural therapy (CBT) and so on. The cognitive approach made the most sense to me but it didn't seem to have all the answers – and neither did I, when patients said to me, "But, if it is my thoughts that are making me anxious, how come I wake up suddenly at night in a sweat of panic?" It felt as if we were trying to fit people's behaviour into neat boxes and had to ignore or discard anything that stopped the lid from closing.

Then I went to a seminar on the human givens approach and, from the broadness of its base, it seemed to answer so many more questions – it felt like a ray of sunshine. Here, through the concept of essential human needs and innate resources, was a simple explanation of what it is to be human and an approach to helping people that was brief and focused on their skills and abilities, enabling them to engage in their lives. I also realised just how damaging some psychological approaches can be to people suffering from depression, if they embed the depression (by getting sufferers to 'explore' it more deeply) instead of helping lift it.

By that time, I had taken a job as a community psychiatric nurse (CPN), working within a primary care team for Coventry Primary Care Trust. Unusually, I work at a GP surgery, sharing an office with health visitors, district nurses and occupational therapists. (Normally, CPNs work from within community mental health teams based, for instance, in mental health resources centres.) My proximity to the seven GPs at the practice, and to my colleagues in other disciplines, means that, obliquely, I have been able to increase awareness of the effectiveness of the human givens approach.

For instance, shortly after I joined, one of the GPs asked if I felt up to seeing a young girl who had been traumatised by a rape a year previously, or whether he should refer her to a psychologist at the hospital. I had just attended a MindFields College workshop on how to treat post-traumatic stress disorder quickly and safely with the rewind technique (see box opposite), so I agreed to take her on myself. Jenny was 16. She had seemed to cope with the awful event that had happened to her until six months afterwards, when the young man responsible was arrested and she had to give evidence in court. The memories and associated fear came flooding back; her behaviour at school deteriorated dramatically and she started drinking, in order to cope with her emotions.

When I assessed her, to her surprise, I focused on her resources, rather than on what was 'wrong' with her. Previously, she had been confident and outgoing, enjoyed school and going dancing. Now she had lost all of her confidence and her friends, was unhappy and habitually binge drinking. The rewind technique had an instant effect. When I saw her two weeks later, the intrusive memories had all stopped and she had re-established contact with some friends. I worked at relaxing her and helped her to identify and imagine achieving what she wanted to do in her life. The third time I saw her, she was completely back to her old, bubbly self. That really convinced me that I *could* help people put something awful behind them and get on with their lives. It wasn't some long-drawn-out process that only psychologists or 'highly trained' psychotherapists or counsellors could do.

When the NICE (National Institute for Clinical Excellence) guidelines

The rewind technique

THE REWIND technique is a non-intrusive, safe and highly effective psychological technique for detraumatising people, which can also be used to remove phobias. It should be carried out by an experienced practitioner and is only performed once a person is in a state of deep relaxation.

When they are fully relaxed, the person is encouraged to bring their anxiety to the surface and then are calmed down again by being guided to recall or imagine a place where they feel totally safe and at ease. Their relaxed state is then deepened and they are asked to imagine that, in their special safe place, they have a TV set and a video/DVD player with a remote control facility.

They are asked to imagine floating to one side, out of body, and watch themselves watching the screen, without actually seeing the picture (double dissociation). They watch themselves watching a 'film' of the traumatic event that is still affecting them. The film begins at a point before the trauma occurred and ends at a point at which the trauma is over and they feel safe again.

They are then asked, in their imagination, to float back into their body and experience themselves going swiftly backwards through the trauma, from safe point to safe point, as if they were a character in a video that is being rewound. Then they watch the same images but as if on the TV screen while pressing the fast forward button (dissociation). All this is repeated back and forth, at whatever speed feels comfortable, and as many times as needed, till the scenes evoke no emotion from the client.

If the feared circumstance is one that will be confronted again in the future – for instance, driving a car or using a lift – the person is asked, while still relaxed, to see themselves doing so confidently.

Besides being safe, quick and painless, the technique has the advantage of being non-voyeuristic. Intimate details do not have to be made public. ■

For further information about this technique, and why it works, see *Human Givens: A new approach to emotional health and clear thinking* (2004) by Joe Griffin and Ivan Tyrrell, p 284–9. For details of the MindFields College workshop which teaches it, call 01323 811440 or visit: www.mindfields.org.uk

for treating PTSD were published, the GPs had little idea what to make of them. They have no time to spend struggling to get to grips with treatments like CBT and EMDR (eye movement desensitisation and reprocessing) – which weren't even defined in the short version of the guide produced for GPs. Contrary to the belief of psychologists and perhaps psychiatrists, GPs are not necessarily well versed even now in what CBT is all about. Having learned from me a little about the human givens approach, and seen how successfully I have been treating people, they feel confident in referring patients suffering from PTSD to me instead of, as per the NICE recommendation, committing them to a lengthy waiting list for CBT. Because I am on the premises and communication is so easy, I can usually make space to see their patient within a week, if necessary.

As a community psychiatric nurse, part of my work is to administer depot injections of antipsychotic medication to those prescribed them and monitor the effects and side effects of medication that patients are taking. I work alongside psychiatrists and secondary mental health services, when my patients are under their care, and I will accompany patients to appointments to support them, if this is their choice. I feel that it is unfortunate that psychiatry is still so firmly rooted within a medical model, with medication the first line of treatment, and I am happy to help patients' voices be heard, if their wish is to reduce their medication. Patients' expectation is often of a 'magic pill' that will cure all their troubles. When one medication fails, another may be tried, or added to the first, resulting in the polypharmacy that appears to me to be fairly commonplace within mental health services.

Unhelpful labels

Psychiatrists and psychologists all too often seem to try and fit people into categories dictated by the diagnostic criteria used within mental health services, so that people often end up with distressing labels such as 'schizophrenic' or 'personality disorder'. One woman, whom I had been helping with anxiety and depression, was shocked and understandably distressed when she was given a prescription by a psychiatrist in the outpatients' department, on which was written a diagnosis of 'borderline personality disorder' and 'adjustment disorder'. These diagnoses had *never* been mentioned to her in her two years of contact with the mental health service! The 'label', I discovered, had been applied by a junior doctor during her initial two-week inpatient admission, when she had not been cooperative with the nursing staff. I know from my own experience of working on a psychiatric ward that patients deemed 'difficult' often end up with this label – and it colours other professionals' views of them thereafter. Therefore, as I didn't, in my own professional opinion, think the diagnosis was warranted, I wrote to my patient's consultant psychiatrist to say so and attended her next appointment with her. The upshot was that he agreed to 'work with' the diagnosis of anxiety and depression, instead of borderline personality disorder, but refused to overturn or change the previous diagnosis because it had been agreed by a consultant psychiatrist senior to himself who, as far as I am aware, had not actually met the patient!

Whereas the human givens approach starts from the perspective of the person, their emotional needs and resources, this simple understanding is missing in so much of psychological medicine, particularly in the way that services are run. For instance, the first time people go to a hospital outpatients' appointment, the psychiatrist may spend up to an hour taking a thorough history. Patients feel heard and, therefore, hopeful. When the psychiatrist prescribes a drug, they often assume that it will cure their troubles. They return for their next appointment, expecting the same amount of time and attention but are sometimes shocked to find that, at best, they receive a 10-minute review of their medication. Very often, each time they go to an appointment they see a different doctor, which again can be very distressing.

The case of Rosalind, a woman in her early 50s, also illustrates how the way a service is organised can feel as though it lacks human understanding. She was referred to me by one of my GP colleagues because she had chronic anxiety and depression. Seven years previously, when living in a different area, she had been referred to the psychological services team, to see a psychologist. Before her appointment, she was sent a lengthy and complicated questionnaire, which she was expected to complete by herself and return. She found the task horribly daunting, and anxiety inducing, but just about managed to make herself do it. On arrival at the assessment, she discovered that she was expected to complete another questionnaire, the prospect of which, this time, threw her into a panic, and she refused to do it. Her case was closed, as far as the psychological services team was concerned.

Working with Rosalind

By the time I met Rosalind to offer her ongoing support, she was on high doses of a variety of different psychiatric medications because, over the intervening years of no progress, it had been continually upped; she is very damaged by all she has been through. I spent a long time engaging with her and she revealed to me that she believed the root of all her problems was that, for all her married life, her husband had been cross-dressing. This was something she had never felt able to come to terms with and they had kept this secret from everyone they knew. She thought of herself as a victim, who had been weighed down and oppressed by this secret for all these years. I helped her reframe her idea of herself as victim by exploring with her the *choices* she had made; the reasons why she had stayed in her marriage and why she and her husband had chosen to keep their secret.

Rosalind had taken early retirement about six years previously, due to her problems with anxiety, and she had not yet come to terms with her loss of status and independence. She felt very angry and let down by the mental health services but she has gradually started to trust me, and this led to my being able to work with her to set some small goals. She had once loved walking and gardening, but a knee problem had curtailed such physical activities, so we worked to help her recall and rediscover the enthusiasms she used to have for other more sedentary activities. As a result, she took up tapestry again. With the help of her GP, we are also working on gradually reducing the medication she is on.

About a quarter of the patients I work with are chronic sufferers from mental ill health. Unlike those who actively choose to seek help, many of these are people who have spent 20 or 30 years shuffling around within the mental health services, dulled by hefty doses of psychiatric drugs. Some are not motivated to make changes in their lives. They identify with their diagnosis – it is what defines them and grounds them – and they would be frightened to move on. However, I'll always try to say or suggest something that might open minds to different possibilities, without threatening their status quo.

Brenda's story

Brenda is 60 and has chronic, active psychosis. She has fixed delusions, such as that her water is being poisoned, and has fantastical, complex beliefs in different godlike creatures and the signs they send her. She lives alone and, although well supported by her daughters, is clearly lonely – largely because she resists people's efforts to help, even when the effects are beneficial. For instance, her support worker took her to a local painting group, which she enjoyed enormously, but she didn't want to go again. I have built up rapport with her and it seems that having someone she can trust, and to whom she can tell the strange things that make up her private world, is a comfort to her. (Her daughters refuse to listen to her 'madness'.) So I listen to her and, when she describes some delusion that causes her panic, I'll normalise it at a physical level by saying, "It must be frightening, feeling that way. What I find really help-ful when I'm fearful is doing something called 7/11 breathing." I'll then demonstrate how to breathe in to the count of 7 and out to the count of 11, and how it calms down a thudding heart. She seems to find such interventions helpful.

Moving on

Sometimes, however, I am thrilled to be able to play a part in helping someone really move on with their life and it is the human givens approach that has given me the skills to do this. Bob is only 50 but has had chronic anxiety for the past 13 years. At that time, he had suffered a mental breakdown, largely arising from overwork, and had ended up in a psychiatric hospital. His experience there had so traumatised him that he was terrified of ever going in there again. He didn't dare do any-thing that might challenge and overwhelm him and, as a consequence, had become virtually an agoraphobic. At the time I was asked to see him, he had managed to collect his wife from work in the car, for the first time in all those years. Usually, he didn't dare, because he feared he would have a panic attack if he was kept waiting.

I congratulated him on what a huge step he had achieved in collecting his wife and the fact that he had achieved that without any help – stress-ing that he clearly had the inner resources and the motivation to move forward in his life. I worked with him over a period of six months, during which time I used the rewind technique to deal with the hospital trauma, gave him techniques for relaxing himself and helped him set goals and believe in his ability to achieve them. The biggest one was to take a holiday with the family in a caravan – he had not been on a holiday in 13 years. He achieved it; he and the family thoroughly enjoyed themselves, and he now has the motivation to set even bigger goals. He is even thinking of returning to some kind of employment, something he was unable to contemplate when I first saw him.

Gradually, my CPN colleagues are becoming more aware of what I can do. When I meet with them to discuss our caseloads, I talk through how I've helped people and what techniques I've used. Currently, I am planning to introduce a needs assessment with clients – to scale how well, or poorly, their needs for connection, status, attention, safety, privacy, and meaning, etc are being met – and, in due course, I'll share that idea, and its impact on patients, with my colleagues. I have planned a lunchtime training session at the surgery to talk about the human givens approach and teach some helpful skills. This session will be for the GPs and other primary care colleagues – health visitors, occupational therapists and district nurses – and may well lead on to other sessions for colleagues in different primary care teams, and maybe the community mental health teams in the city.

My primary care colleagues will come to me for advice if they have any concerns about a patient's mental health. The health visitors will ask me to see a new mum on their list, if they suspect post-natal depression, and the district nurses and occupational therapists, if one of their elderly patients seems to be getting depressed.

However, as the only person in Coventry that I know of using the human givens approach, I do feel professionally quite lonely, in some respects. So I hugely value being a member of the Association of Human Givens Practitioners in the NHS*, which is centred at Milton Keynes. We come from all different specialities but what we have in common is the need to manage NHS bureaucracy, and to find 'quiet' ways to pursue and introduce new approaches within it. I hope, for

---

* To find out more about the Association of Human Givens Practitioners in the NHS, visit: www.hgi.org.uk/sections

instance, that the positive feedback I receive from patients and the speed and effectiveness of my work will continue attracting the interest and curiosity of my colleagues, and show them that things can often be better done differently. Just as I used to think that psychologists and psychotherapists must be so much better trained and equipped than I to deal effectively with human misery, so do many GPs and other health professionals still believe that particular myth – and, like most myths, it is powerful and pervasive. We must patiently keep working and wait while the wellspring of change fills slowly, drip by drip.

* * ✳ * *

Liz Potts *is a primary care community psychiatric nurse working full time in an innovative project in Coventry to provide a wide range of services at a local level. She receives referrals for people with a diverse range of emotional difficulties and 'psychiatric disorders' and has been applying the human givens approach to her work since 2003.*

*"To read without reflecting is to eat
without digesting."*

EDMUND BURKE

Evidence of learning

*Principal of TheSPACE, **Fred Grist**, and director of therapeutic services, **Mike Beard**, describe a unique facility for youngsters who face complex and challenging experiences in life.*

BY THE age of 12, Andy was a regular user of drugs and alcohol. He spent his days and, increasingly, his nights with vagrants on the streets and his single mother, struggling to cope with five children by five fathers, was unable to stop him.

Andy's behaviour became so aberrational and aggressive that, after many failed placements, he was sent to a secure unit. Even there, staff couldn't cope, so his local authority paid for an expensive private placement operated by two burly ex-bouncers, who kept him out of trouble in a house in the country. When Andy became emotionally aroused and frustrated, as he routinely did every day, their solution was to make him work out on the punch bag they had installed for the purpose. Otherwise, he sat watching television or was taken on long walks in remote places. His contact with other young people, or adults, was zero.

Andy was referred to Fellside (Woodlands School, as it was then known) when he was 13. In the three years since, he has willingly engaged in schoolwork for the first time in his life and has learned to relate to others and to find better ways to manage himself. His gradual reintegration into family life means that he is returning to his hometown this summer, where he will be going to college and then seeking gardening and grounds maintenance work, for which he has discovered he has both enthusiasm and talent.

Andy's story is not unusual. Most of the young people who come to Fellside have a background of abuse and a history of placements in care that have seriously broken down, resulting in some desperate solutions. Thirteen-year-old Vanessa had been put into care and then, because of her "dangerous sexualised behaviour" (grabbing at female carers' breasts or groins when she was upset, which often led to her being restrained), ended up in a 'secure house' by herself, where she was looked after by (and was deemed to need) five adult carers. She didn't attend school, also spent her days watching television and had no contact with young people. Another young lad, Miles, had acquired several labels by the time his placement had broken down, including attention deficit hyper-

About TheSPACE

TheSPACE (an acronym for Therapeutic Specialist Providers of Assessment, Care and Education) was established in 2000. Two years later, the first school opened in Kendal, Cumbria, and now there are two schools: Fellside Middle School, which can accommodate five young people aged 7–12, and Fellside Upper School, which can accommodate nine aged 13–19. All live with us for up to 52 weeks of the year. In our extensive and attractive grounds is the Bungalow, where two young people aged 16–19 can live semi-independently (shopping, cooking and caring for themselves) while attending college.

Both schools have their own residential, classroom and office accommodation and are situated on the edge of woods, with spectacular views over Kendal and the surrounding countryside. All bedrooms are en suite, and there is plenty of space for communal activities, as well as places to meet privately with visitors. It is just five minutes' walk into Kendal town centre (15 back up the hill).

TheSPACE/Human Givens Consultancy (known as the Centre), in the centre of Kendal, opened in 2005 as a base for professional staff development, work with our young people and their families, and for offering therapy to the general public and training for health and education professionals nationally. It also offers training and consultation to a wide range of organisations throughout the country.

We have nearly 50 staff in all, a mix of teachers (12), pastoral care staff (17), therapeutic, administrative and ancillary staff, plus Dan, our dog. All staff are given a grounding in the human givens approach, so that our work with the children has a coherent basis. ■

activity disorder, Asperger's syndrome, dyspraxia, reactive attachment disorder and several antisocial disorders, on account of which it was concluded he needed constant supervision.

Unsurprisingly, by the time they come to us, many of the children's difficulties have escalated sharply because so many of their needs are failing to be met: needs for emotional security, social connection, autonomy and control, meaning and purpose and so on. They are commonly overwhelmed by feelings of worthlessness, low self-esteem and the inevitability of failure. Often they don't even know how to enjoy themselves, play creatively, learn, make friends or participate in any group activity and, indeed, even lack the motivation to seek out almost any positive experiences. Most have assumed that it is their fault that their world is such an unhappy place.

Therapy, in its broadest sense, is relief from pain and suffering and promotion of health and wellbeing. At Fellside, we set out to achieve this by creating a safe living and learning environment, where all can share the values of the community, experience the genuine care we have for each other, and come to realise potential. All of our work is underpinned by the philosophy of the human givens approach: when someone is unhappy, unwell or being difficult, emotional needs are not being met in a balanced, authentic way or else innate resources are not being used correctly. This doesn't remove a young person's responsibility for their behaviour, but it does provide an insight into why they are behaving as they are and it may give some clues to the solution.

Living at Fellside ensures an integrated learning experience, through structured education, individual therapy, small discussion groups and shared activities within the home and in the local community. Every year, staff go on holiday with all the children, staying, for instance, in cottages in Ireland, the Isle of Eigg or camping. This way of living allows each young person to challenge what has gone before in their lives, to look for what is missing and to work towards change. It is crucial that our young people *want* to change and have the capacity to do so. We are not about containment; we are about development. As a precious, limited, resource, we opt to help those who have a desire to change and improve their lives. So, choosing who comes to join us is extremely important.

The first step

We refer to this as "Join up". Initial home visits (preferably two, usually made by Fred) are a crucial source of information. Seeing the physical environment generates an idea of a family's values, even if the child in question is already in care. For instance, what do the family members choose to spend their money on? (One home had huge flat-screen TVs but the son's room contained only a mattress and the bathroom walls were peppered with holes, where the father punched his fist when drunk.) And is a visitor offered something to drink (a telling indication of a child's likely understanding of normal social intercourse)? The aim is to meet as many family members as is possible, to see how the child fits into the family dynamics.

How the child reacts to the idea of a placement at Fellside depends upon their history. Those who have already been in a placement that has broken down (and one of our children had had 18 before coming to us) tend to have preconceived ideas about "another crappy residential home". Those who have never been in care are very nervous about what it will be like, especially as most will know at least one child in their street or estate who has been in care and has told them in no uncertain terms the horrors to expect.

Fred brings pictures of children engaged in productive activity and having fun, as well as pictures of the beautiful house and all the rooms in it. He provides as much information as he can to start to set their minds at rest and encourage them to visualise the kinds of things they would be doing at Fellside. He then asks some questions that are completely novel to them. What kind of things do they like doing? What are they good at? What would they like from a visit to Fellside? What are their own expectations – for this placement and for their lives? Do they expect to remain in care? What would they like us to do for *them*? (That floors them.) We also clearly distinguish *needs* from *wants*. If their aim is to become a taxi driver or a builder or a hairdresser, what skills do they think they will need in order to achieve that? In effect, it is the format of a mini-therapy session, building rapport, gathering information and encouraging the child to think realistically about expectations and goals, access their resources and start to rehearse the good things they could expect to experience at Fellside. Young people have such resilience and a wealth of resources that it is easy for the conversation to flow.

Often, they don't know the answers to such questions at that time. At a second visit, it becomes clear how they have processed the information received – or if they have given it any thought at all. Our young people like to refer back to those initial meetings and laugh at some of the things they said or did. It gives them a sense of how much they have moved on.

A visit to Fellside

When children come to visit us for their first time, they are invited to arrive about an hour before lunchtime. Some believe they need to swagger and look confident, to show they are bomb proof; others are clearly scared to death. Our children are brilliant at helping them feel relaxed; they have all been there themselves, and remember it well. Most of the visit is spent with our young people. After a tour of the premises, including sitting in on a bit of a lesson, the new child is invited to lunch, where staff and children all eat together. Our shared mealtimes are a really enjoyable occasion and our kids are skilled at working to include someone nervous and new.

Fourteen-year-old Mark refused to join in the meal on his first day. Staff didn't insist, and just let him sit on the swings outside, warily watching through the window. He had never had a family meal, let alone eaten at a big table. He was unnerved by seeing polite, helpful children, unaware that they had all once been as anxious and out of control as he was. He was a daily drug user and desperately wanted to help himself. But, whereas he knew he could survive on the street, where he had to be hard and self-protecting, being in a place where people cared about him and he had a nice room and exciting opportunities was scary. He was terrified of failure. Mark came back for another visit and still wouldn't share a meal (a prerequisite for acceptance into the school because it demonstrates a willingness to engage with peers and adults). He set up obstacles – "I wouldn't want to come here unless I could paint my room the colours I want". "You can. All the children here paint their rooms as they want them." "Well, then, I wouldn't want to go to class every day." And so it went on, until he was gradually reassured, participated in a meal and joined us, since when he has made stunning progress.

Vanessa's carers were appalled when, on her visit (we had already met her twice by then), we suggested she go down the road with one of our children to post a letter; they expected to go with her, because of her "dangerous sexualised behaviour". But we were confident the brief expedition would be fine, as indeed it was. The "dangerous sexualised behaviour" disappeared within a few weeks, once we had viewed it from a human givens perspective and responded accordingly. Vanessa suffers, as a result of a genetic condition, from a cognitive impairment that left her, as a 13-year-old, with a mental age of seven. She was going through puberty and had become interested in female sexual characteristics but in a childish, inappropriate way – thus the grabbing at breasts and genitals when upset, and subsequently being restrained. She had quickly realised that doing this brought her instant attention, albeit negative, and so had learned to repeat it; in a house where she was the only child and often left in front of a television, any individual one-to-one attention was better than nothing.

If children have learned to respond to frustrations or difficulties by running away, being violent or doing inappropriate things, they are going to do so when they arrive at Fellside, and we expect it. Vanessa duly grabbed at female staff. She also, however, displayed an amazing ability to notice details, such as the fact that the cornicing in the ceiling of one room was different from that in the other rooms. We calmly commented on how good she was at noticing things, such as the cornic- ing detail, and how therefore we had no doubt at all she could remember and recall all that was explained to her – this brought an acknowledging, wry smile. We then 'noticed' the fact that inappropriate grasping at breasts and genitals had, in the past, reliably brought her a lot of attention; but then described some of the more positive ways young people might gain attention. By validating the reasons for her actions instead of criticising, we were quickly able to substitute new, more desirable means of meeting her attention needs.

Striving for goals

Most important, in terms of whether a place is offered, is evidence of the motivation to change – and willingness to strive for goals. All young people already at Fellside also have input as to whether a place is offered.

Mark said he wanted to do something about his drug use and to be respected. But, at that stage, he had no real idea that he needed to earn respect. Similarly, all of our children have failed either to form or to sustain positive relationships with others, yet none could say, at this stage, "I want to get on with people", as none had identified their inability to do so. Most goals initially relate to being safe and happy.

Making children feel safe enough to become happy is a prime goal of ours too. We achieve it through the physical and emotional environment we create. Our children don't want to be somewhere that is chaotic (they've had too much of that); the ambience at Fellside is settled and calm. We are honest with them and respect their ability to make their own decisions. We also have realistic expectations of them, and encourage them to have realistic expectations of themselves – no one feels safe if expected to do what one cannot do. We try to offer accurate feedback, not false praise.

There is a different pastoral care team for every child – two workers who together ensure an integrated care, education and therapeutic programme. One is a member of the teaching staff, who monitors, supports and feeds back educational progress; the other is a pastoral care worker (a post that in other settings might be termed residential social worker), who helps the child with life activities such as keeping their rooms clean, shopping for clothes, and generally being there for them – in effect, being in their corner, whatever the child has done, helping them to view their behaviour options in less limiting ways. Janet Redpath, our registered manager, is developing a strong team with a wide range of professional experience. The pastoral care workers have set sessions with their charges once every week, and additionally as needed. They also sit in on 'their' child's formal therapy sessions when they can (often choosing to do so in their own time), so that they can reinforce what has been learned.

Getting children ready for more conventional learning is an important early task. Having lacked the kind of early supportive psychological experiences that normally encourages children to explore and take risks and develop competence and mastery, our children have a history of failure leading to expectation of further failure. A cycle of perceived inadequacy, anxiety and inability to cope has to be broken. We do this by ensuring that children are calm (stories to engage attention are a wonderful means of doing this), setting small, achievable tasks that are of interest to them, and providing positive, constructive feedback. A small achievement can lead to the 'ripple effect', creating a desire to embrace education.

Although increasingly we are seeing our children sit examinations, including GCSEs, we have successfully been disapplied from the National Curriculum, so that we can concentrate on personal and social development as much as on academic learning – social, practical and vocational skills are valued by us as highly as academic ones. Our heads of education, Neil Nortcliffe and Maggie Scott, and their talented teaching staff work hard to bring learning alive. For instance, project work in a maths lesson led to a great adventure and true learning experience, in which all our young people and four staff planned and then completed the 135-mile, coast-to-coast cycle ride from Whitehaven to Sunderland in three and a half days. Fourteen-year-old Chris, at the time labelled as 'high achieving Asperger's', had broken his collarbone, so was put in charge of the 'logistical support plan'. Among other things, he co-ordinated breaks and helped the riders keep their daily diaries, had a great time and felt fully involved in the whole adventure. The people we met along the way, the experiences we shared (the memory of Paul missing a right-hand bend and ending up, unhurt, in a hedge, still makes us all laugh) and the sights we saw – of such things are memories made and a sense of belonging created.

Testing for evidence

Every day there are two review meetings, one held at the end of the educational day and another at the end of the evening (where possible, attended by all staff). Here, we test 'evidence of learning' – not, in this context, evidence of ability to recite times tables or identify a noun but something much more profound. Our young people will tell us if, when they did good work in class today, they focused on their own work and didn't distract others; or that they had allowed someone else to answer in class, even though they themselves had known the answer and dearly wanted to shout it out; or that they had stayed calm and hadn't reacted angrily when someone else did keep shouting out the answer. One lad recently commented on how he had formed a relationship with a boy who had just joined us, without trying to dominate him. Someone else might mention that they had offered to take a turn at the washing up without a quibble, even though they had really wanted to watch a particular TV programme. Especially important, children will describe an instance of how they had behaved appropriately that day in the face of disappointment or being corrected, instead of kicking, having a tantrum, running away or whatever their old coping mechanism had been. This, in turn, translates to a greater understanding that, when caught out in wrongdoing (such as smoking in the toilets at their old school), it is not the wrongdoing itself that leads to the dire consequence of exclusion but the reaction of punching, kicking or extreme verbal abuse, when caught by staff.

Every child is asked to 'scale' how they feel they have performed each day, on a scale where zero is not at all good and 10 is great. This is an excellent, inclusive method of giving everyone a voice, because, for some youngsters, descriptive language is difficult at the start. As some children are less likely than others to award themselves the highest scores, it quickly became understood that 8, 9 and 10 can all mean excellent, 5, 6 and 7 can all mean good and below 5, not so good. Nothing rides on the outcome except personal satisfaction and pride: the scale is also an educative tool because staff scale each young person's day too, and discrepancies in scoring (whether higher or lower, and what that might mean) can be discussed and reflected upon. Staff also use scaling as part of their own team and self-evaluation. It is extremely useful and helps promote their experience of being reflective practitioners.

Understandings from the human givens approach are common parlance here. All the children know that we have a primitive (reptilian) brain, a still fairly primitive (mammalian) emotional brain and a more sophisticated rational brain, although they refer to this in different ways. Vanessa, for instance, thinks about her snake brain, her dog brain and her 'thinking' brain, while Ryan responded to the image of the Incredible Hulk as his emotional brain (powerful but not overly bright) and Batman as the neocortex (the thinking superhero). They know that over-emotional arousal stops them from thinking straight and makes them stupid. They know about incorrect pattern matching, done by the brain structure

Therapy 'on the hoof'

FOR therapy to be most effective, we need to be in a calm, relaxed state, in which we are open to and can absorb new ideas and perspectives. I might usually induce this calm by inviting people to close their eyes and relax and enjoy some guided imagery, at a beach, a lake or somewhere they find it pleasant to be. But very many of the young people we work with are initially reluctant to give up control in this way. They don't even like to shut their eyes, as they are so used to being on hyper-alert for danger. This means that I have had to learn to be ready to work in a much less structured way.

On one occasion, for instance, when young Colin came to the Centre, he said he didn't want to talk about 'stuff' in the therapy rooms and would much rather look at the training room instead. He was intrigued by the large screen, used for PowerPoint presentations, so while he was absorbed in examining it, I said, "Wouldn't it be great if you could sort out this business about flying off the handle?" He nodded distractedly. "Just imagine if that screen, instead of being blank, had a film showing now," I suggested. "What would it be?" "A football match," he replied, without hesitation. So, I encouraged him to enjoy the football match and to note how confident the footballers were, and how they played as a team, with controlled actions. Then I said, "Imagine if it were a film of one of those difficult times with your brother [with whom he could be seriously aggressive]. Imagine it is going backwards, rewinding really fast..." He looked at me, puzzled. "Whaaat?" "Can you do that, run it backwards?" I asked. Intrigued, he nodded. And then we were effortlessly into the rewind procedure, although it was done conversationally, not only with eyes wide open but occasional direct eye contact between us! After running relevant scenes back and forth a number of times, I was able to encourage him to see himself as calmer and more confident and controlled and to imagine playing with his brother as if they were on the same team.

Once, at Fellside, I saw Andy absorbed in a PlayStation game. On called the amygdala, whose job it is to keep us safe by alerting us to possible dangers (often getting it wrong because past trauma can make it hypervigilant and because it also doesn't know the difference between real and imagined dangers). Ryan's amygdala is a security team in the basement of his brain; Colin (aged nine) has "sentries on duty at the gates of the castle" in his mind.

Fourteen-year-old Shane, who was almost relentlessly disruptive when he first came, had his progress accelerated when Mike described

impulse, I squatted down beside him and said, "All right to have a chat while you're playing, mate?" He nodded, busy. So I suggested that one part of his mind could continue playing and the other could pay attention to my words and choose to see a different scene on the screen. As Andy was anxious about leaving Fellside shortly to start college, I was able to help him 'detraumatise' his imagined fears of starting college through the rewind technique, and rehearse his next life-step, seeing himself starting out keenly and confidently – yet all the time continuing to play his PlayStation game.

A particularly effective time to make an 'on the hoof' intervention is when a child has had an upset. On one occasion, a staff member and I sat on the sofa on either side of Vanessa, my hand gently resting on her forearm to stop her getting up and harming herself, as she had been doing and was threatening to do so again. As she panted and muttered in a trance-like world of her own, I lowered my voice, deepened it and started to talk of future positives and past successes – what she could look forward to doing when calm again, and how quickly she had been able to recover before. I also used 'paradoxical' embedded commands; reassuring her she "didn't have to feel more calm and relaxed unless she was ready", and that "no one would make her want to feel more comfortable and in control", etc. In no time at all, she was in a deep trance, and we could rehearse more positive ways to deal with such an upset the next time.

I call this 'carpe diem' therapy – although it is not just 'seize the day', but every moment. ■

Mike Beard

the amygdala's role in cartoon form and then drew out for him a graph, in which the horizontal x-axis represented the events of his life, the vertical y-axis represented increasing stress and a dotted line running across somewhere in the upper half of the graph represented the level of stress that would effectively 'hijack' Shane's ability to think straight and lead to his disruptive (and often violent) behaviour. They tracked important events in his life and he decided where, above or below the line, to score the stress levels induced. By the end, he could see that some stresses had been beyond his control whereas other times when he had been 'tipped over the top' were of his own making – he could have chosen to react differently, to get his needs met more positively and acceptably within the community. In therapy, Mike used the rewind detraumatisation technique (see page 59) to deal with severe past stresses and then Shane himself decided he wanted to stay 'below the line' in future, so that he would have a better chance of things working out well. As he loves football and can quickly go into trance by imagining a football game, Mike linked cooling his behaviour to the idea of the referee's whistle. Now, when he is threatening to blow, staff are sometimes able to say, "The whistle's gone, Shane", and he regains access to the calmness he experienced in trance, and can lower his arousal. In such ways, our children use their active imaginations to make sense of complex brain responses, and learn to bring them under their own control.

We also talk about the idea of their borrowing our brains when they have temporarily lost their own, through over-arousal. This has a very different feel from being told what to do, because it puts them in charge of what happens next – allowing themselves to be calmed down and listening to what a staff member has to say that may help them process a difficult situation differently.

Living these kinds of understandings makes them second nature. One day, a few boys were going into town with a member of staff to get a DVD. As they reached a particular spot on the outskirts of town, a pained look crossed one lad's face and he mumbled, "This is where I come to when I run away". Vincent is only 10, yet the staff member heard him say in response to the other lad's comment, "But now you can replace that memory with a really good memory of going out with your mates and choosing a DVD".

Our youngsters respond keenly, and usually responsibly, when given a big say in the things that affect them. For instance, a couple of years ago, when we needed to appoint pastoral care staff, we decided to ask the children what qualities such a staff member should have. After lively discussion they came up with: calm (not wind us up); confident (not scared of us); firm but fair (able to deal with things when they happen and not put it off till later); able to listen well (to hear what it is we *really* have to say); able to help us sort out problems and learn for ourselves (give us help with options, not tell us what to do); able to treat us as individuals (not seeing all behaviours as the same); able, most of all, to treat us in the way you yourself would want to be treated. These requirements now appear in every job vacancy we advertise, whatever the position.

Working on their world

Every child has what we term a therapy entitlement. Most therapy sessions take place at the Centre, a very attractive three-floor building in the town centre, which comprises a spacious reception area, training room, office and therapy rooms, all pleasantly decorated and furnished, with comfortable sofas and chairs. We have very talented staff currently working with us: Tracy Watkins is an innovative Manager of Therapeutic Services and Lesley Wedderburn, our Receptionist, is the vital first, calm and reassuring point of contact for people. Mike Beard, our Senior Human Givens (HG) Practitioner, enjoys innovation and creativity, Sue Hannisch brings a wealth of experience and David Grist (also Deputy Manager at the Middle School) brings a youthful vitality and has just completed his HG Advanced Diploma. In addition, Mike Curtis is an experienced Education Psychologist currently undertaking his HG Diploma. Going to the Centre makes therapy something special and nearly all of the children look forward to it – the only exceptions are those whose previous experience of therapy was poor. That soon starts to change, as other young people offer effective advice and support based on their own experiences, and by our beginning individual therapeutic work in more casual settings and informal ways. Then those young people, too, start looking forward to their visits to the Centre. One of our HG therapists will routinely see every child at least once every four

The win-win situation

A HIGHLY effective way of giving our children more control over their lives without any risk to themselves – and stopping them bucking against 'authority' – is to introduce options. Every situation becomes win–win.

Twelve-year-old Angela was due to go home one weekend but, because her last visit had been problematic, her local authority social worker felt restrictions had to be introduced to ensure that this visit had a better chance of going well. The social worker came up to Fellside to discuss what we would do and agreed to the options that I suggested. These were, first, that Angela could go home from Friday until Sunday and that she would agree to a visit from a member of our staff on the Saturday. Secondly, she could choose to go home from Saturday until Sunday, and would speak to a staff member on the phone. Thirdly, she could choose not to go home at all.

Presented with these options, Angela considered carefully and chose the first, as I had expected she would. If, however, I had merely told her that she could go home on Friday and a staff member would visit her on Saturday, she would have objected volubly. This way, the choice was her own.

Fortunately, Angela now accepts that life doesn't always work out as planned and that, for this reason, we never make absolute promises. On this occasion, despite the social worker's recommendation, her team manager decided to veto Angela's returning on Friday. As I am writing this, I have a meeting scheduled with Angela for after lunch to tell her she cannot have her choice. I will say something to make her mindful of her growing behavioural skills, such as, "You've moved on a lot since I first met you, haven't you, Angela?" She will know at once that something is wrong, but an expectation about positive behaviour will also be activated. I'll give her the facts and I may briefly have to hold her back from lashing out. Then I will calm her because, until she is calm, it will be pointless to say any more. Although she will be very upset, to six weeks and, outside of that, as and when required – even three times a day, should there be need.

We also encourage our children's families to come for therapy sessions too (or, if impractical, Mike will visit them), as all of our good work can so quickly be undone if children return to a home environment where ways of relating have not changed. Nine-year-old Colin really started to move forward after we taught his family calming techniques and how to use positive language – giving instructions that described what they wanted, not what they didn't want, and, if Colin was pushing the boundaries, making comments on the lines of, "I notice that you don't find it as easy to do such-and-such [activity or instruction being struggled with] as you do to do such-and-such [activity or instruction successfully carried out]", enabling Colin to pattern match to success and apply those methods again.

We have now been open for five years and it is no exaggeration to say that every child has made huge strides in their development, self-understanding and ability to relate to others. Not a single child is any longer on drugs – which had included antidepressants, Ritalin,

we will be able to talk through it, because of all the hard work she has done so far.

I imagine she will cry and say, "It's unfair!" and I will agree with her. "Yes, at the moment, it does seem unfair, because you are making such great progress." At some point I will ask, "What do you want to do about it?" and allow her to wrestle some control back for herself. I won't expect her to go back to class, unless she chooses to. She might decide to phone to complain to her children's rights officer, or to help in the kitchen, or to go off by herself to tidy her room and have a cry. Most likely, she will arrange to go and help out at the local riding stables, where she is welcome any time. It will be difficult for her for a while but I am confident that she will be fine, and that there will not be a major setback. For her expectation from her work with us here is that external setbacks have temporary effects, if we make good use of our internal resources. ■

Fred Grist

melatonin and antiepileptics (one young person learned how to reduce his emotional arousal so successfully that he no longer needed medication to control seizures) – and Miles has had all his psychiatric labels removed. Even one lad, Dave, who made what he now realises was a poor decision (to leave our school, after which he fell back into crime and is now in a young offenders institution), has responded to a second chance. As part of our commitment to all our young people, we maintain contact after they leave. (They usually phone when they have good news or for advice and support – just like most children who leave home.) Intimidated by life on the main wing, Dave had chosen deliberately to use or threaten self-harming behaviour and behave in a 'mad' way, so that he would be moved to the comparative 'safety' of the hospital wing. Fred visited him there and the difference in his behaviour was so marked afterwards that, when Mike visited a few weeks later, he was invited to explain the human givens approach to the lead psychologist and all hospital and therapeutic staff.

We too have learned new things, since the start, about what works best in terms of equipping our young people for independent life. When Fred set up TheSPACE, the dream was always to provide *effective* **therapy**, **education** that *inspires and motivates* and *safe and secure* **residential care** to young children who badly need a new chance and a fresh start. But he found it took so long to get the healing process going. When he came across the human givens, he realised just how quickly healing could get started – and finished. The human givens approach has freed us up to move even beyond healing and do all the things as a community that we wanted to do. When you are part of a community, you need to contribute to that community. At the Centre in Kendal, there is the capacity to offer therapy to local people, which has had a phenomenal knock-on effect on staff recruitment at the schools. We are now known as the people who do things differently and who have a big effect, and local people want to work with us. We, in turn, feel we have been very much embraced by our own local community in this part of Kendal, known as Fellside. (Just the other day, a few of our younger children were invited to have tea with a neighbour, behaved themselves impeccably, had a great time and stayed there for two and a half hours!) So, when we opened our second school for younger children next door to the first, we decided to change our name from Woodlands to Fellside School, to deepen our links. We are all proud to be part of this community and the children truly feel now that they belong to it too.

* * * * *

Fred Grist is principal of TheSPACE, which he founded in 2000 along with senior administrator (and partner), Jane Leeson. He has nearly 30 years' teaching experience, the latter half spent teaching, or as a head, in residential special schools in the North West of England. For a number of years, he was Chair of the Cumbria Registration and Inspection Unit. He holds the Human Givens Advanced Diploma and is a Fellow of the Human Givens Institute.

Mike Beard became director of therapeutic services for TheSPACE, in September 2004. Mike continues to work in this role alongside development of emotional health-based work within mainstream education in the South West and nationally. He previously worked within Devon Local Education Authority, where his work focused on the development and delivery of training for health and education professionals working with vulnerable young children. He has also worked in the Criminal Justice Service and at a strategic level within the Connexions service. He holds the Human Givens Advanced Diploma and is a Fellow of the Human Givens Institute.

"Not ignorance, but ignorance of ignorance,
is the death of knowledge."

ALFRED NORTH WHITEHEAD

The road to recovery

Iain Caldwell, director of Hartlepool Mind, describes how the human givens approach to helping people in distress has had a huge impact on mental health services in Hartlepool.

HARTLEPOOL Mind is unrecognisable today from the organisation that it was when I started working for it five years ago. Like other Mind local associations (the voluntary groups around the country co-ordinated by the national mental health charity Mind), it offered 'tea and sympathy' to a hard core of 30 or 40 people with severe, enduring mental illness. People could attend 'drop-in' centres where usually they would spend their day drinking tea and coffee and smoking. Sometimes crafts or music or drama teachers would be brought in to offer them classes. Sometimes they would go on outings as a group. Users of the drop-in centre either turned up or they didn't. They never initiated activities of their own, and nothing noticeably ever changed. Today, however, Hartlepool Mind is a dynamic place, helping 500 people a year to discover or recover a meaningful and satisfying life.

When I joined the organisation, the chair and the manager of Hartlepool Mind had been attending MindFields College seminars for over a year and were itching to offer clients a completely different kind of service, based on the human givens approach of identifying and meeting needs, and best use of innate resources. Together they had put together a bid for money from the Government's "New Deal for Communities", a regeneration package for the most deprived areas in the country, and won the funds to start up a brand-new project – a mental health support network. The 'new deal' covers five areas: employment, housing, education, anti-social behaviour and crime, and health. Our funding was earmarked for the mental health component, but we planned to address them all. In the holistic human givens approach, successful treatment for depression may involve helping people build up the skills and confidence that will prepare them for employment or college, or enable them to challenge difficulties such as unsatisfactory housing. Divisions between 'areas' are just artificial and hampering.

Although we still carried on providing Hartlepool Mind's traditional information services to the public about mental health matters and sign-posting them, as appropriate, to other agencies, the drop-in centre had its doors finally and firmly closed. We concentrated our energies on tackling mental health issues in a non-stigmatising way that people would be drawn to instead of shy away from. We went to talk to residents' associations and community groups about stress management sessions and assertiveness training opportunities and set up advertising and poster campaigns. By this time, we had also won 'new deal' money for a complementary therapies project, so we organised joint complementary therapy and mental health 'days' in community centres, sports centres and church halls in our targeted area. Many people were curious enough to come along, and we invited them to attend our centre for a variety of complementary therapies (from acupuncture to Indian head massage) or to discuss practical or personal problems they were struggling with. Although Mind's remit is to work with people with complex mental health problems (eg voice hearing, paranoia, OCD, PTSD, etc) we opened up access to anyone who wanted it. As we know, countless people suffer lifetimes of stress and distress but aren't formally 'diagnosed' with a problem. Others who *are* diagnosed with chronic psychiatric conditions might well have got their lives back on track, had meaningful intervention been available to them at the outset.

Our centre is based in a one-storey building, which comprises offices, a relaxation room, training rooms and therapy rooms. The atmosphere is friendly, informal and relaxed and clients can always be assured of a warm welcome. We employ 11 full-time workers – a director, deputy manager, support network coordinator, people's access to health (PATH) co-ordinator, health/service navigator, recovery support workers and an administrator – and three part time clerical workers. All of them are required to attend a few MindFields College seminars, so that they understand the human givens approach – after all, it is the clerical staff who are the first to meet a patient. We also employ sessional workers, including therapists. Seven members of staff have the Human Givens Diploma and all have attended MindFields College workshops on practical ways to shift anxiety and depression, and deal with anger and addictions etc. All have to agree to meet the human givens' guidelines for effective counselling (see box overleaf).

Hartlepool Mind mental health philosophy

All staff work from one philosophy only. This philosophy integrates the human givens, continuum of mental health, client direct outcome focused theory (based on Dr Milton Erickson's work) and recovery approach. Recovery is defined as living well with or without symptoms.[1] We view recovery as a journey, a movement from the place a person is in to places that are better to be in, learning and making use of new skills and understandings along the way. This recovery approach is multi-dimensional (holistic), taking into account diet/nutrition, medication, environment, social network, culture, personal narrative and so forth.

This is a very different experience for clients who may previously have been shunted from one statutory service to another, where markedly different models are in use. The NHS, unsurprisingly, relies heavily on the medical model for mental health problems. According to this view, the disturbance or dysfunction is rooted in the body, and taking the right medication can cure or contain it. According to recent figures, 91.3 per cent of psychiatrists adhere to the medical model, as do 60.8 per cent of nurses and 47.5 per cent of social workers.[2] More social workers operate from the social model, emphasising the role of family and environment. Psychologists are increasingly convinced by the cognitive model – changing unhelpful thoughts helps eradicate inappropriate emotional reactions and undesired behavioural responses. Counsellors at GP surgeries, meanwhile, tend to favour the psychotherapeutic model, particularly the active listening, Rogerian kind.

In my experience, from talking and working with clients, these models provide convenient 'get out' clauses for professionals, when a particular approach doesn't appear to have anything more to offer. So the psychiatrist who reaches the limitations of the medical model refers on to the social worker, and so forth. Clients take away the perception that it is *they* who are falling short, not the model. And so they do the rounds of

Effective counselling

An effective counsellor or psychotherapist:

- understands depression and how to lift it;
- helps immediately with anxiety problems including trauma (post traumatic stress disorder) or other fear-related symptoms;
- is prepared to give advice if needed or asked for;
- will not use jargon or 'psychobabble';
- will not dwell unduly on the past;
- will be supportive when difficult feelings emerge, but will not encourage people to get emotional beyond the normal need to 'let go' of any bottled up problems;
- may assist individuals in developing social skills so that their needs for affection, friendship, pleasure, intimacy, connection to the wider community, etc, can be better fulfilled;
- will help people to draw on their own resources (which may prove greater than thought);
- will be considerate of the effects of counselling on the people close to the individual concerned;
- may teach deep relaxation;
- may help people think about their problems in a new and more empowering way;
- will use a wide range of techniques;
- may set things to be done between sessions;
- will take as few sessions as possible;
- will increase self-confidence and independence and make sure clients feel better after every consultation.

For more information, visit: www.hgi.org.uk/register/effectivecounselling.htm

the different agencies. The recovery approach, however, takes an over-all look at people's needs and asks how we can help, whatever that entails. It could mean addressing matters such as diet, sleep problems, emotional difficulties, troublesome neighbours, unhealthy housing or side effects of medication that are interfering with quality of life. In emergencies we act on the spot.

"What's the point in going on?"

When Ben walked in off the street, he was suicidal. A young man in his mid to late 20s, he had been 'on the sick' for some while because of depression. He rarely went out or communicated with anyone, and had spent the last few months brooding in his house. That in turn had led his relationship to break down and now he was homeless, because his wife had thrown him out. He arrived at our centre in a highly agitated state and kept saying, "What's the point in going on?" He clearly needed immediate help.

First I calmed him down by teaching him the 7/11 breathing technique (breathing in to the count of 7 and out to the count of 11, which auto-matically slows breathing and reduces panic and anxiety levels). By giving him a simple but powerful skill he could use straightaway, he was able to take back charge over a small piece of his life, which seemed to him to have spiralled out of control completely.

When eventually he was calm and able to engage with me, instead of being overloaded with emotion, we were able to talk about what was lacking in his life and what needs were not being met. Clearly, housing was at the top of the list and I contacted a housing officer and arranged to take Ben to see him later that day. We also ascertained that he could stay with a friend for a short while, until his housing needs were sorted out. This reduced his anxiety further.

In talking with him it became apparent that his depression had been triggered by stress at work and low confidence in himself. He blamed himself for not being up to the job and then for getting depressed over it and causing the end of his relationship. We didn't dwell on his past but he mentioned that he had always been passive and hated confrontation. I was able to explain to him how stress affects the body and emotional arousal leads to black and white thinking, when everything seems so much more hopeless than it really is. He responded positively to the information that depression wasn't a part of his character: it was something outside of himself that he wasn't to blame for but that he did need to take responsibility for shifting. One aspect of doing that, I told him, was through connection with people, instead of hiding away, as we need to be connected with others to be emotionally healthy. We covered this ground quite quickly but I didn't let him leave the centre until I was confident that he felt hopeful that change could occur and would return, as arranged, next day.

Over the next two weeks Ben had two sessions with a human givens therapist, during which she discovered that he found arguments with his wife excruciatingly painful and would withdraw rather than risk them – leaving a lot of unresolved issues within the relationship. The therapist used the rewind technique (see page 59) to take the traumatising emotion out of the memory of major rows, and guided imagery to help him visualise successfully engaging in discussion with his wife, to address differences in needs or opinions. He attended workshop sessions to learn new skills and strategies for managing stress, communicating in relationships, building self-esteem, being more assertive and countering depressive thinking by challenging negative thoughts, etc.

During those two weeks, Ben went to visit his wife and, as he put it, talked to her as he had never talked to her before. He also went to see his employers to say that he would like to come back to work. The end result was that, at the end of two weeks, when he was offered a flat by the housing department, he turned it down because he had returned to live with his wife. He was also back at work, with a new belief in his abilities and strengths, and felt positive about the future.

Getting back on track

I believe that part of our project's success is due to the fact that we are confident about what we offer. We say, "This isn't going to be long term. We'll probably see you a few times, and that will be all the help you need." This is surprising, to say the least, to some clients who have had many years of mental health service intervention.

One such person we worked with was Linda, a young woman in her mid-20s, who had been diagnosed as suffering from schizophrenia. She heard 15 different voices, all of people who appeared to be monitoring her life and giving her instructions on how she ought to be living it. At the time that we met her, she had been hospitalised a few times but was currently living with her young daughter at her mother's home. There she would be visited every week by a member of a dedicated psychosis team, attached to the local psychiatric hospital, and she was also receiving monthly visits from a cognitive-behaviour therapist. Linda's mother acted, in effect, as the mother of Linda's six-year-old daughter Molly, even taking her to and from school, and also took care of all of Linda's physical needs. Linda perceived her as controlling.

When Linda was brought in to see us, having been referred by the psychosis team, she had no expression on her face at all and was silent unless spoken to. Even then, there was at least a six-second delay before she replied, as if she was slowly processing what had been said. She was on quite heavy medication. The therapist to whom I assigned Linda's case quickly established that Linda's wish was to be able to be more of a mother to Molly. Instead, she spent most of her time alone, worrying about her shortcomings and listening to the voices, but unable to motivate herself to get up and do anything different. The therapist suggested that Linda set an alarm clock for 8am and put it across the other side of the room from her bed, so that she would have to get out of bed to turn it off. This Linda agreed to do. Once up, she was able to help her mother prepare Molly for school and make decisions about what Molly would wear or take in her packed lunched. Quite quickly she got into the routine of getting up early, making the packed lunch, taking Molly to school and collecting her as well.

Over a six-month period, she attended sessions with the human givens therapist (she abandoned the cognitive therapy) and also our workshops that show how to build social networks, starting with the importance of skills such as small talk and progressing through to the need for employable skills to gain entry to the world of work. Gradually, Linda established structure to her life. She responded to the suggestion that she might try a hobby to fill time constructively during the day, and started knitting. She soon decided that was unsatisfying and not what she wanted to spend her time doing, but in the process had become clearer about what she *did* want to do. She wanted to be able to take back full responsibility for Molly. She started taking driving lessons. On request, the council provided her with a home of her own for herself and Molly, and she busied herself with decorating it. The voices began to disappear, as she was too busy to hear them, and she was spending less and less time with her overly directive mother.

At the centre, we saw that the emotion had come back into her face. She would smile, show empathy and respond instantly to questions. Although we had never discussed her medication with her, she told us she had been taking six different antipsychotic and antidepressant drugs, and she had now reduced down to one. She said to us, in relief, "I feel like I've woken up." Linda's psychiatrist was so struck by the change in her that he started to refer us more clients, telling them that medication couldn't solve everything!

The mental health continuum

Hartlepool Mind has the philosophy that all mental wellbeing exists on a continuum, from good mental health to mental health problems. So everything from stress to psychosis is on the same continuum, which is fluid. Everyone moves up or down, according to what is happening in their lives at the time and how equipped they are to cope with it. (People in the general population, who have never had a psychiatric history, quite often also have psychotic experiences at some time.) Diagnoses of psychosis are of little value because someone who is diagnosed as manic depressive at one point is quite likely to be diagnosed as schizophrenic at another. It is far more helpful to work to normalise all human experience and support people through the dips. Tom McAlpine, a mental health specialist from Moodswings Network in Manchester, has been vital in assisting Hartlepool Mind in working with this philosophy.

The human givens idea that psychosis is reality processed through the dreaming brain[3] also makes a lot of sense to me and can be helpful to use in explanation when talking to people who are having experiences that they realise are out of 'sync' with those of people around them. One young woman named Sian described how, during a manic period, she had been watching a science fiction drama on television and became obsessed with the possibilities of time travel. She started talking excitedly about it to friends and family. "Part of me could see that people weren't as excited about the idea as I was and that what I was saying didn't make any sense to them. That part of me could see that I was being over the top and yet I just couldn't stop myself," she said. She felt comforted by the possibility that, when susceptible individuals are highly over-stressed, dreaming 'reality' can leak into waking reality. Just as in a dream we sometimes realise that something we are doing is odd or shouldn't be possible, yet can't help but carry on regardless, so, in an overwrought state, the same experience (but in reverse) can occur while awake. By discussing ways that she could lower her stress and thus reduce such occurrences, she ceased to feel so out of control and frightened.

When people experience ongoing emotionally painful or fear-inducing events that they have no control over, they often retreat into their imaginations to protect themselves. It makes sense to think that a pathological amount of such daydreaming (a REM state trance, just as dreaming is) could tip people into psychosis, if their emotional needs are not being met, as a counterbalance.

Nathan, a man in his late 20s, was brought to see me while he was still an inpatient at University Hospital in Hartlepool. (The staff often bring us patients, so that we can become acquainted with them before discharge, when our role is to help them settle back into the community.) Nathan shook constantly and was clearly extremely stressed. He had started to believe that people might be in his home or were coming to look for him, and gradually became able to 'see' these imagined people. This experience disturbed him very much but he hadn't told the nurses, as his parents, with whom he still lived, were putting him under pressure to make a swift recovery and return to work. He was also distressed by certain bodily changes, such as heavy sweating and having a metallic taste in his mouth. He had started to wonder if 'they' were poisoning his food. I discovered that he had debts that he couldn't pay off. He felt pressured by his parents to make something of himself and to do well at an office job he disliked.

Nathan was seeing a cognitive therapist, who was working to help him change negative thoughts and attitudes. It seemed to me, however, that what he needed most were coping skills and social connections in his life and, most immediately, to be able to make sense of the strange physical experiences he was having. During our session, he was quite clearly switching in and out of psychosis – he would frequently appear vacant and then suddenly 'come back' to us and begin talking again. I asked him if he was OK or if something else was happening and he tentatively revealed that he thought he could see things during the night, that people were maybe coming to get him. I asked about his hearing and he looked surprised and said, "I think I can hear people talking about me". When he was rational, I took the chance to tell him how stress affects the body – for instance, that metabolic changes may make the body overheat and sweat, and the rise in cortisol production may create a metallic taste in the mouth. It also wasn't so surprising that he had started to hallucinate pursuers, as his overriding concern was being pursued for debts he couldn't pay. When these experiences were normalised in this way, he ceased to fear them.

We talked about the need to reduce his stress and how this could be achieved. He said he wished he could have a small flat of his own in a pleasant area, away from his overbearing parents, where he could go to a gym and start to mix with people socially again. He agreed, at my suggestion, to tell nursing staff and family about his hallucinations and concerns, so that he no longer felt pressured to try to feign wellness and return to work. We also arranged an appointment for him with the local Citizen's Advice Bureau, so that they could help work out how to manage his debts.

The project team found Nathan a flat with warden-controlled access. Four months down the line, Nathan is managing for himself fairly well. By setting about meeting his needs and reducing the pressures that were causing him to flip into psychosis, we were able to keep him connected to the real world. The hallucinations disappeared very quickly. Without such intervention, they might well have intensified and left Nathan disabled for a lifetime.

Working with people who self harm

The practical needs-led approach we have adopted has given me more confidence in working with people who self harm. For very many people who self harm, emotional distress is a physical experience, and they may cut to prove to themselves that they feel nothing or to bring themselves back from a dissociated state. It is instinctive to want to encourage people to stop injuring themselves but usually counter-productive. When 22-year-old Chrissie came to the centre, she had been cutting herself for three years. It was difficult to build rapport with Chrissie. She found it hard to articulate her emotions or, more basically, even to distinguish between emotions, both in herself and others. To her, emotions felt either good or bad, and that was very limiting.

I at no time asked her to stop harming herself, telling her I respected that that was her private world. One of the centre workers took Chrissie to a café, where they sat and observed the expressions on customers' faces. If any people didn't look happy, Chrissie routinely catastrophised, imagining that they felt suicidal and might be thinking of going home to kill themselves.

So we agreed that she needed to develop an understanding that emotions could be subtle, and how to identify them so that she could relate more easily to others. We encouraged her to mix more with others, at adult education courses, skills development workshops and finally, by volunteering at the local hospital, so that she had more opportunities to engage with and talk to people, and see whether her reading of situations was accurate or needed adjustment. After four months, with the ongoing help of her recovery support worker, Chrissie had considerably enhanced her social skills, and had developed, and continues to maintain, her own social network, which enables her needs to be met. She has not cut herself for some time.

Mood management

Many of our clients join our mood management programme, which helps people to identify the symptoms that may precede a lurch into mania or a dip into depression. These vary from individual to individual, and may be very small. For instance, overly dry or greasy hair or dry or prickling skin or racing thoughts or not wanting to sleep may be a first sign of incipient mania for some. Identifying the tell-tale signs enables a person to nip the problem in the bud – to resist the urge to go partying or to drink or to start a relationship with a person met at the bus stop and to look at what is actually distressing them (such as a too pressured work schedule or a relationship difficulty), and doing something to re-dress the balance – such as taking time out or talking with their partner or a friend. Similarly, a first sign of oncoming depression might be a desire to withdraw from company or to stay late in bed. A strategy to deal with it might include deliberately socialising and keeping to scheduled activities and ensuring sufficient but not excess sleep.

Joined-up thinking

In five years, we have gone from strength to strength. Clients tell us they are extremely satisfied with our service, finding us warm, encouraging and optimistic. We ourselves are enthusiastic about going to work each day, and helping people to move on and make their lives work again. Other professionals who work with us on an occasional basis say they feel energised by our sessions. They love having the chance to work with us because it is so clear that we love what we do.

We now have additional funding, which enables us to cover more than the 'new deal' area of Hartlepool – fortunately, we still can cover all of that, too. The local hospitals, primary care trust and social service department all refer us a lot of clients. In fact, incredibly, we provide more therapy than any other local service, statutory or voluntary (for instance, GP practices, practitioner nurse services and counsellors, and the local health authority). We would like to be commissioned to provide a mental health service for the whole town, and now we don't think that is an idle dream. We have a joined-up approach and we have shown that it works.

* * * * *

Iain Caldwell is the director of Hartlepool Mind. He originally studied applied psychology at Liverpool John Moores University. He is a Trustee of Primhe and a Fellow of the Human Givens Institute. He has an assertive outreach nursing certificate from Teesside University and a postgraduate certificate of education from Sunderland University. He has also studied various therapy skills gaining a certificate in hypnosis and the Human Givens Diploma. Iain has worked variously in outreach, supporting people discharged from a special hospital, and as an advocate and mentor.

It's what's right with you that fixes what's wrong

*Human givens therapist **Chris Dyas** vividly describes how he teaches troubled children to be their own therapists.*

M EG looked at me with eyes that reminded me of the rabbit I had narrowly avoided on the road when I was driving into work that morning. "Are you psychic?" she asked. I laughed. "No, it's just that you're human, and most humans react the same way when bad things happen…"

Meg and I were talking for the first time. She is 14 and her story is depressingly familiar to me. She was sexually abused by her stepfather for a number of years. When she finally disclosed what had been going on, the family fell apart. Her stepfather was charged and bailed away from the locality, but had been regularly seen by the rest of the family driving around the neighbourhood during the 18 months it took for the trial eventually to take place. Meg had been haunted by the prospect that he was plotting revenge against her and had become a virtual recluse during the pre-trial period. She was experiencing nightmares and flashbacks, but hadn't told anyone because she was afraid that they would think that she was mad. Meg's mother had never openly blamed Meg for what had happened, but Meg felt guilty all the same for the depression that had overtaken her mum in the wake of it. All of this had taken its toll on Meg's school performance and ability to make and keep friends. She was feeling isolated and demoralised.

Many children who have suffered prolonged abusive life experiences can end up 'behind the pack' when it comes to social skills. These young people have often missed out on the opportunity to develop these naturally as part of a daily unconscious interaction with a generally positive environment. Even those whose negative experiences are comparatively short lived can lose confidence and feel socially de-skilled. Both groups of youngsters can therefore benefit from an opportunity to learn or relearn these skills consciously (as they would learn a second language), as part of a holistic package of therapy. This does not have to take very long, however, since I have found that the children I work with can quickly understand and make use of psychological 'facts' and techniques – provided these are explained in plain language, using appropriate metaphors, and demonstrated either in front of them or by reflecting their own experience.

Even small children can understand profound psychological ideas. My own experience is evidence of this. I was in no way an exceptional kid in school. However, when I was nine years old, I went into my local bookshop with my pocket money and I decided to have a go at reading *The Psychology of Interpersonal Behaviour* by Michael Argyll. I have to confess that the only reason I picked up Argyll's book in the first place is because it was on a low shelf near some *Star Trek* books. Now, *Star Trek* was a HUGE influence on my early years – the character of Spock in particular. The fascination of Spock was that he was not emotionless as many suppose, but highly disciplined. Gene Roddenberry's concept was that the Vulcan race became the way they were because they knew that they would destroy themselves if they did not find a way to control the expression of their emotions. Spock continually demonstrated that thinking was easier and clearer if one was able to remain calm, despite arousing circumstances. I loved the idea that I, too, could eventually learn to control the way my mind worked.

I first saw *Star Trek* when I was seven. The sheer cleverness of the metaphors and story-arcs in it made me ask quite profound questions as a youngster about what it meant to be human, how the world actually works – and how I could get to be a cool spaceman too. Through *Star Trek*, my mind linked science and adventure together, and probably the only reason I am a therapist now is because a helpful teacher told me that my maths wasn't good enough for me to qualify as an astronaut.

I have no idea how much I actually understood of Argyll's book. I was a good way through it before my teacher kindly pointed out that the book was too old for me, and so I stopped reading it. Fortunately, however, I managed to read enough to absorb the idea of Maslow's 'hierarchy of needs'. Like the metaphors in *Star Trek*, once an idea like the hierarchy of needs locks itself into the mind it opens the door to other levels of perception. I began to see the hierarchy of needs everywhere – especially in my parents. This gave me something of an edge in predicting important things like the best time to ask for extra pocket money! A few months later, I picked up a copy of De Bono's *Lateral Thinking* – but this time didn't tell any grown ups because I knew what they would say. Again, the effect was practical in that I was able to write far more creative essays (and write them faster, an important skill to a boy who considered homework to be a form of child abuse). And so began what has become a lifelong interest in practical psychology.

Patterns in the brain

"Would it help if I explained what has probably been going on in your head?" I asked. Meg nodded. I have a large whiteboard on the wall of the room where I work, and I picked up a set of laminated pictures and began to stick them one by one onto it as I spoke. "What's this, Meg?" "It's a rabbit." "How do you know?" She briefly looked puzzled and then said, "Because it looks like one." "Would you agree that the only reason you know this is because you've seen something like it before and someone told you that the right word for something shaped like that is 'rabbit'?" Meg agreed, with an expression that hinted that she was beginning to feel relieved that she wasn't the maddest person in the room after all.

"Bugs Bunny!" laughed Meg in response to the next picture I put up. "Yep, not just any rabbit, but a *particular* rabbit." I now put up a picture of a pink silhouette that had a rabbit-shaped outline. "You can even see a rabbit in this one because your mind is able to match the shape to the one you keep in your brain for recognising rabbits with. OK, what do you make of this next one?" Meg looked hard: "It's a rabbit … no it's a duck … er – it's a rabbit *and* a duck." "That's right," I said. "Your brain can match the shape to its pattern for rabbits, but it can also match it to the one it keeps for recognising ducks. Now, notice that you can't see both at the same time. You only see one or the other – but you can choose which one to see. So in this situation you are actually *deciding* what to see."

Meg's expression had now changed to one of amused curiosity. My next picture had her stumped. "I don't know what that is. It's just blobs," she said, as she screwed up her eyes. "What happens to the picture if I say 'cow'?" "Oh yeah! It's a cow!" "OK," I replied, "now try and *not* see the cow." Meg shook her head. "I can't. It's a cow." "So," I continued, "to begin with, your brain couldn't find a pattern to match to the picture and so you literally couldn't see anything. But when I gave it a hint as to what to try, your brain successfully made a match to the pattern it uses to recognise cows with, and now won't give it up. This next picture is where I get to the point…"

I put up a picture that at first glance appears to be a hideous grinning skull, but on closer inspection becomes a scene from a Victorian fancy-dress party. The skull shape is only inferred from what is basically an accidental arrangement of the people and objects in the scene. "My guess, Meg, is that this is what has been going on in your brain. Frightening things happened to you and your brain has recorded them as patterns it can use to spot if anything like it is going to happen again. But, it might have been doing its job a bit too well and matching these patterns to things that are not dangerous at all. The trouble is that the feelings that come up for you then are part of the pattern that has been matched inside your brain – not what is actually there outside you. Now, your brain does this pattern matching thing with the stuff you hear as well…"

Instructive words

I reached underneath the coffee table and pulled out a small video play-back machine. "Just watch this for a couple of minutes," I said, as I put in a video of Derren Brown's TV show where he talks to different people on a train in the London Underground. The video shows him using suggestion and double meanings to get the poor unsuspecting travellers temporarily to forget where they are headed. "How did he do that?" asked Meg.

I took the pictures down from the whiteboard and wrote out one of the sentences that Derren had spoken and showed how it could mean two things: one sounded like an innocent question about the traveller's destination, but the other was an instruction to stop thinking about the destination.

"So, Derren asks the man which stop he's getting off at – meaning which station – then talks a little about how easy it is to forget things, then asks the man again 'So what *stop, thinking about it now,* what stop are you getting off at?' What happens is that the man's brain heard both meanings, but went with the one that had an instruction in it – 'stop thinking about it now'." We watched a couple more examples of him using more sophisticated versions of this and Meg rapidly began to recognise the suggestions as they were being said. "If your brain finds an instruction or a suggestion about what to do next, in what you are listening to, there is a part of your brain that feels obliged to have a go at it," I told her.

Once the video was over, I pulled everything together, saying, "Imagine this … you are travelling along in a car. Suddenly the driver slams the brakes on because she's seen a body lying in the street. A fraction of a second later she starts to laugh and says, 'Who left that bin sack in the middle of the road?' Or you find that you no longer want to eat your dinner at school because someone is telling you about the time they threw up on that table. Or you are walking across the living room with a cup of tea. Someone says, 'Don't spill your drink!' Over it goes, as if it had a mind of its own! The driver of the car was probably hot and shaky even though there was no real body in the street. There was no real sick on the table. You tried your best not to spill the drink – but you did anyway. Why? The answer is in the way your brain sorts out what you see, hear, smell, touch and taste *before* you are able to start thinking about it. When you *do* get to think about it, your mind has already linked what's in front of you to something that has happened before, even if that something turns out not to be appropriate. This only takes a fraction of a second – but a lot can happen in that time."

Meg and I talked about times when all of these things had happened to both of us, in one form or another. By the end of the hour we had agreed that we should do something about the way her mind was 'seeing skulls' and maybe acting on accidental instructions embedded in the things people around her were saying. The man who had abused Meg used to drive a blue car and Meg described feeling a stab of panic at the sight of all blue cars as a result. She also realised that she felt particularly bad when her mum tried to comfort her by saying something like

"There's no need to *feel scared of him coming to get you*" and decided she would explain what was happening to her mum, who could then be careful to use different language. We planned to meet again in a week's time to use the rewind technique[1] (a quick, non-intrusive means of resolving trauma, see page 59) to stop the terrifying intrusive memories and nightmares she was experiencing. We would then look at how she could begin to rebuild a set of friends, catch up on her school work, and keep herself realistically safe whilst becoming confident about being out and about in her locality.

Learning the art of conversation

The rewind technique in the following session worked well. Meg reported that the nightmares and flashbacks had stopped and that she felt much better. She was keen to move on to how she could build up a set of friends again, because the reduction in her fear of going out was replaced by a keen sense of wanting meaningful contact with other youngsters. I introduced the following method to her by stressing how important it was that she understood the principle at the heart of friendship: namely, "I like you because you make me like myself". I then talked about how this means that it is important to work at helping the other person to relax, and described the following method for initiating and keeping up a mutually enjoyable conversation:

1. *Copy the other person's body language to create a 'mirror image';*

2. *Ask three questions – but no more than this until you have done the next two things;*

3. *Find something from what you have just learned to pay a subtle and relevant compliment about;*

4. *Find something in what you have found out to agree with;*

5. *Repeat until the conversation takes on a life of its own.*

Teaching young people to follow this formula has the effect of taking their attention away from worrying about "What do I say next?" and "How well am I doing?" The idea is that the formula acts to lower their emotional arousal and enables them to find areas of common ground in order to create a sense of connection and understanding. The process automatically makes them appear more attractive to the person they are talking to, and confidence builds as they receive positive feedback in return. Meg and I took it in turns to run through the sequence until she felt that she could remember how to do it, and I then led her through a guided imagery exercise, where she vividly imagined successfully using the method to begin friendships with certain girls she liked at school. Before she left, I gave her a small laminated pocket card with a summary of the method on it.

Handling insults

When Meg came back to see me again she reported that the conversation skills method had worked, but had led to some unexpected unpleasantness from a girl who, we guessed, was feeling jealous that Meg was trying to muscle in on her friendship group. Despite this, Meg wanted to win her over. I introduced Meg to the idea of 'popping' insults. This involves understanding that a comment is only an insult if it is untrue (or mostly untrue – otherwise it is simply a fact). The power of an insult is in its ability to force the target to react angrily and attempt to prove it wrong. Therefore, the most effective ways of turning the tables on someone using insults are:

1. *Agreeing with the insult (without believing it on the inside);*

2. *Agreeing with the insult and escalating its severity (for example "Yes, you're right, and what's more I'm the biggest * * * * * in the whole school");*

3. *Expressing feelings using a tone of voice that isn't congruent with what is being said (for example "What you just said has wounded me deeply" in a flat bored tone);*

4. *Expressing feelings in an exaggerated, theatrical way (for example "What you just said has wounded me deeply," whilst staggering about clutching chest);*

5. *Thanking the insulter for the insult and writing it down in front of them to add to the collection – murmuring that it's not the best one but it will do for now;*

6. *Complaining that the insult is not good enough and that you can think of much worse things to be called (and giving examples).*

The aim of each of these tactics is to sidestep the insult and to communicate the message that insults are futile. I linked these options to George Thompson's ideas about tactical communication, which he calls 'verbal judo'.[2] Thompson is a consultant to many American police forces, and has developed tried and tested ways of using language that both keep us calm and prompt voluntary cooperation with someone we may be experiencing difficulties with. In essence, this boils down to using positively phrased language (ie telling the other person what you want them to do, rather than what you don't want them to do). We went over the Derren Brown tape again and I showed Meg how she could also use subtle suggestion to gently distract and redirect an annoying person without insulting them or escalating the situation into a battle of wills. One solution she liked was to plant suggestions in the other person's mind while appearing to be talking about herself. For example, "I really need to *go away now* because I want to *calm down* and *find something better to do*. I expect *you, like me,* would agree this is the best way to *end this.*"

The other person is compelled to pattern match to the embedded instructions and experience an impulse to do likewise. We took turns practising both insulting and 'popping' each other (with much hilarity) and then I used guided imagery to give Meg an opportunity to rehearse responding to the girl in question in a positive and controlled way. I backed this up with another pocket card that she could refer to, if she needed.

Another young person I worked with on similar issues took the pocket card idea further. She was anxious that she would forget the method in the heat of the moment. The solution we found was to punch a hole in one end of the card so that she could hang it loosely around her neck when she went to school. On the blank side of the card she stuck a piece of scratchy Velcro. The card made its presence known to her continually, by tickling and itching – causing her to touch it regularly through the day and therefore to stay reminded and ready to use the advice on it. She did not have to look at the card for this to work.

Saying no

Andy is a 16-year-old young man who has been in care since he was nine years old. Although he knew that it was impossible for him to live with his mum because of her difficulties with alcohol and drugs, he had not wanted to be parted from her. Despite living half the country away and seeing her only on an infrequent basis, Andy worried about her. This worry was at its worst at bedtime and he was managing just two or three hours of sleep most nights. He was also running into trouble with his carers for being, as he put it, "easily led" by his friends. We agreed that, given his experiences of losing touch with people who were important to him, it wasn't surprising that he didn't want to risk losing anyone else by saying no to them.

During the course of our conversation, I described to Andy how we can be manipulated into a 'one-down' position by other people when they are able to bring up in us feelings of guilt or fear or uncertainty. "When we feel one-down in this way, it is easier for us to feel that we have to go along with what other people want us to do, because they seem more powerful. The trouble is that your feelings are 'switched on' before you start thinking. There are basically six feelings and humans have had them for a very long time – from way before the time when we had finally come up with weapons to stop lions eating us on a regular basis. There's anger, fear, sadness, guilt, excitement and love. Anger is a feeling designed to make you act quickly to defend yourself (or someone you love) as fast as possible by *fighting*, and fear is a feeling designed to make you act quickly to defend yourself (or someone you love) as fast as possible by *running away*. Sadness is a feeling designed to keep you safe while you get over losing someone or something you loved, because getting over these kinds of things can take a lot of thinking about and you may not be as alert about the dangers around you as you would be normally. So, sad feelings make you want to stay at home and not do very much – increasing the chances of your staying alive until you feel better again. Guilt is a feeling designed to put you off making the same mistake twice (especially if someone else got hurt or upset by what you did). Excitement is a feeling that makes you want to do whatever it is you are doing again, and therefore motivates you to learn things. Love is a feeling that makes us know that we belong to each other and that we will look after each other *because we want to*.

"Your feelings are part of your 'survival kit'. They are designed to keep you alive. They are not necessarily concerned about whether or not you are happy though. Strong feelings tend to make it hard to think clearly. For instance, when you are angry, it is hard to see the other person's point of view and, when you are excited, it is hard to know when 'enough is enough'. The key to dealing with unwanted or pointless feelings is to learn how to calm down quickly."

Andy liked the idea of using guided imagery to help him to become calm at night and restore his sleep pattern. We agreed to meet again, once he was feeling properly rested and stronger, and look at devising a strategy for being able to say no to his friends in such a way that he would not risk losing them. This would include particular skills that he could use to raise his own awareness of where he was vulnerable to manipulation and tactics he could use to guard against this.

Before he left, I talked Andy through a visualisation called 'the sponge' which involved imagining a bath sponge inside his head that soaked up all of his fears and concerns so that he was free to feel calm, relaxed and untroubled. I got him to see its colour, smell its fragrance and feel its texture so that a vivid image was created. I then talked him through moving the sponge through the whole of his body, finally shrinking away to nothing in his left foot – having taken all the stress and tension with it. Whilst he was in the highly relaxed state that this exercise created, I suggested that he could 'sponge' for himself anytime he needed to, and I led him to imagine successfully using the exercise that night and waking up fresh and strong in the morning.

Andy came back the following week and reported that he was sleeping much better, not worrying about his family so much, and taking a keener interest in his appearance. "And I keep waking up with a strong desire to have a shower," he said. It seems the 'sponge' was having an unexpected bonus effect!

Creating 'cool'

Andy placed a lot of importance upon being 'cool'. He liked my idea that he might become the coolest member of his group, because, if he were the coolest, he would not feel the need to be 'led' anywhere – instead he would be doing the leading and his mates would want to follow.

"Have you noticed that the coolest people do not seem to have to put any effort into it?" I asked. "Yeah, it's like people just want to be with them," agreed Andy. "I think this is because there is a big difference between *attracting* attention and *seeking* attention," I went on. "Do you know the old story about the Sun and the North Wind having a bet about which one of them could get some guy to take his coat off? Well, the North Wind had a go and blew his hardest, but the guy just clung to his coat with all his strength. But all the Sun had to do was shine and the guy took off his coat because he was too hot. Truly 'cool' people shine a kind of calm control that everyone else secretly wants, and so they find it attractive."

I introduced Andy to a social skills method I've named 'The Art of Being Cool and Attractive,' designed to help young people develop an approach to others that will attract the right amount of the right kind of positive attention. The 'art' is contained in ten 'laws':

1. *Learn to do with less attention than you would like* <u>*at the moment*</u>*;*

2. *Do not compete with other people for attention;*

3. *Say less than is necessary;*

4. *Learn to behave well from those who don't know how to;*

5. *Do not 'freeload' or overstay your welcome;*

6. *Never whine;*

7. *Appear unhurried;*

8. *Be different – but not too different;*

9. *Appear not to want things you cannot have;*

10. *Exercise courtesy and tact at all times.*

Catching up at school again

Meg came for what was to be her final meeting with me, because she was well on her way to functioning in the world in the way she wanted to. However, she was now acutely conscious that she was a long way behind where she wanted to be academically, and she was finding it a struggle to concentrate in class – mostly because she was focused more upon being worried than upon what the teachers were saying.

I taught Meg a way of developing her memory skills. According to Dr John Ratey, associate clinical professor of psychiatry at Harvard Medical School, "The brain assembles perceptions by the simultaneous interaction of whole concepts, whole images. Rather than using the predictive logic of a microchip, the brain is an analog processor, meaning, essentially, that it works by analogy and metaphor. It relates whole concepts to one another and looks for similarities, differences, or relationships between them. It does not assemble thoughts and feelings from bits of data."[3]

The exercise I taught Meg was designed to be highly entertaining, to provide a vivid demonstration of how good everyone's memory can actually be – provided the information is put into it in the right way – and to show how easy it is to memorise even 'dull' information. The exercise involved learning to visualise a set of 10 objects that can be easily associated with a number from 1 to 10 (for example the number two was represented by a coin with two sides). These can then be connected to other objects or 'facts' in humorous or bizarre ways to create highly memorable pictures or mini-stories – the weirder, the better! I quite often incorporate such practical learning skills into sessions, as they frequently promote other 'therapeutic' outcomes and a generally increased learning ability. This kind of method for enhancing memory is increasingly widely taught, along with techniques such as mind mapping,[4] as they have been found to be aligned with how the brain works best. My aim with Meg was to show her a reason to feel optimistic about her potential at school and to boost her self-esteem. It worked.

Professor Martin Seligman has long stressed the need to protect the future mental health of our children by cultivating optimism. Social skills training of the kind sketched in this article is aimed at doing this by proving the young person's own power to them – in other words, promoting an optimism based on self-efficacy. At the heart of this kind of work with young people is a key idea. It is not simply to undo the effects of an unhappy past, or to help them feel better, or to stop them from behaving in an inconvenient, self-defeating way. As Aldous Huxley once said, "There is nothing wrong with you that what's right with you cannot fix." To put it simply, the idea is to instil in them the knowledge, backed up by the skills, that "It's what's right with you that fixes what's wrong".

* * * * *

Chris Dyas is a human givens therapist working for a children's charity, based in Newcastle under Lyme, which provides help for children who have suffered severe abuse, as well as consultation and support for their parents and carers. He has over 18 years experience working in the social care field. He also provides training workshops in understanding and communicating with traumatised children, as part of the local authorities' child protection training programme for professionals. He has been applying the human givens approach to his work for the past eight years.

"Given the choice between changing one's mind and proving that there is no need to do so, almost everyone gets busy on the proof."

JOHN KENNETH GALBRAITH

Good choices: autism and the human givens

*Headteacher **Angela Austin** describes how the human givens approach has informed her work to create an emotionally safe place where children with autism can learn.*

IN my career teaching children with special needs, I have learned many ways to work with children with autism and have devised many methods of my own. I was thrilled, however, to come across the human givens concept of needs and tools. Its emphasis on identifying and helping to meet needs, and building on innate resources in the process, has given me and my staff a new framework through which to view what we are trying to do. It also reinforces what we are doing by showing why it works. In short, it has created a cohesion to our work and helped us develop a structure to our thinking, rather than merely applying helpful theories and techniques.

Hillingdon Manor School, where I am headteacher, is an independent special school for children aged between three and a half and 19 years of age. Our pupils are variously diagnosed with Asperger's syndrome, high functioning autism or semantic pragmatic disorder. Some children may have a diagnosis of pathological demand avoidance, which means that the focus of their way of being is to resist the demands of everyday life. This can present as panic attacks, which occur as tantrums whenever they are asked to do something.

The school was established in 1999 by parents concerned by the lack of resources for school-age children at the more able end of the autistic spectrum. Local authorities funded the places for the 51 children we were then able to take. In September 2003, we split into two, with a 'senior school' for children aged 13 plus, and were able to take 70 children.

While very many of our children are capable of making considerable progress in school, they demonstrate a wide range of challenging behaviours, arising from the 'triad of impairments' identified by autism expert Lorna Wing (see panel opposite). As a result, many have been excluded from mainstream schools. Children with autism don't understand 'the rules' of engagement unless these are made absolutely explicit, so they almost always find themselves ending up in the wrong. No one likes to be on the receiving end of criticism or blame but children with autism are especially sensitive to it, and so become highly frustrated and emotional about little upsets. Once they are overwhelmed by their emotions, of course, their rational minds can't function and they cannot learn.

People with autism lack a developed sense of self. They also lack the ability to use language to relate to other people or to solve problems, by themselves or with other people. For all human beings, language and communication is key for our connecting with the world and, for most of us, the wheels of our daily lives are oiled by shared perceptions and agreements about the meaning of words at a sophisticated level. Children with autism, however, struggle with language at quite a fundamental level. Without a shared understanding of the meaning of words and how they map to names, actions, concepts and emotions, there is no real way to get needs met, understand the world and relate to others.

The concept of choice

I saw this very starkly in the early days of our school. Tina, an 11-year-old girl, was brought into my office, kicking, spitting, biting, swearing and lashing out at anyone who came too close. We calmed her down by using the holding and calming relaxation techniques we teach everyday. When she was calm and able to listen and process information, I wrote on a flipchart what we describe as the three causes of upset:

A: *you expect something to happen and it does not*
B: *you want to do something and someone or something stops you*
C: *you want to say something and you do not know how to say it.*

Then I asked Tina which of these three upset her most. This supposedly under-achieving girl instantly got up and pointed to B. "And what do you choose to do when you want to do something and someone or something stops you?" I asked her. "Bite and spit," she replied. I showed her a smiley face and a sad face and asked, "And how does that make you feel?" She pointed to the sad face. "And how does it make other people feel?" She pointed to the sad face again. "So did that work for you?" "No." "That's really good thinking, Tina. So what could you choose to do that would work?" And Tina looked completely perplexed. She didn't know what she could choose to do. She didn't understand the concept of choice. And, because she lacked the necessary language to map this concept to her neocortex, she couldn't make that essential switch from her emotional brain to her rational brain.

If you can't make a choice, you have no sense of autonomy or control. Biting and spitting and swearing only give apparent, in the

Wing's triad of impairments

1. **Social interaction:** reluctance to involve themselves with others; socially inappropriate behaviour; one-sided interaction showing seeming unawareness of the needs of others in a social context; lack of ability to understand the intention of others; often display of self-stimulating and repetitive behaviour; lack concept of self and others;

2. **Language and communication:** difficulties in verbal and non-verbal communication, understanding meaning, and decoding facial expression and body language; inability to take turns; lack of meaningful eye contact;

3. **Rigidity in thought, behaviour and imagination:** limited capacity for creative and imaginative thought; struggle to understand and express feelings and emotional responses; inability to read emotion in others; preoccupation with 'sameness' and difficulties in making change; inability to learn successfully from mistakes or trial and error; literal use of language (eg flummoxed by "it's raining cats and dogs"); inability to differentiate between fantasy and reality.

moment, control. It does not last. The price is loss of self esteem or, as Tina saw it, sadness. With no autonomy and no sense of personal control, a vital human need, essential for emotional health, remains unmet. For children with autism have just the same needs as any other human.

What works

I have learned that to forgive and let go is one of the most powerful tools that human beings possess; and that holding on to things really stops us from doing what we want to do in life. But letting go is a choice, and has to be seen as such. So, at Hillingdon Manor School, rather than blaming children or telling them off, we have created an environment where choices, and their consequences, are presented clearly at all times, in a meaningful way, so that children can experience for themselves what works and what doesn't work for them and others. In an environment where upsets between children or between children and staff can be cleared up quickly, enabling them to move on, children have the emotional space to develop cognitively and to enable their needs to be met.

Our good behaviour policy sets out how we maintain clear rules and boundaries through which pupils can, over time, learn to develop thought processes about what works in the world, and the behaviours that promote that end. Teaching and learning support staff receive training in the method. Training is ongoing and everyone supports everyone else in role modelling what works.

Desirable behaviours are modelled so that they can be clearly identified: good sitting, good listening, good speaking, good working, good walking, good waiting, good sharing, and so forth. In the interests of multi-sensory learning, which children with autism respond to best, choices are made tangible to pupils through the use of symbols on choice boards, and are also presented on the palms of the hands. "Karen," says the staff member in an assertive, neutral tone, "You choose to do good sitting and do your work [staff member points at left palm], and you can go out to play with the other children at lunchtime. Or you can choose to not do your work [staff member points at right palm], and spend your lunch break in Angela's office doing the work." Clearly the first choice is educationally, socially and/or physically advantageous to the pupil, and has an individually positive outcome. The other choice is unacceptable educationally, socially and/or physically, and has an outcome less desirable to the pupil. It is also explained to children that not choosing means that they are choosing the less desirable option.

When children make a choice that is not in their best interest, involving loss of playtime or special rewards, they are asked afterwards, "Did that work for you?" This reinforces our basic premise that there is no right or wrong, only what works and doesn't work. It encourages good behaviour from an objective, non-judgemental standpoint, giving children the space to develop their own understanding of right and wrong. When children who have made an undesirable choice have reflected on their behaviour and the fact that it didn't work, staff ask, "What would have worked?"

Even lunchtime assistants and supply staff are given training in the language to be used when offering choices, because the language should never vary. Research shows that pupils with language disorder have to have things repeated to them a thousand times before they fully understand them and can use them. Given the social complexity of autism, consistency and repetition of language and approach are even more crucial – however long it takes.

One boy, at the end of a day, swore, spat and pulled his trousers down. I told him that he could not get on the school bus to go home because he was not calm and that it was dangerous to behave that way on the bus. He carried on, not believing for a moment that I would keep my word, and yelled in disbelief and frustration when he saw the bus leave without him. I let his mother know that I would bring him home later and proceeded to sit it out. For two and a half hours he screamed and screamed. When he finally chose to stop, I took him home and it was a quiet, well-behaved little boy whom his mother greeted. He has never performed in that way again: he knows now that consequences are carried out.

Colin's video

We also train parents in the use of choice and consequences, so that they can support our work at home. One 10-year-old boy, Colin, loves more than anything to watch a particular video at home. He can watch it for hours on end without becoming in the least bit bored with it. Because his behaviour both at school and at home has been very challenging, we incorporated his love of the video into a behaviour plan for him. For Colin the choice is, "Do 'good choosing' [ie choose appropriate behaviours] at school and you'll take home the folder with a picture on it of a smiling mum and dad. Then they'll know that you can watch the video." But if he does 'not-good choosing' (we never use the word 'bad'), he takes home the folder with the picture on it of his mum and dad looking sad, and he doesn't get to watch the video. His behaviour transformed instantly. Now there is a structure and a consequence (visually reinforced), and that has provided him with security.

One day he forgot himself and hit his support worker, Debbie, in the face because he was frustrated with himself for knocking his game over. Debbie didn't say, "How dare you, bad boy!" and put him in the wrong. She said, "Oh, Colin! Sad face!" And Colin instantly put his arms down by his side and wailed, "Oh, no sad face!" He knew at once that he had done something that did not work for him and that he would lose video privileges. He apologised to Debbie, who praised him at once for good calming down after his upset, but the video remained off limits for that day.

Consistency, we believe, is everything. Every child has a pastoral support plan that identifies specific behaviour that doesn't work for that child, and the strategies devised to deal with it. A strategy is spelt out in exact words, which all staff are asked to adhere to. Currently, we are trying to deter 10-year-old Neil from going up to people and giving them a kiss or cuddle without asking, as this will clearly be unacceptable behaviour when he is older. All staff have been requested to be consistent in their language when Neil approaches for a kiss or cuddle, saying, "Neil, stop. You have to ask me for a kiss/hug". When Neil has asked appropriately, the female response is either, "I don't want a kiss/hug now, thank you" or "No kiss/hug, thank you. I will hold your hand." Male staff respond with, "I don't want a kiss/hug, thank you, but you can shake my hand".

Working in this way is not necessarily comfortable for staff. After all, it is quite confronting to have to make an agreement about how you communicate, which cannot be deviated from – especially when some-times empathy urges you to act otherwise. For instance, someone might want to let a child off for bad behaviour at the start of the day, because the child was upset by something beyond their control that had hap-pened at home. But that does not fit with our approach. We all love the children but we don't think that kind of soft-heartedness helps them. Our role is to support them in what works, so that they can better navigate their way through later life. So we say, for instance, "Steven, I'm very sorry that your auntie has been taken into hospital. And these are the rules while you are at school. You can choose to do your work and go out to play at playtime or …" etc. Staff who cannot work with such an approach do not stay with us, but those who have chosen to stay or to join us are enthusiastic supporters. They are in the majority.

Calming down

One of the tenets of the human givens approach that has resonated strongly with us is that emotional arousal prevents us from thinking straight. We cannot reason or learn if we are angry, upset or frightened. Children who become very upset and physically challenging, and there-fore a danger to their own and others' health and safety, require hold-ing for well being, until they can become calm and relaxed again. Any pupil whose behaviour escalates suddenly to a crisis point is held according to the Holding for Well Being Policy, which is physical restraint. Nothing is said to the child after they have been told they will be held until they have calmed down and relaxed, as, while anxiety and fear levels are very high, little or no verbal information can be pro-cessed. Similarly, if a child screams abuse, it is more effective to have no verbal interaction until staff feel the crisis has passed and the child is calm enough to be able to listen. After the upset, children are always helped to identify its cause.

Teaching children with autism to calm *themselves* down provides them with a very powerful tool for getting themselves back on track when emotion threatens to swamp them. We teach relaxation every day as part of the curriculum. Children are also taught yoga breathing exer-cises and can have a hand or foot massage if they want it. Recently, as a result of attending seminars on the human givens approach, we have introduced guided visualisation as a part of our relaxation repertoire. This gives children ways to deal with an inappropriate emotion such as excessive anger. ("Imagine a red ball in your hand that is hard and spiky to touch. Squeeze it as tight as you can and then let go, and imagine it has become a golden star that showers you with light".) We also encourage them to imagine themselves in a safe place where they like being, doing an activity they enjoy. This has the dual benefit of inducing relaxation and increasing choice. A child can think, "I feel upset but I can choose to shut my eyes and think of something I like doing, and let the upset go away".

Needs being met

We know, from the change in the children since they have been at the school, that our methods are working. Looking at them from the human givens perspective, we can now see exactly why they do, and how we can make them even more effective.

One of our basic needs is the need for security. For children with autism, unless everything is made crystal clear, there is no security. They walk on shifting sands, struggling to understand why circumstances make actions that were acceptable at one time unacceptable at another. By using language in a way that provides structure and consistency, children can be helped to feel safe because they have clarity.

Children with autism lack an inbuilt mechanism for giving and receiving attention. This has to be put in place for them, by means of modelling, constant repetition – "look at me" – and not making them wrong. They need to be taught appropriate ways to respond when, for instance, people have been given bad news. Giving and receiving attention is part of our social skills repertoire. Without social skills, it is also impossible to have true autonomy or control, or true emotional connection with others. We use language to strengthen emotional literacy: "What happened that upset you? What did you do? How did it make you feel? How did it make others feel? Did it work?" Constant repetition of how to talk about upsets and solve them allows the children to let go of their anger without feeling they or others are in the wrong, and that, in turn, allows them the space to develop emotional connection with others.

"Good choosing, Jenny"

Receiving constant verbal praise for what works ("Good listening, Jake." "Good choosing, Jenny.") allows children to feel good about themselves, which then leaves them the emotional space to enjoy other people. One five-year-old boy's behaviour is particularly non-compliant at home, so we devised a list for him, with items such as 'get out of bed', 'clean teeth', 'wash face and hands', 'put on coat'. Every time he carries out one of these tasks without fuss, he receives a tick for it from his parents, and then brings the evidence into school. "How many ticks did you get today, Freddie? Four! That's wonderful!" At the end of a week of ticks, Freddie can choose a toy or book from our great selection. It works! Consequently, Freddie now goes around beaming. His relationship with his parents is better and he is happier when he arrives at school. He has gained respect and acknowledgement and has therefore created for himself the space to forge connections with others.

Children with autism lack both a developed sense of self and a sense of status within a social group – another important emotional need. We help develop sense of self through bodywork exercises and physical activities and also through constant praise for doing what works. Praise also takes the tangible form of awards. Children are recommended for certificates, which are awarded during Monday whole-school assemblies. Awarding them on Monday sets the week off to a positive start. Children who gain five certificates win a book to keep.

There is also a kindness award, to be won by pupils who have been seen to be kind to another child. The aim is clearly to distinguish what kindness is, as empathy and understanding of others' feelings is commonly incomplete, or even absent, in autism. Finally, there is a 'good choosing award', a medal which is given by the headteacher to the winner on a Friday. On Monday, the pupil is publicly acknowledged in assembly for winning the medal and receives the school's recognition for the award. Five wins of a certificate lead to being able to choose a book or toy as a prize. Additionally, the class that receives the most 'good choosing' medals in a term earns a cup at the end of term.

All this creates a sense of competence and achievement, another vital human need. We all need to know that we can do certain things well.

The older children take Duke of Edinburgh awards. But a sense of achievement can be inculcated through much lesser successes. One 16-year-old lad had bought from Tesco a set of batteries that had leaked. Having been taught at school how to handle complaints, he was encouraged to return the batteries to Tesco's customer service counter. Although he was shaking with nerves, he managed to approach the counter alone, explain what had happened and ask for a replacement. When he was handed new batteries, he was as thrilled by his success as if he had won a prize.

Achievement comes from challenging ourselves, and from challenging ourselves also comes meaning and purpose. We work to challenge our children, within a secure environment. Our pupils engage in design technology, horticulture, drama, art and music, alongside the more conventional aspects of the curriculum. Doing work experience, striving for a medal, earning ticks – all help create a sense of purpose. But it is only when the language, the security, the attention needs, etc, are in place, that the children can identify meaning and purpose for themselves.

The human givens perspective has given us a clear way of seeing what is missing in terms of emotional needs in autism, and clarifying what needs to be put in place in order to meet them. For, without specialist support, it is unlikely that children with autism can ever have their needs fully met.

Using innate resources

Many of the resources that are innate for people in general are undeveloped or missing in people with autism. Because of their problems with language and with empathy, and the ease with which emotions can overwhelm the rational part of the brain, it takes our pupils much longer to learn both social and cognitive skills. As mentioned earlier, it may take up to a thousand repetitions before a desired behaviour choice is in place. Repetition, consistency and praise are the means we use to help develop children's long-term memory, problem-solving skills and cognitive styles, and also their rapport-building skills and abilities to be intimate with others.

We are now placing much greater emphasis on the innate resources of imagination and the 'observing self', the ability to step back and be objective, as identified in the human givens approach. Children with autism don't find it easy to be imaginative but guiding them through a visualisation exercise is one way to develop that skill. We are planning increasingly to use guided visualisation sessions to enable them to rehearse success. For example, our speech and language therapists now use visualisation of self when they work with older children on appropriate ways to behave in social situations, such as when eating in a restaurant or when approaching a person in a youth club. We also plan to make much more use of 'social stories' – stories which tell the tale of how someone coped successfully with a difficulty that the listeners also face. This again encourages use of the imagination, as the hearer becomes lost in the story, but also overlaps with the role of the 'observing self'. By hearing a story about someone else in different circumstances, it becomes possible to distance oneself from the situation and thus to take from it what is needed, without the emotional shutters of defensiveness coming down.

Because children with autism have a limited sense of self, we are also starting to use video to help them see how they appear to others. This should increase their sense of their own boundaries, and others' otherness, and reinforce the fact that we can only share thoughts and feelings by speaking them or showing them.

Many of the children who are at Hillingdon Manor School today were with us when we opened. But what very different children they were then. Many had been excluded from mainstream schools because of their challenging behaviour. Some had been badly bullied. Unable to deal with continual verbal taunts, they were in a daily state of terror. We started with 18 children who regularly spat, bit, kicked, hit, pinched, threw things and screamed. It took a year for those challenging behaviours to calm down – we had major incidents with some children about three or four times a day – but we stuck to our line of consistency. The more people keep the rules and apply the rules, the more secure they become. Unless they feel safe and secure, they can't give up their controlling behaviours.

The outcome is that we have children who are learning, happy and able to make friends. They feel part of a community – the community of the school – where they celebrate their own and others' achievements. We aim to keep providing them with the experience of success, to facilitate their ability to cope in everyday out-of-school life. The success we celebrate denotes how far each child has progressed from their own baseline (the only comparison we encourage is with their own former behaviour) and includes progress in socialisation, relaxation, ability to organise themselves, turn-taking and personal responsibility. These are big steps for children with autism to take.

We held an assembly recently to applaud the special achievements of four teenage boys who had earned their bronze Duke of Edinburgh awards. To gain the necessary skills, they had attended a youth club and sports centre with mainstream peers, learning first aid, learning how to mix records, going kayaking and carrying out an expedition. They had also raised over £3000 in a charity raffle they had organised with their teacher, taking care of the administration and speaking to people on the phone to organise prizes. Two of the boys even gave a speech to 500 children at a mainstream secondary school about the fundraising project.

These boys – two had been severely traumatised by bullying at previous schools – now had the enjoyable experience of being applauded by the younger students at our school and standing as role models for them. This is an example that shows, I believe, just how far young people with autism can be helped to connect meaningfully with an initially alien world, by working to maximise their innate resources and, in simple ways, fulfil their all too ordinary human needs.

* * * * *

When this article was originally written **Angela Austin** was the first headteacher of Hillingdon Manor School, a school for children with autism and Asperger's Syndrome. Angela has worked in special educational needs for well over 20 years. She has also been deputy head of a school for children with dyslexia, head of a language unit, and curriculum manager in a residential school for children with autism and Asperger's Syndrome. She retired from Hillingdon Manor in 2006 and now works as both a consultant and MindFields College trainer in order to spread her knowledge of how to work in special needs education, particularly with children and adults on the autistic spectrum.

Just vulnerable people: working with asylum seekers and refugees

*Specialist health visitor **Joanne Ashmore** explains her team's innovative approach to care for asylum seekers dispersed to Doncaster.*

FOUR years ago, when asylum seekers first started being dispersed to Doncaster from London and the South East, our forward-thinking public health consultant realised we had to act quickly if we were to be able to meet their many and varied needs. We were given funding for two health visitors, of whom I was one, to set up holistic health assessments and screening for TB, and to forge contacts with different local organisations. We have now become one of the pilot Personal Medical Services (PMS), a Government initiative for a new way to deliver health care. It means that we have the support of a GP, salaried by the Primary Care Trust, but, in our case, we are a nurse-led team.

For two years we worked hard, establishing contacts with social service departments, education and housing departments and a whole host of voluntary organisations and local support groups. We lobbied and campaigned on asylum seekers' behalf, sometimes working as their advocates, as they struggled to negotiate their way through services with little or no English. We gave talks to the community, to counter unrest about the sudden influx of foreign nationals. (Doncaster, an old colliery town, is a largely white area, where there was a lot of prejudice to break down.) Because we got off to such an early start, we are now successfully established, and there are still very few other teams like ours in the country.

Becoming a PMS has brought us considerably more money, and we have been able to expand. We have the services of the equivalent of a full-time GP, two health visitors who specialise in the health care of vulnerable groups, two nurse practitioners, a practice administrator, two part-time practice advisers and, shortly to be in place, two drugs workers and a citizens' advice worker. Two trainee counsellors are available to see clients who need more one-to-one support. But nothing is long term. We none of us know whether an incoming client will be in Doncaster for a week, a year – or for life.

The realities of dispersal

Approximately 90 per cent of our asylum-seeker clients have been dispersed. There are around 2000 in Doncaster and we have about 500 patients on our books at any one time, with 30 languages and countries of origin and over 20 different cultures between them. The biggest influx is of people from Iraq, Zimbabwe and black African countries, followed by those from Turkey, Iran, Pakistan and Albania. Having arrived in England and claimed asylum, many are dispersed after just a day or a couple of weeks. They are given no choice of where to go: they receive a ticket and are put on the bus to the designated destination.

Among those arriving this way in Doncaster are young Iraqi men, aged between 18 and 24, who have probably deserted from the army; families fleeing religious and/or political persecution, for example Iranian Christians; and women, who have been raped and seen their husbands murdered, now on their own with their children. They are met at our end by representatives of housing associations that have a government contract to arrange accommodation. These housing workers take the newcomers to their houses, flats or hotels, check that they are capable of managing by themselves, that they know how to turn the gas on and find the post office, and then check on them once every few weeks, but nothing much more than that. We have worked hard to encourage the housing workers to bring new asylum seekers to our centre so that we can register them immediately. After two years of frustration and repeated requests to this effect, it is now virtually routine for all new asylum seekers to be registered with us within 48 hours. I don't think this is common in dispersal towns and we are proud of the achievement.

A second loss

But there are other asylum seekers who end up in Doncaster who have been living in communities in the south of the country for several years. They are among thousands whose applications logged in the last several years have not been dealt with by the Government. Then suddenly, it seems, someone comes across a file, decides it must be dealt with urgently, and individuals or whole families get dispersed. It is mostly Albanians and Turks who arrive in Doncaster in this way. I am health visitor for those with children under five and am currently working with half a dozen families who are anglicised to a degree, gave birth in this country and had the support of their own communities in London, but who now find themselves uprooted and moved many miles away from any natural social support systems. I find women who are completely devastated (often they have no English as they had felt no need to learn it when still living with friends or extended family in the heart of their own communities), and who cry almost all day long, because they miss their families and friends so much. They are angry too: angry at being dispersed and angry at us, whom they assume to be part of the 'system'. These families are disenfranchised, disconnected, as is true of everyone who has been forced to migrate; but not only have they had to suffer the trauma of upheaval in, and escape from, their own countries, they are once again the victims of loss, as they are forced from the communities they had forged in their new homeland.

No compartments

A lot of health professionals try to medicalise and compartmentalise the symptoms of distress that asylum seekers display. "You are depressed, so I'll give you these tablets." But what people really need is to be heard: "I haven't got family here"; "My dad was shot in front of me"; "I was raped in front of my husband and I don't know where he is"; and their needs need to be addressed. As a health visitor working in the community, I am not one to compartmentalise. It made sense to me to consider emotions, community networks, social inclusion, status and achievement – which is why the human givens approach makes so much sense to me. When first we started dealing with large numbers of vulnerable people,

I trained with the Breathing Space project run by the Refugee Council, with the hope of better understanding the huge complexities asylum seekers were facing, and realised, in fact, that asylum seekers are no different from anyone else. Loss is loss. Trauma is trauma. My families' lives highlight to me how a whole series of basic needs remain unmet, and – albeit with the additional barrier of language difficulties – I work a step at a time to try to help them meet at least some of them.

The here and now

My concern is to keep focused on the here and now. This is where the human givens has particularly helped me – not to go too deeply into the whys and wherefores of people's tragic situations but providing a practical way to work to make things better now. I have to try to uncover the state of mind people are in. Some have experienced huge traumas, including rape, but are so strong inside that they may not need any specialised input at that time. I deal with their health and welfare needs just as I would any other person. Some people who have suffered think they need to appear severely distressed and unable to cope in order for their claim to have a chance of success, so I have to use my judgement. Others just fall apart. I have had women 39 weeks' pregnant put on the coach to Doncaster from London, where they had been living. They may shortly present with apparent postnatal depression but really, I'd say, what they are manifesting is a reaction to the trauma and loss they have experienced, and complete disconnection at a time of greatest need – new motherhood.

Depression is but a word

I used to ask people if they were depressed. But depression is a word that doesn't have the same meaning for everyone. (In human givens terms, it is a nominalisation, an abstract, empty word that can only be given meaning from one's own experience.) Very often interpreters would have no idea what I meant by depression at all. Even Ugandans and people from Zimbabwe, who are English-speaking, would ask me to explain what I was talking about. That led me to read up on how different cultures manage mental upset. Some cultures, where mental illness is taboo, explain it in physical terms and tangible forms: headache, heart pain, stomach pain, lack of sleep and so on. As a result, I've learned to be very explicit when probing people's experience. I ask things like, "When you wake up, do you feel you want to get out of bed or do you just want to stay there?" "Do you dream a lot?" "Do you feel like you have had an exhausting night?" "Do you wake early?" "Do you sit on the sofa and cry for long periods?" "Do you think of the past a lot?" I also ask if people have any suicidal thoughts, even though taking one's own life is taboo in many cultures and religions.

Elijah in distress

Sometimes, there seems initially to be no way to communicate at all. When a young Ugandan man called Elijah got off the coach from the south of England, the housing worker brought him straight to our centre and handed him over into our charge, saying, "I'm scared". Elijah just sat in the seat to which we had led him, eyes wide open without blinking. He made no eye contact with anyone, just sat hunched, almost in a fetal position. I too was terrified that suddenly he would become psychotic and run amok. Apparently Elijah had already been showing signs of distress when he was put on the coach to Doncaster but he was dispersed anyway. By enormous luck, he was carrying in his hand the report of a psychiatric assessment that had been carried out at the reception centre. I managed to extricate and read it, and clearly he needed help. Luckily, because of our fierce networking in the early stages of the project, we were able to contact the psychiatric liaison nurse at Doncaster Royal Infirmary, along with enlisting the help of the Black African Network within the local Catholic Church in Doncaster, from where someone came to support him. Elijah needed to be taken into hospital that day, but now he is functioning well in the community. The church, to which the Network advocate introduced him, was a lifesaver for him.

Lots of Black Africans are staunch Catholics, so I always ask about new arrivals' religion, in order to direct them to the church if appropriate. Usually their faces light up – it's instant connection to something meaningful for them. And they know that there are going to be people on whom they can rely.

A few people have clearly been on the very brink of sanity when they've been brought in to us. We always make it clear that we are nothing to do with the Government and that we will not be doing anything that could harm them. A lot of asylum seekers have had bad experiences with authority, both here and at home. We also have to make sure that they don't have too great expectations of us. They need us to tell them what we can and can't do for them. We've learned that from experience. For example, many clients want a medical report of some kind, to assist their asylum case. I am unqualified to do this and only an experienced and qualified medical officer carries these out, usually on request of the solicitor.

Concentrating on the children

We see it as part of our remit to provide a range of avenues of options people can choose from. When people are dispersed here, the first thing lost is their sense of control over their own lives. Choice helps generate a sense of control. So, too, does concentrating on the things that people *can* exert some degree of control over, instead of agonising over those that are in the lap of others. I try to convey that there is no point worry-

---

CASE HISTORY:

Time for tea

A UGANDAN woman called Victoria came to Doncaster two years ago. Dispersed on a no-choice basis, she felt extremely low, had no real sense of hope and felt isolated from the indigenously white population. Victoria came to see us on the recommendation of her accommodation case-worker and it became immediately obvious she was mentally and physically suffering.

It takes time to build rapport, and this is something that we think it is vital to give. Over a number of meetings, cups of tea, silence and tears, we ascertained she was HIV positive. Through honest and positive consultations, she eventually agreed to refer herself to our specialist service at the hospital. This enabled her to have some level of control.

Two years on, she is healthy, positive, engaged and active within the local HIV support network and helps other women in a similar situation to overcome their fears. She still has no decision regarding her asylum claim. ■

ing about asylum cases that are in the hands of solicitors, but that there are things they can do to help their relationships with spouses (which are very often strained because of all the fear and worry) and their children (who, for the same reasons, may suffer benign neglect). Often, I use children to focus parents' attention away from their own trauma and on to the practicalities of being a 'good enough' parent. That is something I would do anyway, as a health visitor. (However, I refuse to allow bilingual children to interpret for parents who don't speak English. That creates an undesirable power imbalance in the family.)

Even babies pick up on the anxieties of their parents. I see so many babies and children with no sparkle in their eyes, just sitting listlessly, without playing. Because their parents' trauma means that their own needs are unmet, children either retreat into themselves or become complete handfuls. I explain to distracted parents why children in such difficult circumstances so often appear to be naughty. One young boy kept hitting people. I sat and took the time to play with him and, within an hour, he was calm and happy. His parents couldn't believe the difference.

I try to encourage parents to take their children to the playgroups at our family centres. The mother whose son was hitting takes him there three times a week now, and it has been a natural way of helping her integrate into an alien community – by connecting with other mothers. Young children play with any children, and that is lovely for asylum-seeker parents to see and share. They also cope better with their child, who, as a result of the outlet of play, is more tired and ready to sleep at night. But that, of course, is the way I would approach helping any family where adult anxieties are adversely affecting the wellbeing of the child. I also try to get my families to think about setting boundaries for their children's behaviour, and that too is a way of regaining some control over events, when they feel so very out of control of their own adult lives.

One of our most basic needs is the need to feel safe and have some sense of certainty. Alas, this is a need that cannot, with the best will in the world, be fully met for asylum seekers, for a failed claim may mean instant deportation and even a successful one could lead to a further uprooting, to travel to a different designated home. I try to put in place what I can for the families I work with, in small ways. For instance, they know that I am always available to see them at the clinic at a drop-in session from 12–2pm every Friday. I also try to encourage the security of routine, such as school for the children and college for the adults, even if it is only for six months, because it is important to have a structure of some kind to rely on. Doncaster College has responded brilliantly to the huge influx of people applying for courses. Most of our clients are offered a place within a couple of weeks.

Coping with trauma

In our nurse-led team we operate a triage system. We decide whether an individual needs to see the GP or whether we can manage their needs, or whether we need to refer someone to our community psychiatric nurse, who has had a lot of experience with trauma.

I have learned the rewind technique (see page 59) for trauma and phobias at a MindFields College workshop, and can attest to its power – I can now travel on the underground in London without my customary terror – and am interested to explore its possible application with asylum seekers. The method guides people to imagine themselves on a video screen, quickly going backwards and forwards through the trauma as if on rewind or fast forward, as many times as is necessary to remove the emotion from the memory. The therapist need never even know what it was that happened to the client – a particular advantage when working with women from other cultures who have been raped.

Keeping the lid on

Some health professionals in dispersal towns consider it unwise to offer any kind of therapy, as there are so few resources available – better to keep the lid on, in effect, than to unleash an emotional storm that can't be contained. We would beg to differ. There is so much that can be achieved by simple common sense strategies that make such a difference to people's lives.

I always look for people's strengths and encourage them to make the most of them. I regularly recommend exercise and direct them to social settings that enable the dual benefit of generating greater physical and mental wellbeing, and creating connection. Many young men end up going running at the track, join local football teams or head for the gym, where they can have reduced-price membership. The result is that they soon find themselves better able to cope with the demands of their lives. This has worked well for very many people, I have found.

I try to help people find their own motivation. "Look, you are here. You've travelled so far. You've survived. A part of you *must* want to be here." So many have lost their sense of status, having been forced to give up professional careers to flee. Asylum seekers cannot take paid work, but I encourage them to attend college or become volunteers of one kind or another, particularly interpreters, as a means of restoring some sense of status. Similarly, the need for achievement can be fulfilled in many forms – the ability to have survived at all, being one. I encourage those who are struggling to set goals – even just getting through the day without crying or not punching the walls – and ask them to scale how they are doing, from one visit to the next. I also acknowledge what they haven't got. "It must be extremely difficult for you to cope with not knowing where you'll be in three months' time." Once acknowledged, it is often easier to put the uncertainty on the back burner, and get on with today.

Just like anyone else

In the end, my work is not only about helping people I work with to become physically and emotionally healthier, but about trying to help them become more philosophical about their lives: to aim to make the best of what they have got and achieve some kind of happiness, within the context that they find themselves in. What has helped me most in working with asylum seekers is learning to see them simply as vulnerable people and not as a specific sub-set of the population with needs distinct from those of everybody else. Trauma is trauma and loss is loss, however it occurs, and we all react in a range of very human ways, however diverse our circumstances.

* ✳ ✳ ✳ ✳

Joanne Ashmore is a registered nurse who qualified in 1992 in Sheffield. She gradually moved south until she reached London in 1994. Following completion of a health studies degree in 1999, she qualified as a health visitor, working in one of the most deprived boroughs in the country, Hackney. In 2001, she moved back to her home town in order to practise as a specialist health visitor working with vulnerable groups. Since this article was originally published she has moved back to London to take a Masters in public health.

"I saw that most men only care for science so far as they get a living by it, and that they worship even error when it affords them a subsistence."

GOETHE

Why psychiatrists should be more like plumbers

*Consultant psychiatrist and HGI Chairman **Farouk Okhai** opens his casebook to show how using a variety of techniques, as in the HG approach, can best help severely distressed people.*

RECENTLY, with great relief, I closed the file on Alison, a 37 year old woman who was referred to me early this year. She had already had four spells as a psychiatric inpatient and three and a half years of psycho-analytic psychotherapy elsewhere but, after just five sessions of the rewind technique for quick and effective resolution of trauma, she said she needed no further help. It has now been over 6 months since I last saw her and I have been told by others that she is looking extremely well.

Alison's case is just one of many successes I have had through the use of the rewind technique (see page 59) and other aspects of the human givens approach that I learned in the course of studying for my Human Givens Practitioner Diploma. I am one of a small but fast-growing number of psychiatrists using the human givens approach in daily NHS work. The unit where I work as a consultant psychiatrist in psychotherapy has 35 psychiatric inpatients' beds but I mainly see patients referred to me as out-patients by GPs, clinical psychologists, general psychiatrists or other members of our community mental health teams. Half of my patients are viewed as having intractable problems: often, as in the case of Alison, such patients end up receiving a variety of therapeutic help and still keep coming back, their problems no nearer being resolved. Many of them have experienced some severe trauma, which continues to haunt them and leaves them depressed, anxious or changed in their personality.

I am convinced that the rest of the patients I see don't really need the services of a psychiatrist. Professionals such as social workers, community psychiatric nurses or occupational therapists could easily help them in the normal course of their work, but they are often not confident about their psychotherapeutic skills. They would be, however, if they learned the human givens approach, as many are now doing. This emphasises the major changes that can be achieved in the course of a normal conversation. For instance, reframing an unhelpful way of looking at things, directing people's focus outwards away from their difficulties, (by encouraging them to develop an existing talent, helping others, doing sport or other physical activity), and helping people to identify what is meaningful in their lives. Very often small improvements take place quickly and can be built on.

I quickly wove human givens ideas into my working style. I had been schooled in psychodynamic psychotherapy, cognitive behaviour therapy, cognitive analytical therapy, interpersonal therapy and group therapy, required as part of my psychiatric training in psychotherapy. The human givens approach encompasses all therapy techniques that are effective, without being rigidly confined to any single model. As a result, it is efficient and satisfying. I liken it to being a plumber. Plumbers don't stick to a pre-set model: they learn all the different ways to look at a problem and do whatever is most appropriate to fix the one in front of them as quickly as they can.

I should like to share here a few case histories that demonstrate the effectiveness of this approach in psychiatry. As many of my patients' experiences involve trauma, I have found the human givens version of the rewind technique a particularly helpful tool. (Within the first two years of using it, I had used it over 50 times and on only four occasions did it not put an end to patients' flashbacks.)

A good history

One of the emphases in human givens therapy (and solution-focused therapies in general) is the need to find out not just about a patient's problems but a patient's strengths. I have devised a questionnaire for new patients to complete before their assessment session. It contains not only straightforward informational questions about the concerns that are troubling them, when and how these came about, previous psychiatric history, medication, alcohol and drug use, suicidal thoughts, family and relationships etc but more open-ended questions that include a positive slant. For instance, "Describe your childhood. Include everything (good and not so good) that you remember having a great effect on you. What are the high and low points of your working life? Describe how you've managed to keep going in spite of everything. Which of your strong points – strengths – have you used to do this? What did you try that did not work and what were you thinking of trying next? When you over-come all your troubles, what will you be doing that is different from what you are doing now?"

The idea is to focus people on what is going well in their lives, rather than just on what is wrong (as people who are depressed or highly anxious tend mainly to volunteer information about what is going badly in their lives). It also arms me with useful information that I can use as needed to build on past achievements and so enhance confidence and self esteem.

Beth's story

Sometimes, of course, the exercise may reveal an initial inability to identify any strong points. Thirty-two year old Beth, who had been physically abused as a very young child and sexually abused while in foster care, attributed her ability to keep going entirely to luck. "I can't think of any strengths," she wrote. "The way I feel is that I've been fortunate. I just seem to survive."

When she turned up for her assessment interview, I saw a young woman, full of nervous energy. She was clearly extremely distressed and anxious and went into great detail when answering questions. She was afraid I wouldn't take her problems seriously, as she looked well, had a decent job and had just got married, two weeks previously, to a man she adored. She hadn't told him that she was coming to therapy because she feared he would be hurt and also that he might want her to pore over her past with him, which she was reluctant to do. She was hoping her marriage would be a turning point in her life, and wanted to get on top of the things that she was struggling to cope with.

As she noticed that I was not going to be dismissive of her, she calmed down a little and told me her story. Her mother was a drug addict, who had been hospitalised at one time, and her father was excessively strict.

As a young child, she had been terrified of his tirades and his violence against her. At just five, she was taken to hospital with suspicious bruising on her face and was placed on the 'at risk' register. Later, after being badly beaten with a belt and ending up in hospital, she was taken into foster care and then put into a children's home, where she was sexually abused. Eventually Beth went to live with her aunt. Unfortunately, her uncle died a year or so later. Her aunt remarried but Beth did not get on with the new husband and took an overdose of paracetamol when she was 12. She was then sent to live with her grandparents. This was the happiest time in Beth's life. She was devastated, at 15, when her grandmother died.

In spite of difficulties at school, including being bullied, Beth managed to go on to college and, since then, had had a number of generally unsatisfactory clerical jobs. At 21 she became pregnant but her partner was not supportive. After much agonising, she had decided on an abortion.

"These stay"

On her questionnaire, to describe what was troubling her, Beth had said, "I've overwhelming feelings that I find hard to pinpoint one at a time because they are linked together by emotions that have stayed with me – rejection, self blame, failure, insecurity, the feeling that it's me and I deserve whatever happens in my life. These stay." She said that she was often overwhelmed by these emotions, which were triggered by a raised or critical voice, a "look" or a hand gesture that most people would judge to be innocent. She would flinch and feel as if she were a child about to be beaten. She also tended to flinch when her husband came close to her, a response she attributed to the sexual abuse as a child. Although she did not experience visual flashbacks, she would be "back in my childhood with all the emotions I had then". I decided that Beth's symptoms were consistent with chronic post traumatic stress disorder (PTSD).

Six months passed between the assessment and the first appointment (a dismayingly long time but fairly routine within the NHS). At that appointment, we agreed on three goals: to deal with automatic reactions, such as flinching when her husband came close; to deal with the flashbacks related to the bullying and beatings by her father when she was a child; and to deal with the guilt she felt over the abortion.

In human givens therapy, the therapist always does something in a session to make the patient feel better and more hopeful. (There is no such thing as a session devoted to history taking and nothing else.) So, in the first session, I decided to address the flashbacks of the sexual abuse. When I asked Beth to scale them from 1 to 10, with 10 being the worst they could be, she gave them a 10. I then took her through the rewind technique, asking her to visualise, in turn, as many specific incidents connected with the abuse as she felt she needed to. I also taught her the 7/11 breathing technique (breathe in to the count of 7, out to the count of 11) to slow her breathing and thus help her calm down when she was anxious.

Going down the scale

At her next session a week later, Beth scaled the flashbacks of the abuse at between 6 and 7. It didn't surprise me that they hadn't disappeared entirely; the procedure often needs to be repeated in cases involving multiple incidents of abuse. However, she said she didn't want to use the rewind technique to go through the sexual abuse incidents again. She wanted to deal with the flashbacks related to the treatment she had suffered at the hands of her father. The following week she scaled the flashbacks of sexual abuse at 2 and said those relating to her father had eased off to 7 from the 10 they had started at.

We talked in that third session about Beth's guilt and distress over the abortion. It struck me that, even though the guilt felt amorphous and all enveloping to her, she must have been traumatised by the procedure itself. In my experience of working with patients deeply troubled by a past abortion, the memory of the abortion itself remains vivid. So I tried the rewind technique to deal with that. Beth was distressed and felt nauseous during the session but I made sure she was calm before she left.

Two weeks later, Beth informed me that the distressing memories of the abortion had fallen to 3 from 10 on the 10-point scale. The flash-backs about her father were at 4 and those relating to the sexual abuse still at 2. She didn't want to repeat any of the rewind procedures. Instead, we talked about her difficulties with assertiveness at work. I gave her a sheet explaining simple steps to being assertive and suggested she role play some scenarios with her husband, taking turns at being the bully and being Beth.

I reinforced these ideas with a guided visualisation, a very strong feature of the human givens approach in its own right, not just as part of the rewind technique (see "The power of deep relaxation and guided imagery" opposite). First I relaxed Beth and then encouraged her to see herself acting assertively in different settings. While she was still deeply relaxed, I gave her the post-hypnotic suggestion that she could induce relaxation whenever she felt anxious just by gently squeezing together her thumb and forefinger.

Beth missed two sessions because of illness and a conflicting appointment but when I next saw her a month later she said she had successfully put the assertiveness techniques into practice, saying a firm no to a colleague at work, who was often unreasonably demanding. The following session a fortnight later turned out to be our last. Beth looked well and agreed that she was more relaxed in general. She had found squeezing her thumb and forefinger when she felt stressed enormously helpful, and had been assertive in some quite difficult situations, without any longer feeling put upon and victimised. She had stopped having flashbacks of any kind and announced happily that she didn't think she needed to see me anymore. She left my consulting room, highly confident that she was going to be able to put her whole heart into her marriage and her future: she was considering training to be a teacher. It was clear that eliminating the intrusive memories was sufficient to enable her to get on, and be optimistic about, her life.

Alison's story

Alison was a very different sort of person to work with. One of the basic tenets of the human givens approach is to establish rapport at the outset. That begins quite naturally with a smile, being attentive, and encouraging initial small talk rather than poring over notes with bent head when a patient enters the room. But Alison rarely smiled. At our first session her expression was a combination of distress and frustration. I knew from her notes and returned questionnaire that she had been depressed for many years and had been admitted to hospital four times, once for as long as eight months. During that admission she was aggressive and violent on the ward and did so much damage she was threatened with criminal charges. She was now taking an antidepressant and an anti-epilepsy drug, commonly used as a mood stabiliser.

Alison had been with her husband for 20 years and had two teenage boys. She clearly lived for her sons and supported them avidly on the football field but had always found it hard to be physically affectionate. Alison was very bitter about her childhood. She had an older cousin whom her parents treated as the golden child in their extended family, and she felt she was constantly compared unfavourably to him. She wrote poignantly in her questionnaire: "My cousin could do no wrong.

CASE HISTORY:

The power of deep relaxation and guided imagery

LIKE all human givens oriented therapists, I make considerable use of the deep relaxation state. Because emotional arousal focuses and locks attention, it is only when anxious or depressed people are deeply re-laxed, temporarily liberated from the interminable arousing personal worries and concerns that plague them, that they can, metaphorically, step back, take a wider perspective, and be guided to see different outcomes and options for themselves in their lives.

This was a very helpful approach to use with Nick, a quiet, clean-cut, 38 year old American referred to me for depression. Nick's father, a retired landscape gardener, had undertaken to create a garden behind Nick's newly built home, which at the time was just rubble.

However, the project ceased to be straightforward when a neigh-bour dispute arose over drainage and boundaries of land. The dispute became so bitter and Nick's father so dispirited that, quite suddenly, he took his own life. Nick blamed himself for his father's death, and couldn't stop thinking he should have taken his state of mind more seriously. He had been depressed ever since. He had moved back in with his mother, whose life he felt responsible for ruining. She too had become depressed and they had both started to drink heavily.

Before the suicide, Nick had been a well-liked, efficient manager, on the fast track to promotion. Afterwards, he had intermittently been off ill ▶

I was always bad or wrong. I can remember at the age of about four looking out of the window for my real family. I thought I was adopted and my real parents would come to take me away. I felt I never fitted in and could never please anyone."

Her parents didn't know that her cousin had sexually abused her for three years from the age of seven (when he was 14). During her teen years, she was bullied at school and someone she considered a friend raped her. When she was 17, she went to Barcelona as an *au pair* and was caught in the vicinity of an ETA bomb. Although she suffered few

and, for some months now, had been on continuous sick leave for depression. Recently he was shocked to be called in and offered medical retirement.

When I met Nick, he was on 50mg daily (a high dose) of Seroxat (an SSRI antidepressant) and had seen three separate counsellors, none of whom he had found helpful. Their efforts to convince him that his father's suicide was not his fault had particularly annoyed him. He spent his time ruminating about actions he could have taken to prevent the tragedy and worrying about his mother. Gentle probing revealed that his friends had gradually dropped him and he had ceased to take part in activities he used to enjoy, such as squash and rambling.

Calming down

The first step was to help him to calm down. I taught him the 7/11 breathing technique that I had shown Beth and I also took him through a 20-minute gradual relaxation exercise, during which I reminded him of his past work successes and latent talents, and reframed the enforced medical retirement as the opportunity to choose a new career. I asked him to repeat the 7/11 relaxation exercise for 15 minutes three times a day, to help him to think clearly; to start playing squash again and to look into going to an evening class. The aim was to focus his attention outwards and get him mixing with people again. We agreed that he would keep an alcohol diary, so that he could identify his drinking triggers and learn accurately, rather than guess, how much he was injuries, she continually relived the memory of being surrounded by dead bodies.

After she returned to England, she married. She hadn't worked outside the home since the birth of her first child, and described herself as a non-person.

The troubling flashbacks

Alison was extremely downcast in the way she spoke. She had difficulty expressing herself and had always had trouble socialising, but what

drinking. (I was careful not to tell him to cut down. Most people hate being told not to drink, and I hoped that, once he became more aware of his drinking, he would want to cut down.) With the help of his GP, he was going to start cutting down his antidepressant use by 10mg every fortnight or so.

I next saw him eight days later. He instantly admitted that, although he had found the relaxation useful, he had practised it only once or twice. It is important to emphasise what someone has done, rather than what they have failed to do, so my response was, "It's really good that you did it once or twice. It will become a habit that *you will do more and more*", embedding the suggestion that he would do so.

Nick had realised, from his drinking diary, that his alcohol use decreased when he was distracted. He had managed to keep to between three and six units a day, except for once when, in a pub with friends, he drank 13 units. The antidepressant was down to 40mg a day. However, he was anxious as a result of a visit by his immediate boss who had suggested that he fight the medical retirement. We did a relaxation in which, during his deeply relaxed state, I invited him to consider the pros and cons of returning to his old job.

Two weeks later, Nick arrived looking well. His antidepressant was down to 30mg a day; he had reached a final settlement with his employer; he had continued with playing squash; and he was drinking just two to three units of alcohol a day. (He had had another slip when he drank excessively at the pub, and had now decided to avoid ▶

plagued her most were the vivid and intense flashbacks of the bomb blast, the rape and the sexual abuse. It was these, and these alone, that she wanted to work on. The images intruded almost every day, often two or three times a day, and she would feel she was reliving these experiences each time. She was wary of intimacy of any kind, as this often triggered flashbacks of the sexual traumas. Three years of psychoanalytic therapy and 20 weeks of cognitive analytic therapy had not lessened her distress or helped her to cope with it.

In our first session after her assessment, I used the rewind technique

those particular friends, as he couldn't control his drinking when with them.) We discussed careers advice, enrolling in an evening class and the possibility of his setting up as a painter and decorator, which he had an interest in. Again, we did a guided visualisation, in which I invited Nick to think creatively about his future.

More success

And so it went on. Each session he reported, and I affirmed, more successes. His antidepressant use was, first, down to 20mg daily, then 10mg daily, then 10mg every other day and then discontinued altogether. He had started rekindling his relationships and had gone back to rambling.

It was then, when asked if he had any other goals for therapy, that Nick said that he wished he could stop feeling guilty about his father's death. I knew that I should not to try to persuade him that he wasn't to blame. That was what previous counsellors had tried, to his annoyance. So I drew a pie chart and asked him to attribute portions of the blame for the suicide to all the parties involved – the neighbours, the workers, the surveyor, the council, his father and himself. I was careful to leave his portion of the blame till last. By the time we got to him, over 100 per cent of the blame had already been allocated. We did it again – but Nick was not happy with the result. So we did it again and again until Nick said, "I see what you are getting at: it's not that simple". I then told him a story of a murderer being taken to the gallows. Whose fault was it? His for committing the murder? The victim for being in the for the bomb blast. She gave me little feedback, although she left the room in a calm state. The following week she said matter of factly that the flashbacks to the bomb blast had eased off a lot. When I asked what she wanted to work on that day, she replied tersely, "An incident that happened when I was 14". She said no more about it and, of course, the beauty of the rewind technique is that the patient is not forced to discuss openly anything they would prefer to keep private. I took her through the steps, without knowing what experience she was working through. I don't think she said another word, except to thank me as she left.

wrong place? The knifemaker for making the knife which the murderer used? His parents for not bringing him up right? Society for not providing schooling and opportunities for him? The police for not paying heed to the warning signs? The judiciary for not sentencing him for life for a previous conviction? Nick has not mentioned the guilt since that session.

Nominalisations

Nick firmly decided on painting and decorating as a new career but he needed an interim job while he got up to speed on skills, and was worried that he might not be able to cope with the pressure. The human givens approach stresses utilising one's resources. I asked Nick about previous times when he had been under such pressure and coped, and he gave me two examples. "So you do have the resources to cope," I told him. "They just need brushing up." He agreed.

I induced a deep relaxation, during which I suggested that he review all the times he had coped successfully and retrieve all the strengths, resources, talents, abilities, experience, knowledge, persistence and determination that he needed to succeed now. These abstract words are nominalisations, words with no intrinsic or sensory meaning. Positive nominalisations can be powerful because they send the listener on an inner search to recall positive experiences that match their personal understanding of the words. (Negative ones like depression and misery are, for the same reason, to be avoided.) Helping Nick visualise success instead of failure was key to his recovery. ■

At our third meeting, she told me, but only when prompted, that the bomb blast flashbacks, which she had scaled as 10 in severity, were now down to 5. The incident at age 14 she scaled at 7 from an initial 10. She chose to work on another undiscussed incident, which had involved her cousin.

The following week, there was a glimmer of animation in her face when I asked how she had been getting on. "The flashbacks aren't bad at all. I would never have believed it!" That week we did a rewind on "an incident in the park".

Though she remained aloof, she softened just a little with every session. We ended up with what I would call a comfortable understanding. At the next session, she told me all her flashbacks had resolved and chose not to have any further sessions. I know from her general practitioner that she looks well and is much brighter. Though she still has difficulty socialising, Alison did not want to address that in therapy. It is patients who must set their own goals, and Alison felt she had achieved what she wanted from her therapy.

Reluctant to recover

In my area of work, it is not unusual to see people who have been shunted around the mental health services for years, and whom professionals despair of helping. Sometimes people don't seem to want to get better. They don't respond well to setting concrete goals or to challenging questions such as, "When you are better, what will you be doing differently?" However, I have been surprised that, by using techniques from the wide-ranging human givens approach, one can always do something to move such people along. One man for years attended groups at three different day centres every week, regularly saw a general psychiatrist colleague of mine, and was admitted to psychiatric hospitals several times in the course of the previous ten years – all without making any headway with his many problems. The psychiatrist finally decided to refer him to me, to see if I could do anything more.

I despaired when I first saw him. But he has been improving, though very slowly. I first saw him every week but this has now tapered down to every 3 months. I have used the human givens approach of acknowledging but otherwise ignoring his complaints, getting him to amplify what is going well and asking him to explain to me how he has achieved what he has, and the strengths and resources he used to do so. I also work at embedding therapeutic suggestions: "Hello. You look as though you *feel better*. What have you noticed as you *get better* and *become more able to do things? Can you *do more* or are you already able to *do the best that you can?*" Something is happening because he no longer goes to any day centres and has been discharged by the psychiatrist. He is now in a relationship and has taken on a job for two mornings a week. Quite an advance for someone who, for years, had demanded all the medical attention he could get.

* * * * *

Farouk Okhai is consultant psychiatrist in psychotherapy with the Milton Keynes Primary Care NHS Trust. In addition to his clinical commitments he is in charge of the psychotherapy department and teaches psychotherapy to trainee psychiatrists. Following his basic psychiatric training on the Guy's Hospital Rotation in Canterbury and Ashford, Kent he was the Specialist Registrar in Psychotherapy at Addenbrookes Hospital, Cambridge. His period in Cambridge (in keeping with the broad minded approach of the psychotherapy department there), included working with Cognitive Analytic, Cognitive Behavioural, Interpersonal, psychodynamic, group, systemic, and therapeutic community models of therapy.

*"The single biggest problem in communication
is the illusion that it has taken place."*

GEORGE BERNARD SHAW

The mended fin: physiotherapy and the human givens

*Physiotherapist **Jessica Bavinton** describes how the human givens approach has enabled her to empower her patients and herself, and suggests other health professionals could benefit too.*

WHEN I trained as a physiotherapist, a field of therapy where we try to regain, improve or maintain physical capacity and functioning after illness or disease, it didn't seem strange at the time that the training had relatively little psychology input.

After graduating, physiotherapists spend their first two years moving among different health care settings within the NHS, meeting patients from every spectrum of medicine: people with all sorts of pain or fatigue, weakness, numbness, paralysis, too much phlegm or not enough balance, those with collapsing lungs, stiff joints, and false limbs – we wiggle their necks and teach them painful exercises; we advise people on how to live independently, visit their homes and help stop them falling; we remove phlegm from people's chest and help them walk again after having bits taken out of them or metal-work put in. We work in big, old Victorian wards, quiet, beeping intensive care units, raucous schools, sweaty gyms, behind curtains, and in people's homes where we get tripped up by the dog as we go through the door. We work with children, adolescents, adults and elderly people, alongside their carers, doctors, nurses, therapists, teddy bears and pets. We work with people on artificial ventilators, on crutches, and in wheelchairs, helping people with new knees, replaced heart valves, missing fingers, and with those who struggle to walk, hear, speak, understand, feel or talk.

Amongst this whirlpool of real people and their very real problems and needs, it very quickly became clear to me that being a good physiotherapist wasn't just a case of getting on with the physical mechanics of the job. I remember feeling quite a lot like a little fish that found itself, with a broken fin, swimming the wrong way in a very big stream.

In these first intense years, some concerns especially worried me. How was I going to convince Mary that the only way for her to get better after her knee replacement was to go through regular and painful exercises? (And how could I do it quickly so the next patient in A & E could use her bed?) How was I ever going to get Henry out of bed and walking, when he hadn't slept for days and the last time he walked he got hit by a car? (And how was I going to help lift his confidence, so he could go home independently and see his cat?) How was I going to make sure little Anna did her breathing exercises and managed to take part in sports at school, despite her asthma? (And how could I ensure mum encouraged this too and took off some of the cotton wool?) How was I going to be able to tell a nurse twice my age that she couldn't come into the cubicle and change a dressing while I was having a private session with my patient? (And how could I be sure to do it nicely so it didn't upset my patient, the nurse, or me?) How could I help Edna, sitting in the corner, who has lost her leg and lost her smile (and get her other leg moving, so that she doesn't lose that one, too?) How could I look after four hospital wards, full of people who were seriously sick or dying, when I didn't know how to distance myself from the grief and the pain?

Human givens training could have helped – I would have known how to build rapport quickly and influence and motivate change in people; to be able to explain, advise and communicate effectively to a wide range of people; to manage myself, my emotions and my time.

In essence, doing the Human Givens Diploma has helped answer my everyday physiotherapy questions; it has mended my fin and has sent me on my way downstream. It has bridged the gap between the body and the mind, my academic training and the real world, and has allowed me truly to understand the difference between helping patients just a bit and really empowering them to change their lives. It has given me a complementary framework, a safety net, a reassuring guiding hand through the complexities of human suffering and a wider window into the marvels of human strength.

If I'd have known then …

If I had known then what I know now, I would have reframed Mary's pain and given her a visual image to help her make sense of what was happening to her. I would have told her that it was a helpful pain because it signified the breaking down of the stiff glue-like gunge that had built up in her knee as a result of her operation. I would also have emphasised the benign nature of the pain because so often people fear that knee replacements will work loose if they exercise the painful leg.

I would have used as much creative imagery as I could to help little Anna see the importance of doing her breathing exercises and taking physical exercise at school. Perhaps I would have encouraged her to imagine a little man holding a whole bunch of brightly coloured but deflated balloons. The little man was sad because he needed to sell his balloons every day so that he could put away the money to buy the special present he wanted for his little girl's birthday. With her own breath, Anna could help him reinflate his balloons every day and, in her imagination, see them waving about up high, on the end of the strings that the little man was holding, a huge smile on his face … and, of course, more balloons get filled during physical exercise! Perhaps I would have told her of another little girl I knew, who had had exactly the same problem as Anna, and how she overcame it; and perhaps, whilst treating her, I would have told her stories embedded with therapeutic metaphors, all to help her realise that she could cope with the normal school day.

Perhaps I would have engaged Edna in some crafts or reading she could do at her bedside, or told her a story that would have lifted her low mood. I could have been proactive in raising awareness of the clear link between boredom and depression, and the importance of keeping patients occupied with meaningful activity and getting a good night's sleep. I would also have been keen to illustrate Edna's need to move her other leg, perhaps by explaining circulation in terms of a flowing river and dried-up brook, or introducing her to another amputee patient, leading a successful and independent life.

Time is the most precious commodity in the NHS, and patients' needs for privacy are sadly often neglected in the need to monitor this or change that. With my improved understanding that patients, nurses and physiotherapists all have their own sets of needs, I would have learned to handle better the frustration I often felt when a nurse burst into the cubicle whilst I was talking with a patient. I would arguably now deal with this a little more sensitively than I would have at one time.

Nocebo, therapeutic imagery and my cat

Physiotherapists, and other health care professionals, so often have to pick up the pieces of a devastating nocebo comment containing the sting of a self-fulfilling prophecy (nocebo being the negative counterpart of a placebo). I'm sure that health care professionals, especially those with considerable status, do not have any concept of the damage done when telling a patient they have 'a crumbling spine', 'thorny segments' in their knee or that their 'depression will be with them for life'. These patients often come terrified to physiotherapy, knowing with a certainty that is hard to shift that if they bend forward their backs will snap. (I'm sure these careless comments also cost the NHS millions, when patients are led to believe there is no option but to end up in a wheelchair.)

But, while negative imagery can cause so much damage, learning the powerful impact of an inspiring image or story has made me wonder whether so much more could be made of this, to help patients' recovery. One such setting might be intensive care. Physiotherapists are viewed as the respiratory experts and are often called in the night to intensive care units, to help patients whose lungs have collapsed or whose respiratory system is compromised. The unconscious patients are usually attached to artificial ventilators and it is not possible to have a dialogue. However, it is wrong to think comatose people do not absorb the outside world: when restored to consciousness, one patient said that, at every physiotherapy visit, he had had the image that the physiotherapist was an eagle, to whom he was holding on, being ferried to safety. Perhaps, instead of working in silence, meaningful metaphors and stories of recovery could be delivered into that strange, half-conscious world.

I also wonder about the effects of imagery, nocebo and placebo on physiotherapy electrotherapy treatments, in which a patient is given therapeutic doses of ultrasonic or magnetic therapy (invisible waves transmitted though the skin, to promote healing). Our professional obligations require us to warn patients of the potential dangers of electrotherapy (which could have a 'nocebo' effect in itself). How important is it therefore to emphasise, on balance, how helpful most people find this treatment, and explain exactly how the ultrasonic waves are massaging individual cells in an injured ligament, squeezing blood, laden with new ligament building blocks and a healing glue, directly to the site of the injury?

Using imagery and stories therapeutically, as encouraged by the human givens approach, is relatively new to me. However, when I see the impact of a well-placed image or metaphor with patients, it makes me extra determined to find and use more of them. Indeed, I have had to work to develop my metaphor 'muscle'. As it can be a bit scary to try out new stories and metaphors for the first time on a patient, I practise on my cat. By observing difficulties encountered in her usually fairly stress-free life, I try to think up images I could use (if she were human) to help her overcome them. For instance, the other day, she couldn't get through the cat-flap because she was entering it at the wrong angle. She there-fore gave up and miaowed a lot, and became reliant on my partner or me to let her in. That night, I told her a 'learned helplessness' story about a bird that stays in its cage even though the door has been opened. As long as no one actually sees me storytelling to my cat, I can relax in the knowledge that my storytelling won't be judged!

Chronic fatigue syndrome

More recently, my work has exchanged breadth for depth. I am now working solely in one diagnosis – chronic fatigue syndrome/myalgic encephalomyelitis (CFS/ME): a severe and debilitating condition characterised by a profound fatigue, sleep disturbance and often accompanied by complex emotional and cognitive difficulties. This is a setting where my human givens training has helped me enormously – for here a physiotherapist, mostly trained in *physical* assessment and management, must help someone with complex multidimensional difficulties, ranging from panic attacks and the resulting social phobias to anxiety, depression and problems with sleep. Clearly, there is a need to mobilise the mind – to access the patient's resources and motivation, as well as integrate their emotional needs – before we can have any long-term success in mobilising the body.

Most physiotherapists working in this area already have a great deal of knowledge and experience, and often embrace cognitive-behaviour therapy (CBT) principles and holistic mind–body techniques – most learn *en route* and pick up important concepts over a number of years. I feel fortunate that my human givens training has come along early in my career, as it has provided me with the skills to be truly effective, in a shorter timescale than might be expected for my years.

Spare capacity

I truly believe that you cannot be a 'people person' without looking after yourself. I also believe that it is somehow fraudulent to tell patients about the marvels of exercise, relaxation, sleep hygiene, and work/life balance without appreciating them personally. I am proud to be able to say 'yes' when a patient asks me suspiciously if I practise what I preach (or at least I tell them that I try). In human givens terms, this means taking a careful look at needs not being met in my own life, and making efforts to work towards fulfilling them. For me, this means leaving work on time and being cautious about taking on extra work commitments, exercising daily, enjoying my leisure time and appreciating the support and friendship from my partner, family and social network (and cat). It also means consciously trying to manage my time well at work and at home, acknowledging when I need to have a break, and, while always empathising, making sure I stand back so as not to become entwined with and negatively influenced by the emotional distress of my patients, other people around me, or even people whose tragedies are featured on the TV news.

Many human givens principles are not new to physiotherapists – for instance the importance of relevant information gathering, motivating patients, and working towards meaningful goals. However, there are ways in which the human givens approach has developed these concepts and has provided me with a new bank of tools to draw upon. I feel my patients have gained from an improved clarity in my own thinking, and an ability to access their (often deeply buried) skills and strengths.

Keeping within boundaries

When I was suggesting how I might have helped former patients such as Mary, Anna and Edna, I didn't mention Henry. Elderly Henry was frightened of walking because the last time he had gone out for a walk a

CASE HISTORIES:

Karen and her pills

When I first met Karen, she had been trying to improve her health through a series of coping strategies that she had read about, such as trying to get her sleep patterns back to normal and getting back into a leisure activity she had used to enjoy. However, she was convinced that 'time' and 'pills' were the only things that helped (neither being in her control). I was careful to dissect these thoughts, by directing her towards other more likely explanations, and helping her to consider that it might have been her commitment to trying the new coping strategies that had brought about the positive changes she had recently experienced. She was quite clearly amazed: for the first time she could appreciate that the key to recovery might actually be in her hands.

Mike and his video

All Mike wanted was for his fatigue to go away, his pain to vanish and for his life to be back to normal. Maybe in the past, I would have asked him to pinpoint his pain level on a scale of 0–10, recorded his answer and seen whether it could be reduced as we worked together. However, this would not have given him any tangible evidence of recovery, nor any visible clues as to where to go from there. So, instead, I asked him to imagine himself in a video, seeing himself doing the things he would do when he felt well again ('when' not 'if': importance of hope). It was only when Mike could really visualise himself in a better time, for instance walking his children to school again, that he could identify what he needed to do to be able to achieve that state of wellness. He was then able to make specific, concrete, behavioural goals that he could work towards – for instance walking daily so he could improve his fitness, reduce his fatigue, improve his sleep and end up able to walk his children to school.

Rachel and the hot air balloon

Rachel had been ill for 11 years and appeared to carry the weight of her condition on her shoulders. She appeared depressed and clearly found it hard to see any future: she could see only her current struggle. Her self-esteem was crushed through a succession of 'failed' attempts to get better, resulting in the loss of her job, many friendships and the ability to participate in meaningful activity. I knew Rachel had been ▶

a manager in the past, and was clearly a loyal friend to others. During a session of relaxation, I borrowed a wonderful image that I had been quite moved by during my human givens training (my thanks to Mike, the fellow student who employed it). I asked Rachel to pack all of the difficult times she associated with her illness into bags and then load them into the basket of a hot air balloon, taking special care to notice how much lighter she felt. I encouraged her to visualise the balloon ready to lift off, and got her to cut the straps. She then watched the balloon travel off into the sky, getting smaller and smaller until it disappeared. A tear ran down her face: she told me that she had never imagined that those difficult times could ever be a distant memory.

I then guided her through a possible future, imagining how she could use her management and organisation skills to help a friend in a situation similar to hers. (I knew she had been a good friend to many, so I made use of this to help build her self-esteem and encourage her to take advantage of the problem-solving abilities she had employed as a manager.) She was able to explore various options: she could build up a regular routine, consisting of the right balance between activity and rest, try out new relaxation techniques, start walking gently every day and start winding down before bed. Once she was able to explore what she would say to a friend, she herself asked, "Is this appropriate for me?" and could see that she herself had the power to solve her difficulties. I encouraged her to visualise herself doing these activities, to aid her motivation. She had been unwell for so long that she did not believe she could live a different life — now she could see, for the first time in years, a way forward; she felt quite overwhelmed. And, although she has a way to go, she has a positive attitude again.

Helen's piano

Helen, a keen and highly accomplished musician, struggled to understand some of the fundamental principles of recovery. She wasn't quite able to see how important it was to walk regularly in order to make positive adaptive changes to her body. However, it made sense when I asked her how she had managed to learn the piano to such a high level. She realised that, just as she had had to practise and practise in order to achieve mastery in her music, so she must keep walking every day to build up her body strength. ■

car had hit him. Henry had been traumatised by that event and it would have been so easy to help him resolve that trauma by using the rewind technique, which employs mental imagery to help people dissociate emotionally from traumatic experiences. But I have had to accept that this may be perceived as outside my remit. Physiotherapists, like other health professionals, have designated core skills that underpin their scope of practice. Not only do staff have expectations about what physio-therapists do but so do patients, and it can upset or confuse them to be given, in effect, counselling when they are expecting hands-on treatment or a limited 'physical' approach.

To counter these concerns I am working on a 'human givens protocol' for use at work. This helps to ensure I am staying within a role mutually agreed between my physiotherapy manager, the consultant that I work with and myself. It is agreed that any work I do to ease patients' anxiety and depression is 'complementary to the medical management' and that I can use the rewind technique for the resolution of trauma only if the trauma is CFS-specific. One such instance became apparent when I noticed that one young woman, Elizabeth, became quite frightened when her heart pounded during exercise, and she could not make progress beyond a certain point. She explained that every time she felt her heart rate rise, it took her straight back to a traumatic time when she was very ill with CFS, when she was highly stressed and thought she might be dying. Use of the rewind technique detached the emotional arousal from the memories and enabled her to continue with her recovery from CFS.

I have also adapted some therapeutic principles, to make them more appropriate in a physiotherapeutic context. For instance, the human givens approach places much emphasis on encouraging clients to rehearse success in whatever it is that they want to overcome or achieve. This usually takes the form of a visualisation exercise, carried out while deeply relaxed, to improve the likelihood of the desired outcome. If I don't have time to relax a patient fully, or if it seems inappropriate, I usually ask them to imagine the new behaviour and to describe it to me in detail, using prompts such as "When will you go for a walk? Will it be during lunchtime or when you get back from work? Will you go alone to the shop, or will you go with your wife? What will you do if it rains?" I ask them to write their answers down, and to tell their family, friends and colleagues what they are doing, and I also ask them to reward themselves with something pleasurable, to further aid their motivation. I tell them of the scientific research that shows this approach helps patients, explaining carefully how it works, and how it can have a knock-on effect in all areas of their lives.

A vision for the future

Perhaps we health professionals are all finding it difficult to swim upstream, all with fins that are not as strong as they could be. And, until our fins are strengthened, we may continue to swim weakly, with difficulties establishing direction and speed. If the NHS is to be able to fulfil its admirable objectives, I believe that *all* health professionals need to find ways to deal effectively with diverse emotional needs, not only those of our patients, but also our own needs and those of our colleagues. This means everyone working within the NHS taking individual responsibility to notice and to care when somebody is in emotional distress – whether they are ill and dying of cancer, grieving after the loss of a loved one, frightened and in pain, stressed and out of control with their workload, or else being harassed or bullied – and then knowing how to deal with this, effectively, swiftly, and with compassion.

This deeply human approach really is the key to making the difference between being a shining light or burning out, the difference between giving our colleagues a hand of support or a stab in the ribs, the difference between patching someone up and sending them home, and really empowering and supporting patients to take control of their own lives and health.

* * * * *

Jessica Bavinton is currently working as a clinical specialist physiotherapist in chronic fatigue syndrome at St Bartholomew's Hospital. She is currently chairing a nationwide group of therapists involved in the dissemination of CFS treatment principles to therapists, as well as developing a teaching role and taking part in research in the CFS field. In a voluntary capacity, she has worked for the British Red Cross fire victim support unit and supports various rehabilitation and humanitarian projects in India and the Himalayas. She is currently planning additional private work as a human givens therapist and physiotherapist.

This, too, will pass: coping with high arousal in the classroom

Sue Gwinnell-Smith, a learning support unit manager, describes how human givens principles have helped her to help teachers teach and children learn.

RICHARD was a polite, seemingly ordinary 12-year-old boy – outside school. But in class, at the large comprehensive school where I work, he was a demon. He would have angry, unprovoked outbursts against teachers, during which he swore, became aggressive and threw items across the room. He was eventually referred to me at the learning support unit, which we call The Bridge.

When I spoke with his parents about what could possibly be behind this behaviour, they identified a traumatic year Richard had undergone in primary school, when he had a class teacher whose style was to shout and rant. Richard was intimidated by her and gradually changed from a lively, outgoing young boy to a sullen, uncooperative one. Matters had got worse once he transferred to secondary school. Even the sight of a teacher seemed to arouse him emotionally and he had evidently decided to fight back, causing more and more teachers, in desperation, to raise their voices to him.

I would like to say there was a happy outcome to this story. Unfortunately, there was not. Richard ended up being excluded from school, failing to attend a special school where he was given a place and now, at age 14, has an ASBO (antisocial behaviour order) because of the problems he is causing in the community. The experience of not being able to help him to be better able to handle his behaviour, even with my advanced diploma in special needs and my Masters specialising in young people's emotional, social and behavioural development, was what led me to seek further training. After my very first MindFields College seminar (and I have now done many), I started to develop the understanding and the tools which, put together with my own skill set, now enable me to offer much more effective help to both children and teachers. Last year, our exclusion rate was down by 66 per cent. And, when recently I carried out a survey of staff about the services our unit offers, we were almost without exception graded 'excellent' or 'very good' – and even the exceptions were 'satisfactory'.

I started my career as a science teacher in Liverpool nearly 30 years ago and, by a roundabout route, including a stint in a failing school and as deputy head of an alternative school for children excluded, for a variety of reasons, from mainstream and special schools, I came to West Sussex to set up a learning support unit at one of the largest comprehensive schools in the country – over 2000 students aged between 11 and 18. We called our unit The Bridge because that is what we aim to provide – a bridge back into successful mainstream learning.

We deal with children who, in education parlance, are 'school action plus'. They are the ones who are presenting quite a challenge, have already gone the route of being on report and receiving mentoring and pastoral support, and are deemed in need of more intensive input from the school. At The Bridge we may work with them full time for a month – sometimes less, sometimes more – combining school work with lessons in emotional literacy, anger management, relaxation and yoga. Gradually, we reintegrate them into the lessons they find easiest and then into the lessons they find hardest.

The body language of rapport

Teachers often invite us into their classes to observe a child they are concerned about, or we may go into class to see how one of 'our' children is settling back. It was through seeing so many teachers at work, in this way, that I began to grow more and more interested in why challenging children behave for some teachers and not for others. In breaking down and analysing what it was that enabled good rapport between some teachers and children, but not other teachers and children, I realised most of it was about body language. I can almost tell at a glance who will be 'in charge' and who will not.

However, it was only after attending a MindFields College seminar that I realised the degree to which aroused emotions drive us, and prevent us from learning. Those teachers who were not in charge were sending the message, "You can dump on me. I cannot stop you", allowing high arousal to take control in the classroom; and those who were in charge were giving out the message, "I'm in control here; you can relax".

The implications of this were a revelation to me. Teachers who made it clear they were in charge were enabling children to feel safe, an important human need – and children with difficulties, often stemming from problematic backgrounds or a history of failure, too often feel extremely unsafe. In a place and with a person where they perceived themselves as secure, they could relax their guard and, in this state of lowered emotional arousal, be more focused on their work.

Seeing for the first time exactly why good rapport can be so powerful, I started to work with individual staff on ways to enhance it. It is easy to create rapport with people we like – we do it instinctively – but, with challenging children, rapport building needs to be deliberate, and non-verbal messages reveal a lot. Some teachers seem to stoop, without realising it, or to shelter behind their desks, as if making a gesture of submission. However, when I ask what they think is a good teaching posture, they can identify it straight away – very upright, businesslike but smiling, relaxed and confident.

One teacher, in whose class I was observing a child, was reading a book to the class while slouching against a cabinet at the side of the room – as if trying to get away and hide, and sending the message, loud and clear, that she was not going to take charge. It was a simple matter to show her, while role-playing in an empty classroom, the positive impact of coming forward and 'being there'. Other mannerisms that I have role-played with staff include gesturing with palms up and gesturing with palms down. When they see it for themselves, teachers quickly realise that 'palms up' conveys pleading and appeasement, whereas 'palms down' conveys calmness and control.

The most effective teaching voice is strong and centred. Of course, when we are anxious or otherwise emotionally aroused, our voice rises and becomes quick, conveying a lack of confidence and failure to control. Teaching teachers how to relax themselves quickly, with the 7/11 breathing technique (breathing in to the count of seven and out to the count of 11, to slow breathing down) has been extremely effective in helping them hold on to control when being 'wound up' by a challenging pupil.

Once upon a time...

Only after attending the MindFields College workshop on storytelling did it occur to me that telling a story would be a wonderful way to relax all the children at the start of the day, getting them into a mental state where they are ready to learn. At the beginning of every teaching session, there is supposed to be what is called a 'starter' – anything designed to grab the children's attention. It could be a quiz on whatever was learned in the last lesson, a wordsearch to refresh memories on vocabulary learned or a bit of play-acting, such as the teacher pretending to eat a bowl of cereal at the start of the science lesson, and asking what its constituents are. It is often a struggle to keep thinking of something 'grabby'. How natural and beneficial it is sometimes to start with a story instead. I have been encouraging staff to see how this can be a productive start-off point, whatever the lesson. For instance, a language or humanities lesson could start with a story illustrating the cultural differences in the country or faith or period in time being studied. A science lesson could start with a story of scientific discovery, and so on.

I use this approach myself, when delivering a PSHCE (personal, social, health and citizenship education) lesson at The Bridge. I always make a real story of it, drawing on children's visual, auditory and kinaesthetic senses, careful with the timing, and ensuring a gradual build-up, so that they don't know where I am heading, and hang on my every word. For instance, if I am planning a focus on improving attendance, I don't say, "I'm going to tell you a story about how important it is to come to school". I begin obliquely. "A man down my road told me a story this morning about a young man who used to live round the corner from here. He didn't like school." And then I would tell them the true story of a man who, when he was a boy, started truanting from school. But he soon became very hungry because, if he wasn't at school, he couldn't get the free school dinner his circumstances entitled him to. He started to shoplift for food, and then for other things. Quite soon, he was caught. Having left school by then, his conviction for shoplifting stopped him getting a job, so he started doing burglaries. He didn't like what he was doing and, when a friend suggested one big job that would net them enough to leave the country and retire, he went for it. The job went wrong and unintentionally he ended up blowing off a woman's head with a shotgun. He is now serving 23 years for murder.

Sometimes, if, when I have a few minutes to spare, I pass a classroom, hear a bit of a rumpus and see a teacher – especially a supply teacher filling in for an absent member of staff – struggling to settle a class, I may go in and quietly offer to settle the students while she gets her resources sorted. Then I'll say to the class, "I've got a story I think you might enjoy, while Miss P gets her materials ready" and I tell them half of a story. It could be about anything from a classic tale, reworked to suit their interests, to an interesting, relevant anecdote I've heard, which I enlarge into a tale. (I've noticed they are particularly fond of stories in which small animals use cunning to outwit bigger creatures.) I tell them I will come back just before the end of the lesson to finish it off. On the rare occasions when circumstances prevent me from having the time to get back to the class, I may be sought out by hulking great 15-year-olds, the terrorisers of the playground, saying, "What happened at the end of the story, Miss?"

Teaching staff about needs

I am currently planning some in-service training for staff, which covers not only body language, delivery, rapport and relaxation but also looks at our emotional needs, and how we can meet our own and the children's in class, to create win–win situations.

For instance, safety is a huge issue for very many children at the school (despite many people's assumption that, situated as we are on a pleasant southern coastal strip, life will be largely idyllic). Some of our children may be suffering abuse at home, or they may be given too much control, because their parents or carers don't set boundaries. Some may be suffering neglect and thus lack attention and a sense of being cared for. It can help if teachers understand that this is where the challenging behaviour, usually expressed in angry or aggressive out-bursts, originates from. I used to offer a very complex form of anger management intervention, which I learned on a course. It involved weeks of sessions and a great deal of introspection from the children about why they were getting angry, what had made them angry in the past and how angry they considered themselves on a scale from 1 to 10. The result was that the children got even angrier! (It surprised me then; it doesn't surprise me now.) These days, I concentrate on helping children become aware of when anger is welling up, breathing to calm themselves down and then challenging the justification for the anger. Perhaps so-and-so's remark wasn't meant as a put-down to them at all: perhaps they were 'pattern matching' inappropriately to an earlier occasion, when something similar happened but the circumstances were different, and so on.

Using rewind

Most significant in its impact for reducing angry outbursts in the classroom has been the rewind technique (see page 59). I wish I had known about it when I was working with Richard, the boy who was bullied, whom I described at the start of this article.

I have used the rewind to detraumatise a 12-year-old boy whose extremely violent father would fly into sudden blind rages. At the age of 10, Jack had had the especially terrifying experience of being dragged, with his younger brother, up to a bedroom by his father, who was wielding a large kitchen knife. The father locked the door and proceeded to dart from one to the other, making threats and holding the knife to their throats. His violence only came to an end, as far as the family was concerned, when he was imprisoned for grievous bodily harm after slitting someone's throat with a smashed bottle. However, Jack remained in a state of constant high arousal and would lash out at the least provocation by child or teacher in class. One session of rewind made him a changed boy. His brother has now joined the school, and I plan to use the rewind with him too.

Ben was another young lad who also had unpredictable angry outbursts in class. He had been adopted at the age of five. His birth mother was a prostitute and, when he was four, he had seen her while she was servicing a client. She was so angry at being caught that she had beaten him half to death, compounding the trauma of the event. Ben lacked any real social skills. Although now aged 13, he continually obsessed about his mother, telling classmates he was going to find her and kill her when he was 18. "You have no idea how terrible a mother my mum was! Do you know what she did?" he would ask, and then describe the event in full – no doubt, by that time, well-embellished – detail. Poor Ben felt utterly betrayed, both by his mother and then by his classmates, who would taunt him by chanting, "Your mother was a whore!" Unsurprisingly, he would get into a lot of fights.

When Ben was referred to me, I suggested to him that it might not be such a good idea to go into such detail about what had happened with his mum. "I can't help it," he said. "It's always on the top of my mind." Just one session of rewind enabled him to stop obsessing about his mother and to stop disrupting lessons (although clearly he had other problems that we needed to continue working on with him). Another boy who was causing inexplicable ructions in school was discovered to be obsessing about the fact that his father had had an affair with his best friend's mother and had left the family – and the best friend had known about it first and not told him. Again, one session of rewind brought down his super-high arousal and he was able to let go of his anger against his best friend.

Make it meaningful

The human need for meaning and purpose manifests itself very strongly in a school setting. Children need to know why they are learning what they are learning and to feel it matters, if they are to be motivated to do it; they need to be interested, and to feel able. They also need to feel stretched by what they are doing. If teachers deliver their material in a boring tone of voice (perhaps because they are bored or because they are burned out by the myriad demands on teachers nowadays), they destroy the meaningfulness of any activity at a stroke. I believe that, to be a teacher, you have to have a real interest in the children and a real desire to be as good as you possibly can. That is where one's own meaning and stretching comes from.

I try to encourage teachers to think about the outcomes that they are looking for, as some don't seem to have in mind at the outset what they want to achieve from a lesson. For instance, I worked with a teacher who, when stressed, became sarcastic to his class. That led children to complain to their parents about his behaviour; complaints were made to the school and parents started to discuss him among themselves. "Surely," I said to him, "you do not want to get the reputation of being a bad teacher. Yet, while you are resorting to sarcasm, you will get that outcome. What will help is working harder on building rapport. Then children are more likely to want to learn what you are teaching."

Ensuring that children can access the curriculum is a vital aspect of providing meaning and creating a classroom atmosphere conducive to learning. Children who are fearful about their abilities in a particular subject may even enter the room feeling stressed, and thus, with the best will in the world, be unable to work. The simple technique of relaxing the class at the outset does wonders to reduce that.

To get the best out of individuals, teachers must think about enabling them to work in the way they learn best – in effect, ensuring that they have a degree of control over their working. That might mean offering a choice as to how to complete a task. For instance, if a science lesson is covering food groups – which foods fit into which groups and what they are needed for – one child might be happy to read the information and answer examination-type questions to check understanding; another might like to work the information into a poster; another might like to go to the internet for information and then produce a leaflet; another might need a highly structured worksheet; another might want to 'play teacher' and give a presentation to the class. With a little guidance, children can be helped to choose what they want to do, and, building on the experience of being successful, to feel safe enough also to try out other approaches that they don't find quite so easy.

Don't 'diss' me

We all have a need for status that signifies acceptance and, in large schools full of a wide mix of children, the way status is sought can have significant effects. Children, particularly boys, who feel they cannot achieve academically, may seek status through being 'bad' – taking drugs, being a bully, truanting from school, being a vandal, etc. Everyone needs to succeed and no one wants to feel disrespected (or 'dissed'), which is why it is important to move the goalposts so that success doesn't just equal an A in science or maths. I would like to see all teachers do more to give musical, dramatic and sporting abilities true status, not just lip service, and to make more creative use of them in mainstream lessons. For instance, children can work in groups to produce role-plays, write and deliver 'raps' or other musical renderings of information being learned; or create physical enactments of how molecules bond, magnets attract and repel or how fractions work.

Teachers also have a need to maintain status, and may struggle when they perceive that their status as 'the one in charge' is being challenged. When they are stressed or challenged by the behaviour of difficult children, they may cease to see those children as individuals, who often have huge mountains of their own to climb, and view them simply as obstacles to their doing their jobs. Such tunnel vision, caused by emotional arousal, doesn't result in the most sensitive of handling. One young teacher used to shout so much that his behaviour verged on bullying. When I asked if I could help him explore how to maintain discipline in another way, he said, "I thought shouting was what you had to do to be a strong and powerful teacher". If I ask teachers whether they find that shouting or giving frequent detentions, etc, makes a young person better behaved, the answer is invariably 'no'. After all, if children are the sort who are cowed by bullying, they don't need to be bullied. And, if they are not cowed by bullying, they will stand up for themselves, whatever happens, and conflict will worsen rather than improve.

Of course, no teacher should be seen to be soft but, when it comes to behaviour management, I am a firm believer in keeping it simple: I help teachers to achieve assertive discipline – setting boundaries, being firm and using the mildest sanctions that will work.

One person to care

Because, at The Bridge, we know the often deeply troubled backgrounds of the children we help, we know how valuable it is when a teacher shows an interest in them. One boy who came to us was being physically abused by his father but denied the fact to social workers who came to see him because he desperately didn't want his family split up. Tom was also neglected by his mother, whose only interest was her cats. His clothes were never washed and tended to smell of cat urine, as the cats were allowed to relieve themselves wherever they pleased. When he first came to The Bridge, I used to offer him a chance to shower and have a change of clothes, and, although he would have liked this, he reluctantly refused. He feared that, if he took up the offer, his father would find out and know that he had been talking about his home situation.

Tom used to be so depressed. Although, alas, we couldn't change his situation, what we could give him was hope – to show him that nothing lasts forever and that he did have valuable innate resources which would help him, if he got his education, to escape at 16, if he chose, and make a life for himself. We nurtured his ability and he felt, and still feels, cared for by us. Now he waves and smiles whenever he passes our windows. Sometimes it takes just one person to understand, one teacher or whoever to care, to help a young person develop enough resilience to survive and perhaps thrive.

And teachers need to develop resilience too. It is one thing to work all hours and draw on every resource one has in order to pass an inspection. It is another to keep up the vigour, enthusiasm and commitment in the classroom, every day of every term for 40 years. I tell teachers that they must always be on top and, drawing on the human givens, that there are many ways they can help themselves do that. My big five are:

- know how to relax quickly, to calm down;
- make time for themselves, so that they fill their own needs for nurturing and for emotional and social connection;
- direct their attention away from themselves – for inspiration, for recreation, for getting things in proportion;
- bring pleasant or positive thoughts to mind when feeling up against it (for instance how well Sam behaved last lesson, even though he is playing up now) and to be mindful of the baggage many children bring;
- and remember that nothing lasts.

* * * * *

Sue Gwinnell-Smith is the learning support unit manager at Littlehampton Comprehensive School in Littlehampton, West Sussex.

Uncommon therapy

*__Helen Card__, a consultant psychologist and expert witness,
shows how taking therapy outside the therapy room
can often yield extraordinary results.*

"WHATEVER the client brings to the therapy session is grist for the therapeutic mill," said Joe Griffin, co-founder of the human givens approach, when tutoring the Human Givens Diploma course that I attended in York. His words resonated strongly with me. He was referring to the utilisation principle (a term coined by the renowned, innovative psychiatrist Milton Erickson), which means using whatever a client brings into a therapy session, be it resources or symptoms, as a natural way of facilitating solutions.

I suddenly realised that it was a principle that I had been applying for years – and many times it had earned me a questioning gaze and a raised eyebrow from my highly experienced counselling supervisor – a chartered clinical, educational and forensic psychologist, highly respected within the British Psychological Society. As the results had been so successful, she could hardly argue that it didn't work, and had to content herself by designating my therapy practice 'uncommon'. Having believed myself to be out on a limb all those years, Joe's words were immensely reassuring to me. So I thought it might be helpful if I shared some of my experience of uncommon therapy and, I hope, show how, by being creative and sometimes taking therapy outside the therapy room, the results can be extraordinary. My clients' names have been changed to protect their identities.

A young man's dream

Alan worked in the construction industry and, two years previously, at the age of 23, had suffered a serious injury while working on the roof of a house. He had been cutting metal sheets with an angle grinder when the unsecured ladder on which he was standing (he should, in fact, have been working from scaffolding) tipped backwards. He fell with it, landing hard on his back on the garden path and fracturing his spine. The angle grinder landed on top of him, still whirring and slicing through his clothing. It was only because it was winter and he was wearing a thick jacket on top of his overalls that a colleague was able to kick it away before it sliced into his body. As a result of the accident, Alan spent months in hospital on his back, immobilised, while the fracture healed. He became severely depressed and developed chronic pain. After the fracture had healed, Alan's doctors told him that they could find no reason for his continuing pain, that nothing could be done for it and that he would just have to learn to live with it. He felt crushed.

He was referred to me by the agency that was handling his compensation claim and therapy took place in a tiny, not very suitable, office on the agency's premises. In our first session together, while Alan sat opposite me, bolt upright as if he had a metal rod in his spine, I gathered information from him and searched for resources from his life. Before the accident, he had just bought himself his first brand-new car: sporty, black, top of the range – 'a young man's dream'. He had also been working out every evening in the gym, acquiring the definition and body tone any man would be envious of. He had been looking at properties and mortgages, and was planning finally to move out of his parents' home and live independently. Life was good and his self-image was very positive.

After the accident, his brand-new dream car had had to be sold, as his many months off work on minimum basic sick pay made its upkeep impossible. Although he had since been able to return to work, he was reduced to buying an old banger of a car, which at least he persisted in driving, although he found it highly uncomfortable. He no longer dared to risk exercising at the gym, however, for fear of exacerbating his pain and, as a consequence, he had become very unhappy with his body image (although he was, in fact, still an attractive man). He rarely went out socially any more. Four days before our first therapy session, Alan had attempted suicide.

The key to change

When therapy began, Alan was still suffering nightmares and intrusive memories of his accident so, naturally, I attempted to use the rewind technique (see page 59), a non-intrusive method of taking the emotional arousal out of traumatic memories that requires the patient to be in a state of deep relaxation. However, the tiny office boasted only a few hard chairs and, because of the discomfort Alan felt in his back, he could not find any comfortable position in which to relax. There wasn't any room to lie on the floor and even pushing chairs together was out of the question, as the stiff-backed, log-rolling technique which doctors had taught him for lying down and getting up couldn't be applied.

At that very time, I had just purchased a brand new car: a Mini Cooper S in a beautiful metallic blue. On the day I took delivery of it, I had a session with Alan scheduled for later in the afternoon. An idea came to me. When I collected the car, I found on the back seat, as a marketing gimmick, a soft-toy tiny replica of it, in blue and white fur. I brought the soft toy into the office and, when Alan arrived, told him I had got a new car, which I wanted to show him. He looked intrigued and then he saw the fur Mini Cooper S on the desk and smiled at what he thought was my joke. "Actually, that isn't all it is, Alan," I said, and I led him out to the road where my gleaming new car was parked. His sad face was transformed by the most enormous smile. It was as if the sun had suddenly come out, and the pain dropped away from his features for the very first time. "Oh, that's beautiful!" he enthused. "And it's my favourite colour!" (I hadn't known that, of course.) "May I look inside?" Utterly engrossed, he examined the interior and the controls.

"Which would you rather, Alan? A therapy session or a drive in the car?" I asked. "A drive in the car!" he responded at once. He started to move towards the passenger door but I handed him the keys and stepped to the passenger side myself. His surprise and delight were obvious and he responded instantly to my showing that much confidence in him. (Well, he was over 21 and we were both insured.) He didn't question for a minute whether he would be comfortable – in fact, the seats have good lumbar support – and drove my car around the countryside for about an hour, totally focused on, and absorbed in, what was for him a highly pleasurable experience. For the first time in two years he did not feel weighed down by his depression. I didn't mention pain until we were almost back at the consulting rooms and then I said, "How is the back feeling?" He looked at me in astonishment. "It's fine," he said.

"I'm comfortable. I haven't even thought about it!" He had just learned something very important: if his attention was focused elsewhere, he could lift his mood and manage his pain.

With that new learning, his progress in therapy was swift. He was no longer afraid to try relaxing on a makeshift couch I constructed of two chairs, covered with cushions brought in from my home. I used the memory of driving around in my car to induce relaxation, removed his traumatic symptoms entirely with the rewind technique, and then used visualisation and metaphor to help him manage his back pain. Alan is now in a new and better job, is back at the gym, socialises again and is in the process of buying his own house. I doubt that I could have achieved that shift without the uncommon therapy of driving around in my car!

Sleeping with the cattle

Henry's was a complex case. This 30-year-old man was suffering from post-traumatic stress disorder (PTSD), complicated by depression and a polypharmacy of medication. On top of the drugs, he was heavily self-medicating with alcohol to help him sleep. Henry had been in a serious road traffic accident four years previously. His psychological response to the accident and the behaviour induced by the alcohol had left him isolated from family and friends, as he had become extremely aggressive and violent, even stabbing someone at one point. He had been barred from every pub in his locality and his mother refused to allow him anywhere near her house. The only human contact Henry still had was with his GP and his pharmacist. He was so lonely and despairing that, sometimes, he would leap over the railings of a local park where there was an animal enclosure, and, nursing a bottle of Southern Comfort, bed down there for the night with the Highland cattle.

Henry had been referred to a colleague of mine to be assessed for psychological injury arising from the accident. This colleague had written a report for the court, saying that Henry had an extremely severe case of PTSD, which had precipitated the domino effect of events that had ensued. He recommended therapy but was guarded about the prognosis, as earlier efforts at treating Henry's depression and alcohol problems had collapsed because of his erratic and aggressive behaviour. The defendants in the court case (the insurance company of the driver of the car that caused the accident) agreed to fund the therapy. I had trepidation, too, about taking on his therapy. However, when he arrived for his first session, I felt that, despite his medication-induced slurred speech and slow responses, he really did want things to be different, even if, at that stage, he didn't have much belief that they could be.

For Henry, life before the accident had included being a Thai boxing champion, travelling and doing casual work abroad, and enjoyment of playing chess and fishing. He had also, at one stage, been employed as a parks and countryside ranger and held a deep affinity with nature. These, I felt, were excellent resources, which allowed more uncommon therapy!

In our first session, I attempted some relaxation and guided imagery. Henry seemed to respond well as I encouraged him to slow his breathing, breathing in to the count of 7 and out to the count of 11, but then froze as I began to take him on an imaginary journey to his favourite fishing spot. He snapped back to alertness and expressed his fear at revisiting memories of life before the accident, saying, "It's like that person died." With lots of reframing (for instance, I told him about cell renewal – that every cell in his body would be new since then, so in one way he was indeed a different person) and reassurance, I decided to leave things with the 7–11 breathing for that first session and asked him to practise it every day before we met again.

Naming the animals

At our next session, he told me that the breathing was "doing something", but he was not sure what, and he sat with his head in his hands. He said that all he had wanted, and needed, for so long, was a hug. So he asked me for one. I stiffened as I recalled so much previous training in which teachers of various models of therapy and counselling had emphatically advised against physical contact between therapist and client. But at the same time I was painfully aware that my hesitation and potential refusal would be further rejection for this young man. Then I remembered another gem from my human givens training: 'name your animals'. At times, something a patient says or brings to therapy can trigger a pattern match to something similar in our own lives and strong emotions are aroused. Staying with those emotions can get in the way of the therapy we are trying to do. A solution is to 'name the animal': identify the emotion as disgust, horror, grief or whatever, and, by the act of observing it, shift it into the left hemisphere, reducing the emotional arousal. I identified my emotion as shock and anxiety – "You don't do this with clients!" – and then my arousal subsided, allowing me to go with that moment in the therapy session. Henry hugged me for 30 minutes. He was just clinging tightly to another human being while he sobbed out his pain and hurt at everything that had happened to him during the past four years. He didn't speak a word as I made reassuring murmurs of "That's it, that's right", just as we do when inducing relaxation. This proved to be a significant release for Henry and he never asked or needed for it to be repeated.

In our next session I tried again to relax him, so that I could deal with the traumatic memories of the accident with the rewind technique, but his resistance was just as strong. I decided that a different approach was required, so I suggested we play chess, even though I had never been taught and didn't know how. I gambled on the idea that getting him to focus his attention on teaching a novice how to play would be a suitable distraction, and I found that the chess board and pieces became tools to help him map his problems. This dissociation from the emotional content was incredibly successful. For instance, asking him his favourite piece (the queen) and what it was he was drawn to about her (her ability to move in any direction across the board, without restriction) opened the way to using metaphor to show that he too had the power of freedom, and to help him see that he was setting his own restrictions.

The lesson from the cacti

The next time I saw Henry, I took him to the beautiful Botanical Gardens in Sheffield, where we sat for a while in the cactus house, taking a direct lesson from Milton Erickson. Erickson once worked successfully with an alcoholic newspaper reporter simply by suggesting he visit some botanical gardens, look at all the cacti, marvel at how cacti can survive years without water and do a lot of thinking about it. Henry was very knowledgeable about plants, from his previous employment as a parks and countryside ranger, and he proceeded spontaneously to tell me how and where the different types of cactus survive on so little liquid nourishment. I just listened and allowed the metaphor to do its own work. It did.

I had also brought along a bag of peanuts, which I produced as we strolled through the gardens amongst the chattering grey squirrels. Before long, the squirrels were eating the nuts from his hand, renewing his bond with the natural world, and I saw him smile for the first time.

Around this time I had attended a workshop about antidepressants and their side effects, and I began to wonder if Henry's medication was part of his problem. With Henry's consent, I met with his GP and we agreed to wean him gradually off his drugs. After a week – although it is not advised, but Henry is Henry – he decided to go cold turkey. In less than a month, he was free from all medication and side effects, the slurred speech and slowness disappearing at once. I tried the rewind technique again, this time with spectacular results, probably because I could at last get beneath the blanket of medication his brain had been wrapped up in. Henry is now functioning normally again, sleeping like a baby, and training to be a yacht master. He has re-established contact with family and friends and his future looks bright.

Fairground tactics

At the age of 17, Susan had developed severe problems with her body image. Although of normal weight, she thought she was grossly over-weight. She was referred to me, a few years later, because she was be-coming so depressed about herself that her ability to carry out her work as a computer operator was affected. At the time she came to see me, a large travelling fair was in town. So, on our second session, after we had built rapport and I knew she really wanted to feel better about herself, I acted on a hunch and took her to the fair, to the Hall of Mirrors. We both stood there, looking at the various elongated, shrunken, widened and wiggly images of ourselves, roaring with laughter at how ridiculous we looked. Then we looked at ourselves in the ordinary mirror and she sud-denly saw just how normal she was. "Susan, I think you've had a Hall of Mirrors in your own mind," I told her. She didn't need to see me again and her six-month report showed that she was coping well again at work.

The fairground came into use with another client too. Joanne was a self-assured lady in her middle 50s. Her life was working well except for one thing. She had always had a fear of flying, and as a consequence had never flown. Her daughter and son-in-law had emigrated to Australia and had just had a baby, and so now she would absolutely *have* to fly if she were to see her baby grandson. She was completely terrified but there was no traumatic experience to rewind – the fears were just in her head.

Looking for resources, I discovered that she had loved going to the fairground as a child. So, I told her that I would pick her up from her home the following week and we would visit the local funfair. (She didn't seem to find this odd.) I led her to the carousel, with its array of painted animals that you sit astride as they go round in a circle, bobbing up and down, and suggested we each get on to one. There we sat, two mature women, on a giraffe and a horse. It was in the middle of the week on a working day, and no one else was around. I took the opportunity, while we waited for the ride to start, of getting her to slow her breathing and then, as we took off, suggested she shut her eyes and really get into the experience. Soon she was completely in the moment, removing her feet from the stirrups and thrusting out her legs, and letting go of the pole with one hand. "You know, Joanne, this is just like flying!" I yelled across to her. "We could be on a magic carpet now. Or a plane. Going up and down like this is just how it feels to be in a plane during turbulence. Wouldn't it be lucky if you hit some turbulence during your flight and you could shut your eyes and imagine yourself back here, having this wonderful time on the carousel!" Joanne booked her flight the next day and had no trouble flying.

Uncommon but not instant

Devotee as I am of unconventional therapy, I have never done anything of this kind on the spur of the moment and certainly not in a first session. An idea might spark but I always wait to be sure of rapport with my client and that we have a mutual understanding of where we want to go with the therapy. I might also need to think about my 'hunch' quite a bit, considering ways to put it into practice effectively and safely. That said, I would encourage all therapists to use the utilisation principle in imaginative, unique, or uncommon ways, when it feels right.

* * ✳ * *

Helen Card is a consultant psychologist, expert witness and human givens psychotherapist based in Sheffield.

The human givens manager

Mike Hay, a senior manager within local government, shares some thoughts about putting the human givens approach into practice in the workplace.

AS a manager in the public sector, keen to give my best, I have read my share of management theory and studied management practice, in the hope of doing a better job. The art (or science, depending on your perspective) of management rests heavily upon theories of human behaviour. Yet there is a tension between how, as humans, we normally behave and how we are obliged to behave once we are squeezed into organisational structures, like components in a machine.

While management theory and application have relied particularly on findings from psychology for an understanding of how people 'tick', the focus is on how performance can be enhanced, cooperation ensured and workforces motivated. Much management development still relies upon the work of Jung and his anecdotally based ideas of personality archetypes, rather than on modern understandings of how the brain actually works. Personality (psychometric) tests now so heavily used in recruitment and development activity can be seen to box people into 'types', the descriptions of which are peppered with subjective statements such as 'seeks unity', 'hides difference', 'action oriented', 'challenges current thinking', 'talks more than listens' or the opposite. They read suspiciously like astrological charts, which is interesting, given that astrology was the only topic that Jung tried to analyse statistically. Consequently, the knowledge we use to manage others, despite a plethora of Masters in business administration (MBA), and organisational development courses, will be deficient if not holistically based in what we now know to be the givens of human nature.

The human givens approach focuses on crucial human needs, which a mass of health and social research has now shown to be essential for mental and physical health, and the innate resources we have to help us meet those needs. It is not widely recognised that ways of meeting essential needs, such as those for emotional connection, meaning, attention giving and receiving, control, privacy, safety, even fun, need to be built into organisational structure. While status and sense of achievement are two important needs that we quite commonly look to our work lives to fulfil, the means by which these must be earned, in some organisations, may preclude other needs being met, and/or the needs of other people being met. I am now convinced that the holistic nature of the human givens approach can enhance our management of others, to the greater benefit of staff and the more effective realisation of company goals. In other words, everyone gets their needs met.

For instance, my own behaviour as a manager has changed considerably, since I became aware of the role that attention needs play in our lives. We all need to give and receive attention in a balanced way, if we are to stay healthy. (Indeed, if we are starved of attention, we die.) But much human activity is undertaken as a means of getting attention needs met, rather than for the sake of the activity itself. That is, attention-seeking activity often masquerades as something else. I wonder how many chief executives, perceiving themselves to be leading from the front in meetings, during negotiations and so on, are actually feeding an addiction to attention.

Much bullying behaviour may be an ill-judged effort to meet attention needs: likewise, angry outbursts in meetings or the passive-aggressive act of sitting silently, declining to participate. The heart-of-gold employee who always volunteers to sell the raffle tickets, clear up after group lunches, organise outings, etc, may also primarily be motivated by the attention benefits. When we do notice the person who always has to question every aspect of what a presenter is saying or the person who is always claiming to have a headache or to need assistance with their work, we often accuse them of being attention seeking in their behaviour. It is helpful to recognise, instead, that we all seek attention at times, that this is a *bona fide* human need, and that the good manager/humane organisation can find proper channels through which it may be met.

Attention to others should be appreciative, respectful, and polite. Curt comments, instructions issued brusquely and irritable responses are indicative of impoverished attention giving. It is like fast food: it might achieve the end required in the short term, but it is not a diet to be taken regularly. The idea of respectful attention might seem basic, but it can be surprisingly absent, I have realised. In my own case, I have recognised that, when I am anxious, I become brusque. (To my chagrin, this was confirmed in appraisals completed by my staff.) If I am meeting new people, anxiety may lead me to hold back and say little, which means I don't always make a good first impression and may appear to be uninterested. Since studying the human givens, I have learned the importance of making positive efforts to stay relaxed – calming down my breathing, physically taking a quick break, never responding instantly and, therefore, in anger – so that I can better give respectful attention, because disrespectful attention is a failure to acknowledge others as human beings, with needs of their own.

Disrespectful attention

Little things can so easily diminish the quality of attention exchange. Managerial over-use of email has served to lessen direct personal contact and may seem domineering: instructions issued over the ether in peremptory fashion. I wonder whether such an abrupt, blunt, impersonal style of communication then seeps into face-to-face communication. In fact, does it actually reveal more than it conceals about our true attitudes towards colleagues? In the past, I have sat in senior management meetings where the directors of the organisation have been disparaging both about peers who are not present, and about everyone else 'below' them in the structure. Yet no one outside that meeting room ever knew, because people are generally highly skilled at concealing their true feelings about others; we do it all the time, as part of the oiling of the social machine.

Just as disrespectful, I feel, is the increasing tendency, in open-plan offices, for managers to give an employee critical feedback about their performance in full earshot of everyone else. If the managers themselves work in the open-plan setting, they may forget that sometimes the need for privacy is overriding – automatic instead of conscious behaviour.

The human givens manager will set up workplace structures that encourage positive exchanges of attention: team meetings, in which all contributors are valued; conversations instead of emails and tele-conferencing; an open-door policy; a mentoring and nurturing attitude to colleagues, whoever they may be. I think, too, though others may question this, that part of good attention giving is being interested in a person 'in the round', rather than just in their work role. Some managers, and certainly devotees of political correctness, might think that asking personal questions is probing and intrusive and could lead to awkwardness. For instance, might questions or comments about family life lead to discomfort for someone who has not chosen to reveal that they are gay or that they are in the middle of a divorce? I think that managers have a degree of responsibility for satisfying themselves that people's needs are being met. If certain people are lonely and isolated outside of work, they may put greater, perhaps unhealthy, investment into workplace relationships or, conversely, find it difficult to relate to others. This has a bearing on how they do their jobs, and how happy they and others are.

Also, not everyone looks for the satisfaction of all needs through work, if those needs are fulfilled elsewhere. I once had a secretary who flatly refused to engage in any training or activity designed to 'develop' her for a next step up the ladder. In management manuals, development is what you are supposed to encourage. However, Joanna was building up a new business with her husband. Her secretarial role provided, for the time being, their bread and butter, and she did her work in exemplary fashion. But her interest was in the small business, not climbing the corporate ladder.

Our own attention needs

While becoming aware of the attention needs of staff, we also need to acknowledge our own. I think wandering down the corridor to chat to a colleague, ostensibly about that new project but in reality to receive some personal attention, is a perfectly valid activity. It would be even more empowering to recognise that this is what we are, in fact, doing – then attention needs can be separated out from business discussions, and better-quality decisions might be made. In other words, if we need attention, we would do better to briefly discuss the film that was on last night or the football results, and save the business discussion for when our attention is fully on it. However, a knock-on effect of acknowledging attention needs is that we then tend to need less – so fewer excursions down the corridor might need to be made at all.

In public sector service provision, the overarching organisational requirement is to pay attention to the needs of the most vulnerable members of our community. At an organisation where I used to work, which was concerned with provision of residential care for older people, a human givens audit was undertaken to see how well managers' needs were being met at work and how well service users' needs were being met. On a scale of 1–10, where 1 signified very poorly and 10 very well, managers mainly scored themselves between 8 and 9 – and service users at 1 or 2. As one shocked manager commented, "This is completely upside down!" Clearly, caution is required in assuming that, if the needs of staff are met, then the needs of customers will be better met too.

The need to feel safe

While there are strict guidelines to ensure that workplaces are physically safe, no environment feels secure if threatening and bullying behaviour is rife. A human givens manager will never shy away from dealing with these issues, for they are corrosive in the extreme. As we know, bully-ing can occur at any level in an organisation and is an illegitimate way of getting needs met. It is not uncommon for various cabals to spring up in workplaces; people may be 'sent to Coventry' in unpredictable ways, and there are many subtle social rules about 'pecking orders' – who gets which perks and who is in charge of distributing them. Two senior human resources professionals once told me how they used to 'work' the informal group dynamics within their industries: jobs were only ever given to members of specific ethnic groups, and the leaders of these groups chose who got the jobs. There was, in effect, an official and unofficial (but more powerful) recruitment process. The managers both complained to me of the demise of this tribalism, as "everyone knew their place and there wasn't any trouble" – a satisfactory outcome, as far as they were concerned, but at what cost in human potential?

Whatever mechanisms are in place for stamping out bullying, people commonly fail to use them. They are frightened of the possible consequences, whatever assurances they receive, especially as bullying may be endemic. To be vigilant about bullying means developing good intelligence. It means keeping in touch with what is going on in one's workforce, perhaps even 'going back to the floor', so that knowledge is authentically gathered. But, ultimately, I believe, the only certain way to eliminate bullying is through building an emotionally mature work environment in which it is seen as important that *everyone's* needs are met – something that may become possible as human givens principles spread. Ethical behaviour is not contextual, as some managers may maintain, but is our own internal guidance, which is available to us naturally, if we remain calm and centred and do not focus on our own needs at the expense of those of others.

Taking back control

The increasing application of technology to processes previously carried out with a degree of autonomy is frightening. "For God's sake, let us be men [sic], not monkeys minding machines," as D H Lawrence put it. The ubiquitous computer dictates how we apply a process and won't let us deviate: we have to fill in or okay the displayed fields before we can move on. It is no surprise that the workplace that has embraced this technology to the highest degree, the call centre, has the highest turnover of disgruntled staff.

We must feel some degree of control over what we do, even if that control is more apparent than real. (We think we are choosing Tesco over Sainsbury, or *vice versa*, even though the bottom line is that we are still being herded to the supermarket.)

Of course, technology is here to stay (and can be radically transformative to a business) and other routines performed without variation can be just as deadening. So I have been trying to pay attention to how, even in such circumstances, some autonomy can be introduced at work. Control doesn't have to be in the big things – it may be a peripheral activity for which an individual could be responsible. Being in charge of the office plants, the milk money, the lottery collection, organising an outing or out-of-work social activity, perhaps raising money for a chosen charity, etc, all help our sense of volition. Inviting suggestions for improving procedures can result in some creative ways to introduce more autonomy, as well as offering autonomy in itself – as long as suggestions are acknowledged, looked into and feedback delivered. Flexible working is a powerfully simple tool for creating control, at least over arrival at and departure from the workplace.

Self-esteem and status

Status is strongly linked to self-esteem (which is derived from a sense of competence) and we measure it by how valued and appreciated we feel in the various social groups to which we belong, many of which are work centred. We can be appreciated for what we do, whatever our place in an organisation. Our car park attendant is highly valued, for example, and was recently entered into a national competition for employee of the year (by an organisation with over 13,000 employees). His pride in this was reflected in his demeanour. He is valued because of the way in which he carries out his duties – being pleasant even when required to be negative – and is invariably helpful. Recently, he refused me entry to our work car park (because dignitaries were using it for the day) and, as I huffed and puffed about having to pay to park somewhere else when I had no change, he pulled a £2 coin out of his pocket and offered to lend it to me. It was quite a humbling gesture, one that I shamefacedly declined, as, of course, I only needed to dig a bit deeper into my own pocket.

In our kitchen at work, I overheard a (female) colleague praising our (male) office cleaner (an Eastern European with limited English), saying what a pleasure it was to come into the kitchen on a Monday morning, when he has spent time ensuring that every surface gleams and all is neat and tidy. It was a genuinely meant comment joyfully received – he went beaming down the corridor. I make sure I acknowledge my boss for giving praise and being welcoming (ie non-threatening) to less senior colleagues, because sometimes the contributions of people more senior to us get taken for granted. Whatever our role, we can be appreciated for the contribution we make, and our sense of status will be enhanced.

Congruence

In certain organisations, it is required that every member of staff uses certain language or behaves in a way that befits the aims of the organisation. For instance, the modelling of 'pro-social behaviour' (actively demonstrating positive social behaviour at all time), currently being explored in the prison and probation services, requires all who come into contact with offenders to be trained in the method. It is just as important that cooks, cleaners and caretakers act in the required way as it is for key workers and managers. Everyone is viewed as an integral member of a team. Similarly, the Nurturing Programme, run by Oxford-based charity Family Links, to create calmer, more caring and creative atmospheres in primary schools, requires every single member of staff, including 'dinner ladies', to undergo a two-day training to learn how to offer the children positive discipline, and describe choices and consequences. The thinking in these cases is that, for an ethos to have meaning, everyone in the organisation must espouse and demonstrate it. By involving everyone, such an approach quite naturally increases everyone's sense of status.

It also increases sense of belonging. All the staff at the Hillingdon Manor School for children with autism [see page 111] are taught particular responses and language to use with the pupils, to create a sense of consistency and safety for the children. One supply teacher was amazed to be taken aside and taught these methods when she arrived for a few days, to replace a sick staff member. Her experience, in mainstream schools, was that supply teachers are just "dumped in the deep end" and left to get on with it. So inspired was she by the methods of the school that she applied for a full-time job and is now a valued, experienced member of staff.

This principle of embracing an ethos might well have wider application, especially in work cultures where mission statements such as "our staff are our most valuable asset" are much vaunted but not congruent with actual behaviour: staff feel treated with disdain. Matching behaviour to rhetoric would be a much more powerful way of demonstrating company mission and appreciation of vital staff contribution.

A human givens manager will look for a variety of means to ensure due appreciation is always shown. (The converse of this is that poor performance or behaviour must be tackled at once, otherwise appreciation loses its currency.) Even seemingly meaningless and trivial gimmicks work, because they aren't really meaningless or trivial at all. In one organisation I know of, where parking space was at a premium, the chief executive elected to relinquish his prime-position parking spot, right next to the main entrance, so that its benefits could be enjoyed each month by whoever earned the 'employee of the month' accolade. Competitions offering chocolates as prizes, even a plastic gold cup for the worst joke of the week, or stories about staff published in the staff journal, accompanied by fully captioned pictures – all these work on enhancing status, which is a powerful motivator. If we feel appreciated, we tend to put a bit more effort in. My organisation has just given five days' extra holiday to the employee judged to be best at customer service – no mean reward.

Emotional connection

People can feel lonely and isolated at work (managers most of all, if they operate a closed-door policy and make themselves inaccessible, as it compounds the truism that management is a fairly isolating activity if one is to maintain appropriate distance from those one manages) and the need for connection and for fun and friendship can go unrecognised. I once received a memo from a director, stipulating that, although we should be polite to each other, work was not the place for friendships and fun. Going to the pub together after work, for instance, was taboo, because we never knew when we might have to take action against a colleague. Certainly, on occasions, conflicts of interest might arise – if someone from another team gets a contract from your department, was it – or could it be thought to be – because you two go drinking together? But I personally believe work is a legitimate place to forge emotional connections. Cogs in a machine do not require relationships, while people do.

Work should not, however, primarily be a source of emotional fulfilment, nor engage people emotionally rather than rationally. Ideally, the human givens manager will act as an emotional thermostat to guard against strong emotion which clouds thinking and judgement, leading to poor relationships and bad decisions, and to ensure that people are not conditioned by high-emotion motivational techniques – such as the pep talks, rallies and road shows that are used to boost sales figures, promote development programmes or just bind individuals to the company – which generate less thinking and can lead to cultish behaviour.

Being stretched

We all need to be stretched, to feel that what we do has purpose, and managers can ensure this through proper appraisal. Stretching does not mean breaking. I have found that some staff prefer to be stretched in ways that do not necessarily relate to their job – as in the case of a man who,

at the age of 50, had decided to learn the saxophone and was determined to excel. While not being stretched leads to stress and/or harmful behaviour, people in less senior positions often prefer to stretch
themselves by running clubs of one sort or another at work or by being
involved in their local communities. I make a point of never assuming
that the more junior employee has neither the skills nor motivation to
'get on', nor to assume that 'getting on' must be work related.

Non-hierarchical project work may be a wonderful instrument for
meeting a cluster of needs: autonomy, positive goals, connection, esteem,
status, attention, as well as stretching and therefore providing greater
meaning. I imagine this may explain the rising popularity of project
working. In an environment of seemingly continual change in organisational structures and business targets, it allows for the positive and
creative renewal of project teams, and the combining of people in a whole
cornucopia of configurations. However, just being on a team cannot be
assumed in itself to confer all the above-mentioned desirable outcomes.

Imagining how it could be

The term 'human givens' comprises both the needs we must have fulfilled to ensure mental and physical health and the innate resources that
help us achieve this. Such resources include our cognitive abilities to
analyse, plan and step back to see the bigger picture, which managers
make much use of. They take less advantage of the wonderful facility
of imagination, restricting its use, perhaps, to brainstorming or developing ideas. A human givens manager will explore the potential of deep
relaxation and mental rehearsal of success – the kind that sportsmen are
now routinely encouraged to do and some forward-thinking companies
practise too. I do this now routinely myself: when I am going to be
attending an important meeting, giving a presentation or facing any
kind of challenging activity, I take the time out briefly to relax and
imagine myself performing confidently and competently whatever the
situation requires. When we rehearse mentally in this way, the brain's
expectations are fired, and we seek to fulfil these expectations for real.
So what we focus on is often what we get.

I haven't yet been brave enough to suggest a group relaxation session
with colleagues, to rehearse a shared goal, but I do plan to introduce

individuals to the idea and show them how to do it for themselves. Unfortunately, a more usual workplace habit, especially in Britain, is to rehearse failure ("I'll never get this done", "I'll start stammering as soon as I begin the presentation") – the very last thing a human givens manager should support.

As readers of the *Human Givens* journal will know, stories and metaphors speak directly to the imagination and offer wonderful opportunities for changing perspectives and empowering people. Some companies 'train' people in the use of motivating stories, but stories are not utilised anywhere near as often as they might be, in day-to-day work life. Yet stories and metaphors naturally abound within organisations, and staff will fill a vacuum with their own images, if managers do not. The nautical metaphor of a sinking ship was heard very often in some that I have worked in!

I have learned to keep my ears open, to discover what metaphors are current in my organisation and note whether they compound cynicism or are healthy and constructive – for instance, metaphors of embattlement using martial vocabulary, or of evolution and growth, using horticultural terms. I have also tried to develop a good stock of positive metaphors, to counter what I might hear, and the ability to think metaphorically on the hoof. For instance, talk of chaos and being overwhelmed or drowning can be construed as a short period of intense activity prior to solution, or a crucible from which is forged creativity. Sometimes, in difficult circumstances, we have to find our way in uncharted waters, working together with our trusted colleagues. Or, if someone is complaining about unethical behaviour, I might relate true stories of particular senior managers who face challenges in an ethical manner or protect staff from unfair criticism. (Of course, metaphors cannot be used to avoid tackling genuine issues that concern staff. This would be the fastest way to lose personal corporate 'capital' or credibility.)

I also look for metaphors which appear to have meaning for particular individuals or use what I know of them as a person to inform the metaphors I choose. For example, if someone is a keen gardener, I might talk of a sturdy plant thriving even in hard soil or of 'rooting' ideas. On one management course, I was taught that a good manager should be like a swan: calm on the surface, even if paddling away like mad underneath. Those of us who were on that same course would often say, "Swan! Swan!"

if one of us was panicking about something. Metaphor is powerful. Is your ship struggling in stormy seas, about to be swamped by the tidal waves of a hurricane, or are you sailing in a sleek racing yacht, the crew focused on their exciting and stimulating tasks with the latest sailing technology? Or perhaps your vessel is a futuristic space ship, containing the best and most disciplined minds education can produce, exploring unknown territory with confidence and courage...

Why should we bother to pander to the whims of our workforce? Because we all go to work to meet our needs, and there is nothing amiss about this. If employees are enabled to get their needs met, they will be more balanced, productive individuals and we will value the richer perceptions we have of them. There is also the stark reality of the hard-pressed recruitment market – if we don't provide an environment which helps employees with their broad range of needs, they will simply move on elsewhere. A quick search on the internet will reveal the "Directors of Fun" (yes, that's right) who are being employed in commercial settings. A report issued by the Health and Safety Executive just before Christmas headlined that "staff have to be happy, healthy and here". Developing a human givens workplace makes complete business sense, and even the most hard-headed boss will need to consider all this if their business is to survive in the 21st century.

It is said by some that management is a fairly amoral activity, as it concentrates on the attainment of organisational goals, not on what those goals actually are. Following the human givens approach would indicate otherwise. Once such ideas spread, if an organisation's products or goals become meaningless to us, we may be less inclined simply to take the cash. We will have ceased to operate mechanically as managers, and both we and the staff we manage will have a more curious, questioning, and less conditioned set of responses to what we do. Beware, the human givens approach may be harmful to acceptance of the status quo!

* * * * *

Mike Hay *is a senior manager within local government, although writing in a personal capacity. He holds the Human Givens Diploma, is a Fellow of the Human Givens Institute, and a member of the Chartered Institute of Management.*

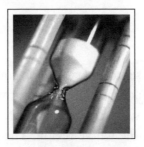

When time's not on our side

*James Hooton describes how human givens principles
help him in his work as one of the new mental health
practitioners in primary care.*

SOMETIMES, when people ask what I do for a living, they look
bemused when I reply that I'm a mental health practitioner. For I am
one of a relatively new breed, spanning the divide between secondary
and primary mental health services, in a role which has been developed
as part of the drive to improve primary mental health care.[1] As the
rationale for my presence in primary care is to help more patients receive
effective treatment quickly, I am highly grateful for what I've learned
from the human givens approach, which enables me to accomplish a lot
in a limited time.

Two years ago, in Bognor Regis, where I work, two mental health
practitioners were appointed for a pilot six-month period to work across
four GP surgeries and see all patients within a fortnight of referral. The
idea was to find out whether providing direct, speedy access to specialist
workers in primary care would be clinically and cost efficient and result
in a cut in referrals to secondary care, reducing the over-burdened community mental health team's workload. As I was overseeing the project at
this stage, I sat in on a number of sessions with different GPs in different
surgeries, to gauge just how much of their work involved dealing with
mental ill health. Without exaggeration, poor mental health was an
issue – whether directly or indirectly presented – for 90 per cent of people
consulting their doctor. GPs know only too well that, if someone keeps
coming in with different small ailments every other week, something
bigger is the problem – whether home or social circumstances, lack of
employment or family difficulties. But not only do they lack the time,

and perhaps the expertise, to manage these concerns themselves; most haven't had access to quick and efficient treatments.

Our pilot project was such a huge success that there was no question but to roll it out across the whole region. The project was carried out with no extra funding – we had just reconfigured the service by moving secondary care workers into GP surgeries – and brought such financial as well as emotional health benefits that it received the instant blessing of both the primary and secondary care trusts. By this time, one of our mental health practitioners had moved on and, as I wanted to be a full-time clinician again, rather than a manager, I applied for the position and was really pleased to be offered it.

It is hard work. If people have any image of Bognor Regis at all, it is as a run-down seaside town, with, as its greatest claim to fame, King George V's disparaging cry, "Bugger Bognor!" In fact, the area is a mix of urban and rural, of all social classes and income levels. What is notable is the huge gap between the better off and those living in the very deprived areas, a mix that could predict a higher level of dissatisfaction with life circumstances. As we still have just two mental health practitioners to cover the whole area, we had started out as a triage service. We'd see patients for just 20 minutes, looking at symptom management and prior-itising referrals – to the psychiatrist for someone hearing voices or to the clinical psychologist for someone with obsessive-compulsive disorder (OCD) – or directing them somewhere else ("The Citizens' Advice Bureau is really good at helping with debt" or "Your husband died two years ago and you still see him sitting in his chair. Have you thought of contacting CRUSE, the voluntary organisation that helps the bereaved?")

But it became clear very quickly that this was not what people wanted. Although we do still refer people with employment and debt problems to experts in those areas, most people see us because of depression, anxiety and post-traumatic stress, along with phobias, OCD and eating disorders, and they want us to be able to help them. With trial and error, we have settled on 45-minute sessions per patient.

Negotiating NICE guidelines

I feel comfortable about treating most people but, because I am not a private practitioner, I have to follow the NICE guidelines where appropriate. So, for someone who is moderately depressed, I have to go along with the prescription of antidepressants by the GP. If someone has severe OCD, NICE tells me I must refer the person for cognitive-behavioural therapy. I satisfy NICE guidelines in the following way. When people see me for eating disorders, moderate to severe depression, OCD, post-traumatic stress or severe phobias or anxiety, I tell them that the Government recommends cognitive-behavioural therapy in their cases. I then offer them the choice of seeing me for a few sessions, to see how we go, after which I'll make the referral, or my making the referral straight away but still seeing them for a few sessions in the interim. The usual outcome is that either I no longer need to refer or the referral gets cancelled. This seems to me an efficient approach, with clear cost and health benefits and well within the guidelines.

I also see some patients with psychotic disorders and do not make the assumption that, just because someone has the written diagnosis of schizophrenia, I must instantly refer them on. People labelled as schizo-phrenic get stressed, depressed and anxious, just like anyone else. How-ever, if people are hearing voices telling them to harm themselves or others, I involve the crisis intervention team, which can offer immediate help and protection. Similarly, I would involve them in the case of some-one with severe depression who is having seriously suicidal thoughts, or in any case of high risk.

The friendly approach

I have to make the most of every minute of my time with patients. Some come in looking calm and almost businesslike, but I know that they are anything but calm inside, and that this will get in the way of any work I try to do. Some are obviously distressed. So I try to lower their anxiety straight away. I don't sit behind a desk, even though I use a doctor's surgery for my sessions. I approach people to welcome them, make eye contact, and match my actions to theirs, to start building rapport. My aim is to be professional but friendly – as if I am about to serve them a drink. I've experimented with dressing casually (but not in jeans) and with wearing a suit and tie, and both seem to work equally well. My feeling is that most people are so relieved to be able to talk that it doesn't matter what I'm wearing; it is the friendliness that counts.

When working in such short sessions, I find it useful to normalise people's experience as quickly as I can. The tension can drop right down for an OCD sufferer when I tell them that most people have some kind of obsessional behaviour or that, in psychiatry, we come across their problem a lot and that, although it feels as if it is ruling their life and will never let go, we know treatment works, because we've done so much of it. Commonly, people with OCD have had it for years before they seek help and they are terrified that there is something seriously wrong with them. It helps at once simply to talk of OCD as a gremlin on their shoulder or a bully. Similarly, if people tell me that they are having panics, I will deal with that straight away, by explaining the causes and showing them how to cope.

People in difficult life circumstances that aren't magically going to vanish tend to be close to the end of their tether by the time they see me. They may complain that it all gets so much that they can't think straight or that they get completely overwhelmed and confused. In such cases, of course, learning effective anxiety management techniques is key. I like to use the image of an egg-timer to help calm people down: "All that pressure in your head, making you giddy and confused – imagine it as sand in an egg-timer that has just been flipped up, so that all the sand is scrunched into the top. And you can let it start running down, be-cause that's what sand in egg-timers does, just run down, so that you feel more safe and supported and balanced, and you won't topple over."

Guided imagery

When difficult circumstances can't be changed, I really value guided visualisation as a means of helping people get back a true sense of their strengths and resources and motivating them to carry on (while also trying to build some respite into their situation). In other cases, I have been amazed to find how guided imagery alone may prompt someone into a life-changing decision. One patient, Ruby, was 46 and had been married for 23 years, for most of which time her husband had been an alcoholic. She had stayed with him because they had three children and she hadn't wanted to break up the family. In the last few years, however, he had lost his job because of his alcoholism and had started to drink and behave drunkenly in front of their teenage children, which had shocked and upset them. He had refused all help and made Ruby's friends unwelcome at the house.

Ruby took care of her appearance and had a responsible job as a school secretary but she was in a constantly heightened state of emotion and her sleep was badly affected. At the time she came to see me, she was in a terrible state and trying to decide what to do. I had never met anyone who was so unaware of her own worth and abilities as a person, because her self-esteem by that time was so low. After calming her down, I used guided imagery with her to bring to the fore all of her considerable achievements – keeping the family together, emotionally and financially, at the time when it mattered, having children who had grown up feeling safe and confident because of her, holding down a job that demanded both efficiency and kindness, having and keeping friends, caring enough to keep up appearances for the sake of others, and so on.

Swift changes

I am still amazed that she changed so dramatically after that one session. When I saw her again, she had got her husband to leave the home and had contacted her solicitor, to start divorce proceedings. I saw her four times over a couple of months and, by the last, she was open to thinking about the future and meeting someone with whom she might want to share her life.

The quick reframe or new perspective, so integral to the human givens approach, is always a wonderful tool in a setting like mine, where I am so time limited. Twenty-three-year-old Nick sweated so profusely in his extreme anxiety that he had to take paper towels wherever he went. His anxiety, which had started at college, had gradually escalated, until he became a virtual recluse and spent much time alone smoking cannabis. Speaking on the phone was so anxiety inducing that he avoided doing even that. He wanted to work in IT and had been offered a job on leaving college, but had turned it down because he was so anxious about it. His goals were to be able to make phone calls and to feel okay going out.

Making the phone call was the hardest thing for him to handle. I said to him, "If you pick up the phone and call someone, what is the worst that can happen?" That simple question opened something up for him. He couldn't even think of an answer, except that perhaps the person at the other end mightn't reply. It enabled him to view his dilemma from his 'observing self' and get it into perspective. The last time I saw him he had been to a gig with friends – a huge achievement – and had totally reduced his cannabis use, although we had never directly addressed it.

100 per cent improvement

In a mini-survey that I carried out with patients, to rate the difference between how they were at the start of treatment and how they are at the end, there was a 100 per cent increase in improved feeling on a scale from 1 to 10, a rise of 4 to 5 points not being uncommon. What was most noticeable was that it was the whole process that made a difference, including the quicker access and being seen in the familiar GP surgery, and the normalising affect that this had.

One of my biggest challenges, however, has been Evelyn, a 60-year-old widow who has had a lifetime of treatment for anorexia. In a period spanning more than 40 years, she had experienced several episodes as an inpatient, forced-feeding, drug treatments, dietary measures and weigh-ins, and different behavioural approaches, a great deal of it in specialist mental health services. The people who worked with her no doubt did their best to help her, but she experienced it all as abusive. This highly intelligent woman, formerly a solicitor, still struggles emotionally with her appearance and her weight. If anyone she meets says, "You are looking really well! Have you put on weight?" she feels almost suicidal, and usually reacts by shutting herself away for a while. That makes her feel worse because her way of keeping her mind off how badly she feels about herself is through busying herself with voluntary work. Evelyn's GP, who has known her for many years, referred her to me, after she had failed to cooperate with the community mental health team, as she had felt dissatisfied with her treatment.

Knowing this, I asked Evelyn, when I met her, what she thought or hoped I could help her with. She gave a deep sigh. "What I want is to be able to sit in my garden and read for half an hour without a negative thought," she said.

At her worst, she told me, she felt just one step away from killing herself, although she knew she would never resort to that. "When was the first time you felt that way?" I asked her. "When chubby little Evelyn had been naughty again," she said. She had felt her parents were cold and critical of her and had cared more for her brother than for her. The messages she internalised were "You are fat because you are naughty" and "You are naughty because you are fat". Whenever doctors and dieticians asked her to stand on the scales, she felt like a naughty child and experienced the terrible anguish all over again.

Undoing old damage

I felt that I had to take it very, very carefully with Evelyn. I would have liked to use relaxation and guided imagery with her, and perhaps the rewind technique (see page 59), to deal with the memories of all that 'abuse' and to uncouple the pattern match between weight and being bad – so strong that being told she looked well could spiral her into despair. I had a hunch, however, that in her many years in the mental health system, relaxation techniques might have been tried in some form or other, and, therefore, form part of her memories of abusive treatment. I was right. She loathed being made to relax.

I have, therefore, concentrated on inducing trance indirectly, slowing my voice and working hard to focus her attention. (She tends to jump around a lot in her thoughts and her speech, perhaps to protect herself from the bad feelings.) I learned that she was interested in redecorating her home, so I told her the true story of a friend whose relative bought an old nuclear bunker and transformed it from being a place where people would hide away, fearful that, when they came out, they would find their world had become an ugly, frightening place, into a beautiful home, with huge windows spreading light and looking out onto a peaceful landscape. She seemed to enjoy it.

We have also talked about how, if she feels bad about a compliment or chance comment, she can choose to pause, slow her breathing and reflect on the fact that her bad feelings might not be appropriate to the current situation ('looking well' does not mean 'fat').

Even with this limited approach, I have seen marked changes in Evelyn in just a few sessions. I have asked her to find out information about the rewind treatment (she has a curious mind and enjoys learning about things), in the hope that she may, as a result, choose to undergo it, rather than experience it as something 'abusive' she is subjected to. It is a work in progress. Evelyn has had 40 years of treatment and she is still the same weight as she was at the start, and still emotionally disabled in many ways. She has been doubly traumatised – by her childhood experiences and by her experience of the mental health services. I come across many people whose experience of an unwieldy and unsatisfactory psychiatric system has set them back rather than moved them forward, and I am glad to be part of the new approach to meaningful care.

Many years ago, I was a plasterer. I did what seemed, to outsiders, like the same job every day and yet each job called for something individualised because of the nature of the materials I was working with. It's something like that with people, I think. Everyone has a different surface and a different interior, and there is an individualised human givens approach that is appropriate for each.

* * ✳ * *

James Hooton *is a primary mental health practitioner, working for Sussex Partnership NHS Trust. He has worked in mental health for 22 years, mainly as a community psychiatric nurse and community mental health team service manager. He holds the Human Givens Diploma.*

When the lightbulb doesn't really want to change...

*Senior social worker **Richard Brook** shares some insights into working successfully with clients compelled, but reluctant, to receive help.*

HOW many therapists does it take to change a light bulb? One is enough, provided the light bulb really wants to change. But what if it doesn't? What if the light bulb is dragged kicking and screaming into the therapy room, ordered by the court, sent by someone in authority or subject to the statutory powers of a child protection conference or a mental health tribunal? What if the light bulb scowls at you from under its cap and, in response to your friendly welcome, just shrugs or snarls?

This is the daily lot of countless social workers, youth workers, substance misuse counsellors, probation and youth offending workers, to name but a few. Burdened with the expectation imposed by the body that sent them – "improve your parenting", "change your attitude to offending", "overcome your addiction", "manage your temper" – clients come to us cynical, angry, sarcastic, often embarrassed and anxious, decrying our profession and challenging us to make a difference. What follows is a collection of thoughts, ideas and observations derived from my own experience and that of colleagues who strive to help the light bulbs that don't really want to change.

But they must want to change!

It is worth restating the principle we all know to be true – that, before they can change, people must want to change. It is common knowledge that, no matter how persuasive and compelling our arguments or how enticing our presentation of the possibilities, the momentum and agency for change comes from the individuals themselves. Those of us who continue to get up in the morning to work with the unwilling rely on the assumption that, somewhere inside them, most people do in fact want to change. It is, after all, a human given that people are programmed for progress.

It has been well documented in the *Human Givens* journal how brain chemistry prompts us to seek fulfilment by stretching ourselves and developing our competence in new areas, and we all have experience that bears this out. Furthermore, in my experience, many of the people who come to us via some statutory process tell us they have been knocking on the doors of the helping agencies for years, asking for help, or, at least by the time they arrive in our offices, they are painfully aware of the need for change, and hardly need us to point out that something in their life is not working. It is, then, a reasonable assumption that the clients we work with, reluctant as they may be, have a strong sense of need and an appetite for change. Our task is to overcome the resistance and connect with the resources that will make a difference.

Getting started

So, the client has arrived, thanks to a strongly imprinted fear of reprisals, and sits, arms folded, in the chair furthest from the door, looking at you sitting in the chair nearest the panic button. What do you do now?

Reluctant clients come to us without much interest in either telling us what is bothering them or listening to what we have to tell them. If they were pressed to express a preference, however, I'm certain that most would opt to be listened to before they are talked at.

Agencies in the statutory sector, without exception, have a procedure for gathering essential information, embodied in an 'assessment framework', which usually has to be completed in the first session. It requires us to ask about family history, health and education details and, in some cases, details about drug and alcohol use and mental health history. Clients under duress often find this process extremely intrusive, and feel that it threatens their right to autonomy and control over their personal information. The result is that people 'clam up'. Spending a little time simply building rapport and relaxing the pace allows workers to invite their clients to offer information without pressure, and therefore to retain the dignity and self-respect which is implied when we refer to someone as a 'client' rather than a 'case'. The outcome is usually richer and more useful information than we get by simply rushing to tick the boxes, although it covers what is required by the statutory agencies too.

Human givens practitioners know that attention is a strong, non-negotiable human need. If we avoid the temptation to interrogate, but listen carefully and respectfully to our clients, offering them our attention rather than demanding theirs, they are far more likely to say the things we really need to hear. I have worked with numerous parents who, having being allowed just to talk about their concerns for their children and their experience of parenting, have answered their own questions and found they did not need my expert advice. Listening really is a great way to help people talk.

Let's look at it another way

Reluctant clients will usually have our interaction set in a singularly un-helpful frame. They may see us as persecutors or punishers, or simply as people aiming to get them to do something they don't want to do, and are intensely aware that the balance of power is in our favour. It is important that clients feel sufficiently empowered to make informed choices about their treatment, and the art of reframing can help achieve this. I have found that a simple statement such as "The court has ordered me to see you twice a week for the next six months" puts an unexpected spin on things and causes clients to relax a little.

There is, of course, no formula for this process, but creative therapists are always looking for ways to frame a problem as an opportunity, so as to raise the levels of optimism and enthusiasm in our therapeutic conversations.

Where are we going?

Paying clients usually come with a fairly clear idea of their goal for therapy, or at least see the point of being asked to consider it. By con-trast, those who are sent to us often look blankly when the subject of aims is first raised. Our clients' goals are often at odds with our own. "To get you and your organisation well and truly out of my face" is generally the gist of it. So, where do we go from there?

The only satisfactory answer I have found is to do what a mathematician would do, and seek the lowest common denominator – ie the first point at which you and your client can agree to agree. With young offenders, this point is often to prevent the young person going to prison, get the police off their backs or prevent them from getting killed. Clients of social services are often surprised to discover that the organisation aims to preserve and reunite families, and, once enlightened, can consent to a plan in which this is the ultimate aim. People who are sick can usually assent to a goal that involves their getting well. The process by which this initial goal can be agreed usually involves bids and counter bids, until a satisfactory position can be reached.

"I'm sorry, Darren, but, if I just p*** off and leave you alone, I will get the sack for not doing my job properly. What do you reckon is the best result we can hope for that doesn't end up with me unemployed or you in prison?"

Calming down and using the mind's eye

Goals of course only become real, attainable targets when we can visualise them and test them out in our imaginations. Very few people go straight from the stage of longing for a holiday in the sun to the experience of it without first collecting the brochures and savouring the prospect in their minds. Likewise, clients of therapeutic agencies, willing or otherwise, rarely experience tangible change until they have been able to visualise whatever their new situation entails. This becomes a problem for those of us in statutory services, as imagination does not mix well with the high emotional arousal associated with coercion and compulsion. For this reason, it is sometimes necessary to hold fire on the 'goal setting' stage until the strong feelings have cooled off.

A mum subject to a statutory parenting order recently came to me proclaiming, "I've thrown my son out, and nothing you can say will make me take him back!" It took half an hour or so of listening to her story and acknowledging her strong feelings before she began to hint that she would welcome a reconciliation. Reasonable and agreeable goals tend to emerge in states of calmness and composure. The therapist's energy is best expended in lowering arousal so that these conditions can prevail, rather than forcing the issue or arguing with provocative statements that are uttered in states of high emotion.

Once I am satisfied we are in a position to think about goals, I almost always ask about them in a way that appeals to the imagination. "How do you see things improving for you over the next few months?" or "Just imagine it's our last session, and you are actually feeling these meetings have been helpful to you. I wonder what would have to have happened for you to feel that way?"

Setting the sights even further ahead, I find that young people are often quite accustomed to imagining their adult lives, and I am pleasantly surprised by how seldom this seems to revolve around crime. Some of the most habitual offenders, when asked to describe their ideal lives 10 or 20 years hence, come up with something more straight laced than the most conservative social worker could dream up for them: career, home, family, all things in moderation, youthful excesses spent. The aims of our intervention can be framed as stepping stones towards the positive long-term futures our clients want and deserve. Thus, 'anger management' work is not so much about avoiding getting into fights at the weekend; it is about learning the skills that will make someone a good parent when the time comes, or help them make a success of the important relationships in their life.

I find it is important to acknowledge when clients have a low level of motivation and, with young people, I sometimes use a diagram of a target to illustrate the three possible outcomes of our sessions. A 'miss' is a clear failure, which results in a return to court, and the ways this can be achieved are clearly spelled out: failing to attend, or otherwise not complying with the rules. A 'hit' is what I call 'getting by' or 'scraping through'. Here, the intervention programme is successfully completed, but it has been tedious and tiresome. A 'bull's-eye' is something quite different: here, real benefits are enjoyed and our sessions end with a warm handshake and a sense of achievement. I explain that this outcome is always my aim, although I acknowledge it might not be theirs. All the same, I invite the young person in front of me to imagine such a scenario and tell me what might have to happen for our sessions to deserve a top rating. I am amazed how often the warm handshake has occurred and by the positive outcomes that can be achieved when the imagination is engaged in setting the goal.

Keeping going

Once rapport is established and goals are clearly defined, we are on the road to success, but there are still obstacles to overcome. Culture, peer pressure and anti-authority sentiment can all serve to remind our clients they aren't supposed to be cooperating with us. Furthermore, chaotic and disrupted life circumstances can confuse plans and take our minds off the original goals. So how do we keep the ball rolling?

I firmly believe the fastest progress is made when we pay rigorous attention to strengths, successes and solutions. Talking about these matters often unsettles clients, who expect they will be repeatedly dragged through the mire of whatever misadventures have brought them to our attention in the first place and are pleasantly surprised to find themselves talking about the time they didn't lose their temper, or when they behaved decently or parented positively. This helps people to see that they may be nearer to a solution than they realised and might motivate them to go the extra mile. Reluctant participants can sometimes be encouraged to rouse themselves, if the task can be made to look sufficiently easy.

Many of the most problematic clients I work with seem to me also to be the most resourceful. It is salutary to realise the extent to which basic emotional needs are met in the context of criminal behaviour, be it the sense of belonging to a pro-criminal peer group, the ability to assert one's autonomy by challenging the law, or simply the rush of adrenalin that comes with being chased by the police. Most descriptions of criminal activity I hear about are laced with bravery, initiative, vision and determination – qualities that sit cheek by jowl with violence, disorder and stupidity. Solution-focused workers recognise the need to seek out the strengths that clients bring with them – even the ones that seem inextricably bound up with the problem that brought them to us.

Many professionals in statutory agencies nod assent to ideas like this but, in practice, express horror at their practical application. Domestic violence is a particularly provocative example. The notion that violent behaviour towards a partner might be a misguided but sincere attempt to solve a problem is regarded as virtually unutterable. Any attempt to acknowledge the offender for his efforts and encourage him to direct his good intentions in a different direction is seen as collusion and a failure to grasp the seriousness of the offence. The emotional arousal that this dilemma provokes in many professionals just forces us back into black and white thinking, and our punitive and judgemental positions, where we feel intellectually and morally safer.

Affirmation, affirmation and affirmation

The practice of affirmation requires that we compose ourselves and genuinely seek out the strengths and resources that are present even in dangerous and antisocial behaviour, for here is the material that will lead to a solution. Thus, I often reflect to a client, whose gang is terrorising the neighbourhood, "Your friends are the most valuable part of your life at the moment, aren't they?" or suggest to a heavy-handed parent, "Discipline is really important to you, isn't it?" Acknowledgement of the resourcefulness and good intentions behind bad behaviour does not amount to collusion, and does not negate the need to challenge harmful beliefs and actions, but it invites the client into a collaboration whereby the expertise of the therapist and the energy of the client have equal value in resolving the problem.

A television programme I saw recently provided me with a fantastic metaphor to use with young people. A group of successful entrepreneurs was mixed with a group of ordinary workers and, in the course of a number of tasks and challenges, a group of behavioural psychologists attempted to distinguish who was who. The programme provided a fascinating insight into the mind of a successful business person, which turned out to be capable not only of problem solving and creativity but also of cheating, risk taking, rule bending and intensely individualistic reasoning. Towards the end of the programme, we learned that a second group in society shares almost exactly the same psychological profile – convicted criminals. A number of the young people I have discussed this with were fascinated to discover just how close they could be to a successful and lucrative career. They might not aspire to a multi-million-pound business empire – some would say, neither should they – but looking at the stories of entrepreneurs can inspire a glimmer of that elusive elixir – hope. They are able to see that their own deficits might not need all that much fine-tuning to be converted into worthwhile attributes.

Going with the flow

Reluctant clients tend to come to us at times when their lives are particularly chaotic and their circumstances prone to change. It is easy to lose the plot unless we possess the flexibility to steer round the obstacles and move towards our goals via a circuitous route, taking in unexpected challenges and opportunities on the way. For instance, it is pointless insisting that people complete a project on 'victim awareness' or 'social skills' when they arrive clutching an eviction notice. Circumstances might demand that we abandon our cerebral activities for a while and concentrate on more concrete ones – job seeking, benefit claiming, or conflict resolving. These are all important at times, and help further to build rapport by demonstrating commitment to the client's needs. The positive angle is that sometimes a crisis offers us an unexpected opportunity – a fight that has occurred might present an opportune moment to deal with 'anger management' or an arrest might prompt a useful discussion about citizenship.

CASE HISTORY:

Respect tinged with disgust

SCOTT, at 15, had no intention of going to school. Anticipating that education was about to give up on him, he had given up on education. He had learned that 'the authorities', including his mum, were powerless against this degree of resolve, and so he spent his days engaging with the PlayStation and his evenings getting drunk and causing mayhem with his 'crew'. I was the authorities' last resort.

At our first meeting, sensing a dead end to the obvious line of enquiry, I gleaned as much as I could via a conversation about music, skateboarding, computer games and Manchester United. Scott was clever enough to understand why I had come, so he raised the subject of education. "I can't see the point of school any more," he pleaded. Seizing on his implication that there was a point, albeit unseen, I mused, "I wonder what would be different for you if you could". Scott drifted into thought for a moment and smiled. He then gave me the look usually reserved for an

One of my most inspiring experiences, as a social worker, was the observing of a lesson in a school for young people with behavioural difficulties. The teacher had responsibility for half a dozen pupils, none of whom seemed able to concentrate on anything for more than about five minutes. One was reading a book; one writing a paragraph about frog-spawn, while a pair together grappled with some maths problems and another looked blankly into a computer screen. The reader began to rock on his chair and shout out obscenities, which unsettled the mathematicians, so roles were reversed. The computer inspector was provided with paper on which to draw a computer and one of the readers, who had begun to fight, was asked to aid the naturalist by looking up some information on newts. "F*** off! Do you think I'm gay or something?" was the retort, to which the teacher immediately called the class's attention, wrote 'sexuality' on the blackboard and kicked off a lively discussion.

In the break, by which time I was exhausted, the teacher explained that he keeps in mind the individual work targets for each pupil and

adversary at chess when you have been lured into a trap and have just seen the inevitable checkmate: respect tinged with disgust.

Subsequent sessions revealed a pattern whereby Scott's ambivalence to school was more to do with being hung over than disaffected, and his drinking was not so much about having a good time as blotting out the pain he felt at being rejected by his father. We embarked on some practical exercises, looking at how Scott could communicate his feelings to his dad and maybe reinstate contact. We looked at Scott's aims for the future and discovered gateways to his various career aspirations, with or without qualifications. Scott's most pressing need was to be able to sleep at night, so I helped him via relaxation and guided imagery exercises to learn how to shut down the stress factory and regain control over his level of emotional arousal.

When I last met Scott he was drinking less, sleeping better and had written to his dad. He had also commenced a part-time programme aimed at restarting his education.

The light bulb was not burning brightly, but it was beginning to glow. ■

the requirements of the national curriculum, but knows his class is unable to learn in traditional hour-long segments. He told me that, in each session, every pupil usually covers four or more curriculum areas and that classroom discussions take place every few minutes. By the end of the year he is confident all targets will be attained and everyone educated to the satisfaction of the government, but how he went about it was truly breathtaking. It has occurred to me since that many of us, in the course of our work with those who live disorganised and chaotic lives, require a measure of the flexibility and spontaneity I witnessed in that classroom. There is a big picture and an ultimate aim, and many ways to get there.

Real life

Life outside the therapy room is where the rubber really hits the road, and all effective therapists look for ways to connect the work they begin with clients with the real world – using the imagination to envisage and raise expectations of a solution, and suggesting practical steps to initiate change. With reluctant clients, this is another point in the project where the wheels can come off. Those who are compelled to attend sessions may see it as their inescapable duty to be present, but that is all – the idea of performing tasks or attending to concerns in between times is like being asked to do homework, and few of the people I work with have ever done homework. Exercises to engage the imagination seem a bit like 'therapy', and we are unlikely to be calling it that, so how can we keep the ball rolling right over the end of our session and into real life?

Following the leader

The first principle is always to go with whatever momentum the client already has, and direct your efforts there. For instance, young people might be quite unmotivated in most areas of their life, but are eager to get a job, a car, a girlfriend or a qualification of some description. If this is the case, I always move on to the practical strategies for achieving these ends, and gently suggest a phone call, application form, visit to an advice centre, or whatever seems appropriate.

Following the leader means suggesting strategies that involve the part of the client's life that they really want to work on, even if whatever that is seems to you to be a lesser priority. For example, young people with an over-active temper might be reluctant to tackle this in the places it most badly effects them – school, family life etc, but might be prepared to do some work on their temper in the context of sports that they play, and are intrigued when I suggest we use some sports psychology techniques to improve their performance. A keen young footballer I worked with, while unwilling to work on his temper problems in school, did say he would like to be more composed in front of goal, as he tended to panic and shoot over the bar. After a simple rehearsal technique using relaxation and visualisation, he told me, the following week, that he had kept his cool and scored twice. He grew gradually more willing to widen his focus, as he came to have confidence that his temperament was not destined always to be his master. Other specific events in someone's life, such as a forthcoming job interview, a family occasion, a flight, a court appearance or a driving test, might equally well provide the starting point for guided visualisation. First-hand experience of the benefit of mental rehearsal, or 'performance-enhanc-ing daydreams' as I sometimes refer to them, can increase confidence sufficiently to stimulate interest in tackling the big stuff.

Bargaining

I have on occasions employed some devious tactics to move a client into the strategy stage. Recognising that the important events in a client's life are the ones that happen outside of our sessions, I sometimes capitalise on the fact that they didn't want to come to me in the first place by making a deal. "Our sessions are supposed to be an hour long, but I will make it half an hour if you will promise to use the other half hour today and tomorrow practising the breathing exercise I have taught you/ filling in the form you sent off for/visiting some education sites on the internet ..." A handshake seals the contract, and the task is often carried out as promised. Even if it isn't, the message is subtly conveyed that application in the real world is necessary to make our work effective.

Sometimes, the way to move into the rehearsal stage is to invite the person you are working with to suspend their disbelief just for a moment. If the rapport is good, they will often indulge you, just out of curiosity. I recently invited a young man, who had told me that he wanted to be decent, honest and respectable but just couldn't find it in himself to be that way, to imagine finding a wallet in the street and taking it to the police station intact. He insisted that he could not envisage this, as it would be entirely out of character, but he went through with the exercise nevertheless and told me afterwards it felt great to imagine such an outcome. He visualised a police officer who knows him well dealing with the transaction, and laughed at the thought of the look on his face. Time will tell whether fantasy converts into reality, but the point is that rehearsal of such behaviour in the imagination is a more powerful agent than many of the cognitive methods we might otherwise resort to, that don't engage the emotions.

Compulsion

Agencies with strong statutory powers can use their authority to push things forward. For example, attendance at school or a careers inter-view can be made a requirement of the statutory programme and en-forceable by the court; leverage can be applied by a child protection conference for attendance at a parenting course. Care needs to be taken when mixing therapeutic goals with enforceable compulsion, but some-times a sledgehammer is needed to crack the nut, and occasionally it helps to apply a little force to those areas of our clients' lives where we feel small changes will make a big difference. Statutory powers can be used as a 'carrot' as well as a 'stick' – the prospect of early discharge of an order or a favourable review can act as an incentive for clients to get on with the programme they have been assigned to complete. Thus, reluctant clients can sometimes be guided unwittingly into beneficial changes and, before they know it, they are feeling better and enjoying the taste of success.

The bottom line

It may still seem that some clients, in spite of our best efforts to engage with them, cling on to their resistance and do not accept our invitation to change. My personal view, however, is that those who are angry, hostile and outwardly resistant are not nearly so difficult to engage as we might first imagine. Their restlessness and agitation strongly hint at a perception that things are not right, and respectful, intelligent strategies of engagement can help us form an alliance to work towards a goal. If this were not so, there would be little hope for those of us employed in statutory services or for the clients we meet there. It is my belief that the model of therapy inspired by the human givens approach is not just for motivated, focused and fee-paying clients. It offers something of value to all who contend with difficulties associated with unmet needs, including the ones who think they don't really want to change.

* * ❋ * *

Richard Brook is a social worker with experience of child protection, family placement work with children with special educational needs and their families. He is currently senior practitioner with Norfolk Youth Offending Team. He holds the Advanced Human Givens Diploma and also works as an independent trainer in brief therapy using the human givens approach for working with children, families and young offenders.

*"I can't understand why people
are frightened of new ideas. I'm
frightened of the old ones."*

JOHN CAGE

Working with stroke from the human givens approach

*The emotional impact of stroke is profound, but degree of impairment is not necessarily the most crucial factor. Consultant clinical neuropsychologist **Jim Tapper** explains the part played by met and unmet needs.*

MR D was 53 years of age when he was referred to me by a physiotherapist. He had suffered loss of movement in his right arm and leg, left facial disfigurement, and had difficulties with vision and speech after a stroke eight years before. Previously a large, strong, active man who worked as a specialist painter and decorator, he now used a wheelchair and was unable to work.

Despite the passage of time, Mr D was still traumatised by the stroke. He was a virtual recluse who was jealous of people who could walk, and he continually ruminated about his circumstances, experiencing frequent disturbing dreams. He had not been into his town centre for eight years for fear of being seen by anyone who knew him, was afraid to eat in public and would not have close relatives or his son's girlfriend to eat at his home. He had not renewed his sexual relationship with his wife and was distraught by the burden that he felt his needs placed upon her. He had clinically significant symptoms of depression and post-traumatic stress and above average anxiety on the Depression Anxiety Stress Scales (DASS)[1] which I use as an outcome measure.

I saw Mr D on six occasions for assessment, treatment and review. I treated him with the rewind technique (a simple, non-intrusive method that involves visualising the traumatic event at one remove, and in an unemotional state; see page 59) to detraumatise him of the effects of the stroke, and with guided visualisation to rehearse his achieving his goals of taking part in community activities again. Afterwards, he was quickly able to start going out, visited various towns across the North West, and went to crowded places, such as retail parks for Christmas shopping, and family events, such as wedding anniversary celebrations. He recovered his sexual relationship and developed a renewed social life with his wife and immediate family, as well as being able to eat in public again and to play host to his wider family and his future daughter-in-law. For the first time since the stroke, he and his wife went on a foreign holiday. At discharge seven months later, according to the DASS, his scores for depression, anxiety and stress were all within the normal range.

Two years later, with the help of his enormously supportive wife, he has maintained all of his gains. But Mr D might have remained without this life-changing psychological help had it not been for the recent development of specialist stroke services.

Guidelines by the Royal College of Physicians[2] and the Government[3] recommended the establishment of dedicated stroke wards, as research showed that people who suffer strokes have a better chance of survival in specialist wards than in general wards. They also recommended that a clinical psychologist should be a member of the specialist stroke team and that there should be access to neuropsychological expertise, to deal with problems affecting intellectual/cognitive function or mood. About 110,000 people in England and Wales have a first stroke each year (around 1000 are aged under 30 and between 250 and 400 are children), and 30,000 go on to have further strokes. Aside from cognitive impairments, up to half of patients in hospital for stroke and a quarter of those in the community are thought to suffer from mood disorders, such as anger, denial, anxiety, depression and post-traumatic stress. Such states are associated with significantly worse outcomes.

Although many NHS trusts do now have input from a clinical psychologist in their stroke services, I am unusual in that very few have a neuropsychologist dedicated to stroke services full time. Dr Diana Forrest, then director of public health for St Helens and Knowsley Health Authority (as it was, at the time) championed the appointment of a consultant clinical psychologist when our acute stroke unit was set up. I am a member of a multi-disciplinary team, comprising medical consultants, occupational therapists, physiotherapists, general nurses, specialist stroke nurses and family support workers from the Stroke Association. I have the help of a voluntary counsellor and I have trainee clinical psychologists from the universities of Liverpool and Lancaster on placement.

We admit around 650 stroke patients a year. A further 250 people in the district experience a minor stroke or a stroke-like event that does not require them to be in hospital, but which still may have psychological sequelae. Nearly half of the patients referred to me are of working age, so it isn't a service just for the elderly.

After a stroke, people are admitted to the acute stroke unit until they are medically stabilised. People who survive go straight home, if the stroke was mild, or move on to our specialised stroke rehabilitation unit. A stay in the acute unit is usually around seven days. The average stay in the rehabilitation unit is 26 days, ranging from a few days to six months. This doesn't always depend on severity of the stroke but on how quickly the person's social services department can arrange the necessary home care.

Essentially, a stroke is an interruption of the blood supply to the brain: even a brief interruption (transient ischaemic attack or TIA) can cause temporary changes in neuronal activity; an interruption of over five minutes will usually cause irreversible damage. There are two main types of stroke. The most common is caused by a blockage (an ischaemic stroke), when an artery carrying blood to the brain is blocked by a clot of blood or a fat globule. The other (a haemorrhagic stroke) is a burst blood vessel that causes bleeding either inside the brain or between the brain and the skull. Besides seeing stroke patients, I see those who have had a TIA, which I define as a stroke that nearly happened, and also people with vascular dementia, in which the arteries in the brain become gradually clogged with a build-up of lipids, not resulting in stroke but still causing loss of cognitive abilities.

How the human givens approach helps

The human givens philosophy underpins all of my work with patients, and I teach it to the trainee clinical psychologists on placement with me. With its emphasis on psychological needs, it is an ideal approach for any rehabilitation service for long-term medical conditions or for services for elderly people, because it details the essential components of a person's life.

When I first came across the human givens approach, the emphasis on the meeting of essential needs was already familiar to me, as I had worked in the field of learning disabilities, with the ideas of Wolf Wolfensberger. He had developed the concept of 'normalisation', which he renamed 'social role valorisation' because some service providers wrongly assumed what was meant by normalisation, whereas they hadn't a clue what social role valorisation meant and so had to study exactly what he was talking about: the components he defined as essential for a normal life.[4] I also found valuable (and still do) the concept of the family life-cycle – the idea that people most commonly develop psychological problems at transition points in the life-cycle.[5] However, the human givens approach struck me as more ecologically valid than both of those concepts. Although there is great overlap, the latter were approaches based on sociological or clinical observation, whereas the needs delineated within the human givens approach are more evolutionarily based: needs – such as those for safety, connection, attention, status, meaning and purpose – that have developed as we have evolved as human beings.

Over the last five years, almost 900 people have been referred to me. I find that there are three levels of complexity of psychological problems in this work depending upon the extent to which a person's human needs were being met.

'Needs met' – first tier

The first tier comprises those whose needs were met before they had a stroke. Perhaps they had a job they enjoyed, a supportive family, a challenging career, stimulating hobbies, a secure sense of themselves, and so on. Then the stroke or TIA occurs and threatens everything. For the lucky ones, the stroke may cause just mild effects or even no apparent after-effects at all – in brain terms. However, the experience of having a stroke or TIA can itself be traumatising; then, finding oneself in the acute unit, connected to monitoring equipment, being told one has had a stroke, seeing others with severe impairments, being aware of others dying, and seeing posters and leaflets about strokes can all generate further fear. One trainee clinical psychologist carried out research which showed that 50 per cent of people attending our stroke review clinics had clinical levels of psychological disorder and 22 per cent had symptoms of post-traumatic stress.

Some people who have had a TIA or a mild stroke, from which a full recovery is expected, may appear to their relatives to undergo a 'personality change': they may develop specific phobias – of watching soap operas, for instance, or going into any bathroom with white tiles. They know they were watching *Coronation Street* when they had their stroke, or that they had their stroke in their bathroom at home, but they think they must be going crazy if, on these subsequent, seemingly unrelated, occasions, they go into a state of extreme emotional arousal. They don't know anything about the power of pattern matching and how the amygdala, the small structure in the brain that has evolved to be on the look out for potential danger, triggers panic mode if it recognises anything crudely similar to the original circumstances in which trauma occurred.

This can manifest as a fear of losing complete control or losing one's mind. Because stroke affects the brain, and people relate the brain to the concept of mind, that fear may be all the greater. Fortunately, I can quickly help those I see by using the rewind technique to deal with the intrusive trauma memories. I usually only have to see people in this tier for a few sessions.

'Needs met' – second tier

A larger group of my patients are those whose lives were also working well before their stroke (their human needs were largely met) but who suffer major forms of disability after their stroke, which impede fulfilment of their needs thereafter. This is much longer-term work. Cognitive impairments, which can range from difficulties in planning activities, concentrating on a task and remembering things to co-ordinating movements, orienting oneself in space and having a sense of time, can have a huge impact. Verbal impairments may make it hard to communicate with others, to ask for what one needs or to join in meaningful activities with other people. Physical disabilities may prevent people not only from feeding themselves or being able to go to the toilet alone (common causes of shame and disgust, which exacerbate individuals' distress) but from satisfying their intellectual needs. Someone may not be able to put on the radio, get a book or answer the phone, if their carer is not there, resulting in frustration and isolation. On top of this, these people, too, may be traumatised by the experience of the stroke, if they can remember it, adding to their already high emotional arousal. The ability to meet basic physical and diverse emotional needs thus becomes severely impeded.

Many people experience sexual problems after stroke. For men, this may be as a result of medication, but psychological difficulties are common too. Women who have had strokes are particularly often ashamed

CASE HISTORIES:

Stroke-like symptoms but not a stroke

SOMETIMES people are referred to me with symptoms suspicious of stroke but which turn out to have other causes entirely. One young woman was admitted to our stroke unit after suffering sudden temporary paralysis of her left arm and leg. Brain scans showed that the paralysis was not caused by stroke, and she was referred to me. When I asked her about her life and her relationships, her breathing became shallow; she started to shake, and her left arm and leg became rigid. The paralysis was a symptom of a panic attack. I was quickly able to calm her, and she then told me about her violent marriage. At the time of the previous panic attack, she had been going through a particularly bad period both at home and at work, where she had had the attack. What had initially presented as a suspected stroke was, in fact, the effect of extreme emotional arousal.

Mr A was a young man, in his 30s, who collapsed at a social family event and, because he had poor coordination of one arm and leg, a stroke was suspected. A brain scan revealed no sign of a stroke, but the corpus callosum, which bridges the left and right hemispheres of the brain, was only partially formed. This explained, for the first time, why he had less control over one side of his body than the other and had had to struggle all of his life to do the kinds of things that most of us take for granted. His mother had tried in vain, when he was a child, to get some help for him but had had her requests rejected – he was just seen as slow and clumsy.

of their changed appearance or physical awkwardness. Partners may be reluctant to make a sexual advance, for fear of seeming insensitive (although the stroke sufferer might well yearn for the assurance that they are still sexually attractive). Sometimes, people fear that sex will induce another stroke.

All of these concerns can be addressed in the human givens approach to therapy, with its emphasis on empowerment and making the most

The result for Mr A was that he suffered a lifetime of rejection and bullying, by schoolmates, teachers and employers, because he didn't do things quickly enough. His self-esteem was rock bottom, and he had never had a really satisfactory intimate relationship – one he did embark on broke up quickly, which devastated him, and he attempted suicide when it finished. It was two years later, at the family gathering, when subjected to ridicule by a neighbour, that he reached the limit of his endurance and collapsed. His tremor and strange gait led to the suspicion of stroke.

I saw him shortly after his arrival at the acute stroke unit and found that his constant exaggerated tremor disappeared after a relaxation session. It was clear that so many of his needs were not being met: he lacked autonomy, intimacy, sense of competence, status and challenge. He was extremely anxious in the presence of females of his age. His life was meaningless. I arranged to see him as an outpatient, to help him learn to handle his deficiencies and prevent another collapse. Although, against all odds, he had qualified as a printer, he has been reduced, because of bullying, to supported employment in a factory, screwing on bottle tops – and even there was shouted at for being too slow, because he didn't use both hands. Over the three years that we have worked together, his assertiveness, confidence and self-image have all improved immensely; he is more socially able and there is more going on in his life. He has developed friendships with both sexes. He is better able to make his own choices and has recently been arranging a house move entirely by himself. Like Mr D, he was fortunate that he had a supportive family, who were able to be less critical of his failures once they understood his needs fully. ■

of one's resources. It is not an approach that engenders false hope: resources are based in reality and include not only one's own skills and mental attitude but also the support available from others. Teaching people how to relax and calm themselves and use visualisation helps lower the emotional arousal; it can also help with emotionalism that sometimes results from stroke – the tendency to laugh or cry at inappropriate times.

'Needs met' – third tier

The final group of patients comprises those whose human needs were not being met even before their stroke. They might be long-term unemployed, be trapped in a violent relationship, have children who have turned to drugs or they might live near to antisocial neighbours. They often have additional medical problems that exacerbate these challenges. Perhaps they have a drink problem, in their attempt to self-medicate. They are in a state of ongoing emotional arousal caused by unremitting stressors, to which is then added the trauma of a stroke or stroke-like event, whether mild or major. After their hospital stay, they return to the loveless relationship or the estate where they live in fear of gangs or where used syringes and other rubbish are dumped in the hallways, but now they have anxiety and depressed mood and post-traumatic stress to deal with on top. And they may well find that they are at the limit of their coping ability, unable to handle those original stressors – challenging unruly youths, minimising marital discord – in the way they managed to before.

As Merseyside has an above-average incidence of stroke and of death from stroke, part of which may be attributable to the effects of social exclusion,[6] this is an important group to work with. The rewind technique can be used to take the continuing arousal out of stressors that are still impinging on the present, despite being in the past (such as being sexually abused or bullied as a child or the victim of violence or accidents), thus releasing precious energy to find resources to cope as best as possible with ongoing day-to-day difficulties.

Mostly, I see people when they have returned home. During rehabilitation, the emphasis is on medical needs, physiotherapy and occupational therapy. People are referred to me while still in hospital only if they are distressed (for instance from a fear of falling or being in such a low mood that they are difficult to motivate) and so cannot benefit from the rehabilitation services. As a result, the prescribing of antidepressants in the rehabilitation unit has decreased substantially. More usually, however, while people are in the rehabilitation unit, they seem to be under the impression that life will return largely to normal, once they get home. Even though they are struggling to re-learn old skills and to manage as best they can with day-to-day living, they very often have an image of themselves going up and down the stairs, having everything to hand or getting things from the kitchen just as they used to, when even these simple activities are now well out of their ability range. It is only when they get home that reality hits horribly, and the emotional difficulties really kick in, often alongside relationship difficulties – exacerbated or new. Visiting a loved one for a set length of time each day, and not being in charge, is a very different matter from living with them and being the main carer.

As our stroke service follows patients up for a year, in their own homes and in follow-up clinics, it is within this period that our specialist stroke nurses or the family support workers will quickly pick up on distress and refer people to me.

Hidden stresses

When I ask my patients about stresses in their lives, either ongoing or else in the past but still affecting them in the present, they commonly mention sexual or physical abuse. Sometimes they deny anything traumatic has happened to them, but their stress levels are far higher than those you would expect from whatever stress it is they admit to – such as worry about a daughter's exams or a work concern. I draw a timeline, marking on it major events, such as the stroke and an earlier depression, and bring it up to date and then point to the empty space between the beginning of the line and the depression and say, "Are you *sure* nothing happened in this section?" Seeing it visually in that way usually prompts people to reveal some kind of trauma. Then I'll say, "Let's see if we can do anything about lowering the arousal that is still around that". I will tell them how relaxation helps and, when they are sufficiently relaxed, move on to the rewind technique.

Little Ted

IN AN initially mystifying case, a woman of 59 who had been admitted to the acute unit because of a suspected stroke was referred to me when brain scans cleared her. Mrs A had been traumatised by the terrible death of her engineer son G, while he was working on a ship in Singapore harbour. He had been decapitated by a metal cable that suddenly became taut. She learned of this by telephone one night, when she was in bed. She talked of the difficulties they had had, sorting out the return of his body, how terrifyingly impersonal the process had been and how long they had had to wait for the post-mortem report, which seemed cold and impersonal too.

I used the rewind technique with her, and it seemed to help, although I was unable to review her because she was going abroad to stay with her daughter for three months. However, she returned after a couple of weeks, because she did not want to be away from reminders of her son, and was referred to me again. She was clinging to any connection with her son: his school, the paper shop, an ex-girlfriend. Her son had, as a child, had a teddy bear called Little Ted, which he had kept as an adult as a mascot. It arrived home, to her surprise, with his other effects and she took it everywhere with her. She had bought a small rocking chair to sit Little Ted in and then bought a girl teddy as company for him. She dressed them both up, buying or knitting clothes for them.

As I probed to find where all this had come from, it emerged that she had had a stillborn daughter when she was 20 years old. As was the custom at that time, the dead baby was whisked away, and she was given no chance to see her or christen her. It was an impersonal and heartless experience, and she had clearly pattern matched to it in the aftermath of her son's death. When I asked her why she hadn't mentioned her daughter's death before, despite being asked about prior bad experiences she said, "It didn't seem respectful to G. I was here for him." We carried out another rewind, this time on the still-birth. At our next appointment recently, she volunteered that she had stopped taking Little Ted and his girl companion everywhere with her, and she was working up to recovering the physical intimacy that had ceased on that fateful night. ■

One elderly man, who had had a minor stroke, was referred to me because of extreme anxiety levels. All three scores on the DASS were at ceiling level. His hyperarousal turned out to be nothing to do with the stroke. It emerged that, 10 years previously, he and his wife had been returning from an outing and, while they were ascending on an escalator in an underground station, he had playfully tickled her. Laughing, she had twisted away from him, lost her balance and fallen back to the bottom of the escalator, breaking both legs very badly. He felt deeply responsible for, and upset by, her difficulty with mobility and the sight of her scars. He ceased to be outgoing and lively and became nervous and withdrawn. He hadn't slept properly for the last 10 years and was being treated unsuccessfully for apnoea in a sleep clinic.

After learning all this, I rewound the original trauma. He told me, at the next session, that, when his daughter had driven him home, he had fallen asleep in the car – an unprecedented event. Then he fell asleep over his tea. And he had been sleeping properly at night ever since – to the great joy of his wife, who had also had her own nights disturbed by his continual jerking.

A more complete service

I feel very privileged that I am able to help people with problems such as these, which come to light incidentally, as a result of strokes or near-strokes. I am also grateful for the freedom to work with stroke patients in the way I find works best. Most stroke services use the concept of post-stroke depression, but there is no neurological evidence that stroke lesion can generate depression.[7] When people's lives catastrophically change in an instant, and they can no longer do what they used to do, they may well ruminate about what they have lost and so the cycle of depression[8] starts – with ever-mounting worry and arousal leading to unnaturally extended dream sleep (emotional arousal is discharged during dreams[9]) and resultant exhaustion and lack of motivation the next morning. Fortunately, this cycle can be interrupted quickly, using human givens therapy skills.

In five years of working with stroke patients, I have seen only a handful of people who had clinical depression and were very difficult to motivate or expressed ideas of suicide as per the archetypal symptoms laid down in the diagnostic manuals – loss of appetite, apathy, loss of interest in sex and other activities, and so on. For most people, their post-stroke emotional disorder is caused by a whole mixture of things – such as anger, guilt, shame, stress, panic, fear, sadness, loss of confidence, shock. When the stroke effects are mild, they can be helped to overcome these emotional effects. And when the stroke effects are more major, working to identify and address unmet needs and make best use of remaining resources (such as using the imagination positively, rather than negatively in replaying what is lost) can free people to make the most of the lives they have now, however different that is from their original expectations.

It won't surprise human givens therapists that research now shows that undergoing rehabilitation at home rather than in hospital seems to empower patients and improve motivation[10] – they take the initiative and express their goals more often than those undergoing rehabilitation in hospital. Also, there is likely to be less problem with unrealistic expectations of recovery, of the kind described earlier, and consequent distress. So we are currently establishing a new community team to enable some people to be discharged quickly from the stroke units to receive rehabilitation at home. This team will have a dedicated clinical psychologist, who will initiate the human givens approach as soon as possible after people are medically stable and back in their own environment.

* * * * *

Jim Tapper is consultant clinical neuropsychologist at St Helens and Knowsley Hospitals NHS Trust in Merseyside. He is a member of the Human Givens Foundation Advisory Board and current chair of the Association of Human Givens Practitioners in the NHS. (For more information about the Association; please visit: **www.hgi.org.uk/sections**)

Human givens and the NHS

Sandwell PCT's mental health strategy is entirely based on human givens principles. The challenge now is to translate them into practice, says **Ian Walton**, *GP.*

D ESPITE the current horrendous climate in the NHS, in which every mental health trust in the country is being forced to make cuts, here in Sandwell, in the heart of the West Midlands, known as the 'Black Country', we have managed to plant the human givens flag and are gradually embedding its base in concrete. However, it will be no easy task, and I write this article in the hope that others can benefit from our experience. For, although Sandwell's primary care trust, social services and mental health trust have all embraced human givens principles, incorporating this approach into Sandwell's mental health strategy, anyone who works in the NHS will know that we are top heavy with strategy documents and guidelines produced by well-meaning administrators, who fail to connect with front-line clinicians. If we are to mainstream human givens into the NHS, so that it underpins practice as well as strategy, there is an enormous challenge still ahead.

Over the period that it has been in power, the Government has created a number of large organisations, including the Modernisation Agency, the NHS University and the National Institute of Mental Health in England, all costing millions and yet now defunct, to force through improvement and change. As each of these failed to produce the desired effects, it was re-branded or disbanded: the current 'change organisation' is called the Care Services Improvement Partnership. All of these organisations have produced large, long reports, toolkits for improvement and 'new ways of working' documents, which overwhelm service commissioners, who are forced to set clinicians targets related to the strategies written about in these documents. Alas, for the commissioners of services, reaching targets is all important, as their future depends on it. Indeed, the policy writers and Government are so focused on the meeting of targets that regular inspections by various agencies take place, requiring form filling and huge amounts of time: time which could have been spent focusing on local needs but instead is spent producing the documentation required by the inspectors. Though intending to force improvement, this has probably had the opposite effect, as minds are continually focused on not failing the next inspection, rather than on a broad view of improving services.

Meanwhile, clinicians have been disengaged from the whole process, and so feel powerless when they are told that they must conform to a strategy that they have not been involved in producing. Even more frustrating to clinicians is the fact that we must focus on the things deemed important by politicians in any particular year. Thus, we have less time to take a whole view of the patient and may neglect aspects of care that are not deemed to be 'targets'. Indeed, a recent study has confirmed that, as mental health was not a major focus of the new GP contract, it became neglected because attention was focused on collecting "Quality and Outcome Framework points" in the target areas, principally diabetes, heart disease and lung disease.

In the health service roughly 90 per cent of consultations take place in primary care but this absorbs just 15 per cent of NHS funding. Secondary care has soaked up the lion's share of the funds, while primary care has generally been deemed less important, because hospital medicine has always been the more glamorous and hospitals are thought of as the places where lives are saved. However, it is an alarmingly little known fact that, when there is an increase in the number of GPs, death rates fall, but an increase in hospital doctors has the opposite effect. For years, in primary care, we would plan developments of our services and, each year, our developments were pulled at the 11th hour, as secondary care overspent. I remember complaining about this to the health authority's accountant one year and being told that it had always happened this way and it always would! So far he has been totally accurate.

Balancing the books

Now, however, the Government has realised that, despite doubling of funding for the NHS in the last few years, the secondary sector continues to overspend, and it has told them that they must balance their books. Last year the acute trusts, which run the medical hospitals in the country, were bailed out in the usual manner but, as it was deemed that deficits could no longer be carried forward, mental health services, in particular, were hit hard to pay for the medical sector's overspend. Although mental ill health is a major cause of mortality and morbidity, mental health remains a Cinderella service, and there was hardly any time to decide where the cuts would have to be made. Some areas have made psychologists redundant to protect hospital beds because, in the 'new' NHS, keeping beds open will protect income for the new foundation hospital trusts. Sandwell had actually balanced its books overall, but was still forced by the West Midlands Strategic Health Authority to bail out other primary care trusts in the area to the tune of a few million pounds.

At least our mental health trust kept its psychology services. Instead, it closed a ward of the local mental hospital sooner than planned and before we had the workforce in place to support the patients at home. The trust then transferred this work onto the primary care mental health teams, which meant that patients in primary care lost out. (Primary care teams in the medical sector have also shrunk, as nurses put into the community, and often paid for by primary care to provide local services, are pulled back into hospitals.)

But of course this only saves money in the short term and for the hospital trust, not for society as a whole. If we in general practice do not have the expertise in our local team, we often have no choice but to refer to the hospital, inconvenient for the patient and expensive for the country. If we want to reverse this situation, we need a whole-system, not a piecemeal, approach. We have already shown in Tipton, one of the most deprived areas in the country, where I am a GP, that a relatively low level of investment in general practice and the community sector can produce major health gains and reduce referrals to far more costly secondary care.

For the last six years, I have had the privilege of leading the Tipton

Care Organisation that we formed to bring all the local GP practices together. The Government was steering resources towards deprived areas and, with funds that we received to compensate for the shortage of doctors in the area, we showed how we could greatly improve outcomes for our patients, simply by asking the patients and those working at the coalface the best way to invest the money.

We have found that the most effective way of improving services has been by education, particularly the way that we impart information to patients. For instance, we discovered that 76 per cent of our diabetics did not understand why they needed regular blood tests and what the results meant. Also, we needed better communication between agencies, so that services augment each other, rather than work alone.

Perhaps most importantly, we measured and audited outcomes of care. It may seem incredible to outsiders that this is relatively new to the health service but, in general, things have always been done in the way they've always been done. Mental health is even slower than other specialities to measure outcomes, as there is no simple way to do this. It has been very satisfying to know that we have a number of diabetics who, but for the extra care we put in by paying chiropodists to do and chase up foot checks, would have required amputations. Our death rates from heart disease have significantly declined, which is especially satisfying, as part of our area had the highest rate of cardio-vascular disease in England. Sadly, at first, we were seen as a threat by our primary care trust because, instead of following their directives and guidelines, we did what we felt would be most effective for the patients, treating them as individuals and focusing on empowering them to learn about their illnesses and lifestyles, and then proved its value. Because we had outcome measures, eventually they had to take notice and later they took our work as a model to spread to other areas of Sandwell. In these kinds of ways we can stop the ever-increasing drain of resources into secondary care. I plan to continue to provide evidence that investment in mental health and wellbeing has both health and cost benefits for all patients, and that is why the human givens approach is the foundation of our strategy. When our patients have their needs met, it is not only their mental health that improves but their physical health too.

Needs met

This is the message that we really need to get through to the Government. We have already researched a wellbeing programme introduced in my practice, in which the top users of the service, including people with diabetes, hypertension and asthma, were taught mental health skills to enable them to take more control of their lives. We have demonstrated significant improvements in both their mental wellbeing and their physical health that continued to increase for at least two years after the course was completed (the time when our follow-up for the study ended). The results show clearly that, when patients learn the mental skills to be able to steer the direction of their lives, even if burdened with illness, they get better and better at doing it. Not only that, but their use of health services significantly declines, which was not the case for the control group, those who declined our invitation to participate in the programme.

It is a major breakthrough for us that, as laid down in *Everybody's Business: Sandwell's Mental Health Vision 2006–2015*, commissioning on mental health will for the first time be linked to outcomes. A major part of our investment in the human givens approach to therapy will be research to ensure that our investment is effective and that outcomes for our patients do improve. We expect that we will see reduced need of hospital services in both the mental health and the medical sector. And it will be in the medical sector where the most significant gains should be made. For a generally little known but very important fact is that half of the patients seen in hospital outpatients' departments have medically unexplained symptoms. These are the patients who won't do the right thing and get the diseases written about in the medical textbooks! They are not, of course, making up their suffering, but tests and scans fail to show up physical illness.

Most of us accept that a headache is most likely to be due to underlying stress or life circumstances. Our brain itself can't hurt as we have no pain receptors in the brain; the brain can even be operated on without anaesthetic. Yet it seems that, as a society, we do not want to accept that aches and pains in other parts of the body could also be psychosomatic, despite the rise in illnesses such as irritable bowel syndrome, now affecting up to five million people, and chronic fatigue, for which psychological approaches have now become treatment of choice. It is well known that you are twice as likely to be depressed if you suffer from diabetes, but recent research shows that depression causes metabolic changes that are often the precursor to type two diabetes. So depression may be a cause of diabetes and not always the other way around.

As we understand more and more about mind–body links, so it becomes more and more apparent that, for good health, we have to look at the whole person. This is something that has been lost in secondary care, as our hospitals become increasingly specialised in looking at less and less of the individual. A recent audit showed a decline in hospital referrals by GPs in Sandwell but, overall, outpatient appointments increased, as consultants refer between themselves, each looking at a different part of the person. It is not uncommon for the patients then to be sent back to us, totally confused after seeing a number of specialists and angry at being told that there's nothing wrong with them, although they still have the symptoms and may actually be feeling even worse.

Increased capacity

Another reason that we need the human givens approach in Sandwell, and throughout the country, is that mental health specialist services are at capacity. This means that, even when a patient has an urgent need to be seen, there may be difficulties getting them into the system. Some of this lack of capacity in the specialist mental health services is due to the fact that, once you do get into the system, it is very difficult to get discharged from it. Our service mapping has shown that there are a number of reasons for this, including a common belief that those with "severe and enduring mental illness" can only be maintained and not cured, and that they may need a fast route back into the system, which they may not get if they are discharged. Another reason is that a major national measure and target for mental health services is reduction of suicide. Though devastating, suicides are fortunately relatively uncommon, yet every suicide is closely scrutinised by the public health doctors and blame apportioned. There is, therefore, a reluctance to discharge from secondary services and many patients are even brought back to outpatients every few months to ensure that they are all right – though

I would have thought that continually reminding people that they are mentally ill might have the opposite effect from that desired. A final reluctance to let go of patients is accounted for by the secondary services' lack of faith that GPs have the correct skills to manage mental health, even though GPs deal with the vast majority of mentally ill patients who are seen in the NHS (about 93 per cent). It should also be noted that about a third of those with the more severe mental illnesses – generally thought to be the province of secondary care – choose to stay with their GP. They prefer a family doctor whom they already know and trust, who may not be as experienced in dealing with their illness as psychiatrists but who, they know, will seek help and advice if needed.

Skilling up primary care

Once diabetes, blood pressure, raised cholesterol and asthma were the preserve of hospitals; only the specialist was seen to have the skill to treat these conditions properly. Since the treatment of these problems has been transferred mainly to primary care, the standard of treatment across the country has improved, because, through training, we have created the capacity in the primary care team to carry out 90 per cent of all NHS consultations. By giving primary care the skills it needs, through training and education, and by moving services into the community, we can create the same capacity in mental health. This means providing effective counselling services and training psychiatric nurses to work alongside GPs and their teams. In Sandwell, we now plan to have link workers trained in the human givens approach, who can assess any patient the GP is concerned about, advise the GP on how to treat if appropriate, direct to the appropriate agency in the community or to counselling, or get rapid help when appropriate from secondary care.

One of our inspirations has been a visit to Hartlepool Mind, which I undertook along with the chief executive of the Sandwell Mental Health Trust and the chair of the Service Users Group. Here we saw for ourselves how human givens is the recovery model, which in theory the NHS is signed up to. We have a model now to copy, and we plan to pilot it by opening a wellbeing centre in Smethwick,where patients can self-refer, or to which we can refer. It will have its own therapists, and, if successful, we will expand it to the other six towns in our area. This should solve the problem of how we get patients out of secondary care services and rehabilitate them into the community. [For an account of the way that Hartlepool Mind works, see 'The road to recovery' by Iain Caldwell on page 85.]

There is still a very long way to go. Without one commissioner in particular, who has battled away almost single-handedly, we could not have achieved what we have achieved so far. (It was her brainwave to run meetings where service users met commissioners and were able to help us shape the future of mental health services.) Yet, without my being on the team, she would have got stuck long ago, as I frequently have to bulldoze us through dead ends she runs into, because she is not a medical practitioner and so can be ignored by clinicians and managers.

We also still have the challenge of winning over the psychologists and psychiatrists. Farouk Okhai, chair of the Human Givens Institute and consultant psychiatrist in psychotherapy for Milton Keynes Primary Care NHS Trust, gave a talk to the psychiatrists. The junior doctors loved it, but the consultants have not really fed back. We have had three human givens training workshops, at which we offered free places to any staff that the mental health trust wanted to send but, despite promises to work with us and to release staff for training, there have been significant numbers of no shows. The trust has promised to look into this, but we have varying support from their different departments. Meanwhile, some of the psychologists say that training has to concentrate on cognitive-behavioural therapy, as this is the recommendation from NICE guidelines, and they have a limited number of training days. We will plough on regardless because, with every training, we win new supporters.

The human givens trainers have not found it all easy either. The service users, key to forcing through our redesign, have insisted on attending the training. They tend to be an angry bunch, as many feel that they have been let down by the services in the past and are still desperately seeking help and see the training as a possibility. Similarly challenging are those medics in the audience who ask about the evidence base for human givens. To fully win over the NHS, I think it is vital not so much to challenge existing practice as to concentrate on showing how the human givens approach can meet NHS needs. I plan to do this by demonstrating that human givens is the key to rehabilitating and discharging patients from secondary mental health services into the community and is an effective means of treating those with medically unexplained symptoms. This should help produce the evidence base that NHS medicine insists on. We already have two studies on the go in Sandwell. One, on the effectiveness of the rewind technique, is being led by Vinay Kumar, a community psychiatric nurse in one of our primary care mental health teams, and a second is being carried out with Stafford University, on the effectiveness of human givens for the treatment of depression. These should lead on to further studies.

I believe we are past the point of no return, and that is exciting. I have been fortunate to work in a primary care trust whose chief executive had the vision to support the development of primary care mental health services and who has allowed me the resources to do so. In the latest shake-up, he has been replaced, luckily by another chief executive with the same vision. Currently, we have identified 19 general practices in Sandwell keen to spearhead and research investment in primary mental health services with a human givens approach. We have a couple of protected learning days planned, where we close the practices for the afternoon and can concentrate on finding out what other further training and resources are needed and how to deliver them.

So it is an exciting and challenging time for us, and potentially a coming of age for the human givens approach within the NHS. If we prove it to be as successful as we expect, MindFields College will need to have the capacity and the flexibility to cope with the increased demand for training. But we can expect continued resistance from the psychiatric and psychology establishment, which we will continue to need to win over. Experience has told me, however, that there are a large number of clinicians out there desperate for the training and the tools to help them help all their patients. If we add the human givens model, which seeks to cure ill health by meeting unmet human needs, to the medical model, which seeks to cure ill health with surgery and medication, then the medics will have added a powerful tool to their toolkit.

Speaking out

Sadly, there are only a few places in the country where mental health is a priority for health service provision. Through Primhe (Primary Mental

Health and Education), a charity which I chair, we have started to train specialist primary care practitioners – mainly GPs but also some nurses, commissioners and voluntary sector workers. We need leaders in primary care to be able to lead the commissioning and development of improved mental health services through 'practice-based commissioning' (the latest directive and direction for the health service), an initiative in which GPs will hold 75 per cent of NHS funding and so manage a large proportion of the finances of the NHS. Many psychiatric nurses working for the mental health trusts are frustrated with the current system and are keen to change things, but are afraid to speak out, as this would be seen by their managers as denigrating the services they work in, and could result in their being disciplined. They need leaders such as those we are training to speak out for them. As a self-employed GP who cannot be sacked for speaking his mind, I can tell the truth, call a spade a spade and say when the emperor has no clothes on.

Until our service is focused on patients' individual needs and can continually be challenged with regular audit of outcomes, which is certainly not the case in mental health services at present, it will frequently look pretty naked to many of us.

* * ✳ * *

Ian Walton is a GP with special interest in mental health, working in Tipton, in the West Midlands. He is chair of the charity Primhe (Primary Mental Health and Education) and GP lead for the Birmingham and Black Country Mental Health Network.

Common ground: diplomacy and the human givens

*Former diplomat **John Bell** suggests that only a radically different, innate needs-based approach to conflict resolution can bring a possibility of peace to the Middle East.*

DIPLOMATIC intervention seems, in this day and age, to be less and less effective as an instrument of managing frictions and conflicts between states. This is particularly so in the Middle East, where venture after diplomatic venture has failed; indeed, they have possibly even exacerbated the troubles there.

At its core, the Middle East conflict speaks to the ancient human need to protect against outside threat. The irony is that the methods the region has developed to do so now propagate those threats by blurring the need for security with other unidentified essential needs, no longer meeting any of them clearly and, as a result, exacerbating problems with outsiders. If diplomacy is to offer any useful answers, it needs a fresh approach and a clear understanding of human needs, how they manifest and how to meet them.

Classic diplomacy is fundamentally based on the notion of state interest. It is a tradition that arose and thrived, from Metternich to Kissinger, as European nation states developed and solidified: professional statesmen were mandated with the mission of managing their nation's interest through dialogue, negotiation and treaty. The premise behind it is that state interests are consciously rational. That is, 'professionals' or elites could determine what was beneficial for their state, pursue this through rational means and so achieve equilibrium states with other nations, often called 'peace'. This approach matured during the European Enlightenment, a period marked by its appeal to 'reason' as the saving grace of humanity. A few 'wise men' full of reason, fundamentally disconnected from their fellow citizens, decided the fates of millions. This was successful in some periods, such as the Congress of Vienna in the 19th century, and unsuccessful in others, the First World War being a case in point. Conflict resolution and 'diplomacy' remain to this day the realm of 'the few' operating under the premise that reasoned argument and negotiation among 'the few' can lead nation-states to greener pastures and end war and disputes.

It may be, however, that the problems between nations today are so complex, and so misunderstood, that such 'rational' procedures don't have a chance to resolve longstanding or deeply rooted conflicts. We are in an age where unknown factors and the apparently 'irrational' may be playing into decision making at the international political level more than is accepted or recognised. Much money is thrown at diplomatic efforts and much authority vested in individuals, often with little result. Indeed diplomats, and professionals in conflict resolution, of whom I am one, may be at risk of being charged with professional incompetence and social irresponsibility.

My own experience as both a UN and Canadian diplomat and now the Middle East director of a global conflict resolution organisation, called Search for Common Ground, is that new 'starting points' are necessary in order for this field to deliver the goods and bring peace and stability to long-suffering peoples. The area of my knowledge, the Middle East, is simultaneously the most intractable of conflict, yet also the most telling of how wrong humans can go. Its excesses speak loudest to our failures and to a 'missing piece' in the equation.

A few years ago, along with some former colleagues in the Canadian Foreign Service, I began a project on the lodestone of the Middle East problem, the Old City of Jerusalem. This is where the Temple Mount, or the Haram Al-Sharif, is found, a space holy to both Jews and Muslims, as well as Christianity's Church of the Holy Sepulchre. In 2000, the Camp David talks failed partly because of a focus on the sovereignty of the space (what belongs to whom). As a result, we decided to pursue a new 'needs-based approach' to the problem: identifying the needs of all parties interested in the Old City and how they could be met. At the very time the Old City project began, a close friend directed me to a book called *Human Givens: a new approach to emotional health and clear thinking*.[1] The similarities between the practical approach we had set upon and the paradigm in this book were obvious; the parallel between the individual and the collective level clear: if humans did not have their innate needs met in a society, conflict would inevitably ensue, just as mental illness would ensue, in an individual.

In the Middle East, needs are not being met because decision-making systems do not address or even recognise them, and often intentionally and wilfully ignore them. This certainly leads to poor decisions, because a possible set of answers are not factored in. The inherited systems of organisation, such as tribe, nation, religious identity, even centralised government or ideology, that bind groups and motivate behaviours limit responses and conflate needs into a blur that is not easily disentangled.

Human needs in the Middle East are so confused, through the admixture of religion, traditional politics and belonging, that no one can distinguish what their needs actually are – or the way forward. Furthermore, collective unrecognised and unmet needs, whether for security, autonomy, or meaning, can lead to things going very awry. In the Middle East region, religious heritage plays an especial role: it provides simultaneously a reason for pride, an instrument to bond the group for the purpose of survival, as well as, theoretically, a mechanism for pursuing greater meaning and purpose in life. The result is intermingled needs which, together with archaic instruments for managing modern problems, create a sure-fire recipe for conflict. So, in the Middle East, we have people clinging to land that others have, rationalising behaviour through ancient scripture, and sticking to political answers that have no evidence of efficacy. Attempts at new solutions or understanding matters anew often result in outright disbelief by adherents or the risk of attack or censure.

Disaggregating needs

Over millennia, the people of the Middle East have learned to rely, for their identity, on belonging, particularly to a religious community, thus enabling them also to pursue meaning (especially through the collective pursuit of the 'divine' and meet needs for survival and security (as in "I live or die by my group"). In actual fact, these dimensions need to be disaggregated and understood as separate, in order for needs to be met practically, in this day and age.

It is because of this deep conflation of needs that the Middle East 'feels' existential to any one who works intimately with it. The parties appear to be uncompromising and will apparently throw away seemingly sensible deals, or roads leading to them, such as at Camp David in 2000, because, in the end, the sacrifices involved threaten these essential needs all at once – or at least *appear* to. Arab Muslims today feel they cannot compromise because their heritage and survival is threatened and at stake. Jews, too, hold on dearly to all they have nurtured through the millennia as life-vests of the spirit and body.

Testing each side's readiness to compromise is volatile exactly because any step touches on the most basic and existential parts of each group's identity. Conflict is certain and conflict resolution almost impossible because the society does not believe it can violate what it holds most dear in the name of compromise. *Belonging and its fruits matter too much.*

This 'existential' attitude towards heritage and identity can be recognised in extremis in the almost suicidal tendency, on both sides, to fight. Within the space of one week in Jerusalem, I was told by an Israeli and a Palestinian that they were ready to let their children die and their futures disappear because they "had nothing to lose" and all about them was threat. The Middle East has a track record of radical suicidal behaviour, from the siege of the fortress at Masada in AD72, when nearly 1000 Jews sacrificed themselves rather than submit to the Romans, through the revolt in the 2nd century AD against the Romans by Jewish rebel bar Kochba and his followers, also ending in mass suicide in the same fortress, to the suicide bomb attacks of Palestinians of recent years. This latent tendency, currently exhibited by a few radicals, may be more intrinsic to the region's habits than may first meet the eye. It is also demonstrated in the regular failure of negotiations on core issues – because they are 'core' to the very existence of the peoples of the region: rather go to the wall and fail than compromise.

Indeed, for thousands of years, the organising principles of tight belonging to family, tribe and religion made sense. The Middle East is the grand pathway of invasion: Europe, Africa and Asia meet here and many a bold conqueror swept through the Fertile Crescent, annihilating locals in his path. From Alexander the Great, to Babylonian king Nebuchadnezzar to British General Allenby, the path of conquest between Cairo and Antioch has been well trodden. 'Tight belonging' was essential under such conditions; there was simply no other way to survive.

What the people of the Middle East seem to have discovered, however, is that combining this need for belonging and survival with religious beliefs and ideals cemented the group more firmly. The identity becomes 'jetfuelled' by faith, uncompromising, idealised, full of the glory of meaning, while simultaneously assuaging the anxiety of survival. It is a cultural emotional cocktail that is not easy to give up. Indeed, sometimes it produces a strength of purpose and will that takes a defensive principle – belonging – and transforms it into successful offence: thus the Arab Muslim expansion of the 7th and 8th centuries or the Zionist success in establishing a state in the 20th century.

This may even seem a relatively efficient way to achieve societal goals. In actual fact, it is dangerous because of the basic attitude it engenders: exclusivity to the group becomes essential for survival. The very principle that provides life and meaning *excludes*, and harshly so, for the group's integrity cannot be threatened. This intermingling of the needs for survival, meaning and belonging leads naturally to conflict, both because of the aggressive exclusion and because, in the end, the conflation is not an efficient means to meet those needs. Exclusivity spontaneously generates conflict because it often denies the needs of others and survival is threatened by the very mechanism that is supposed to maintain it; the pursuit of 'greater meaning' is confused with other needs such as the need for survival and identity and thus is largely unachieved; and, while belonging is indeed achieved, at what cost does it come and could it not be achieved in a less risky way?

An example of this dynamic in today's Middle East politics is the Israeli settlement enterprise in the West Bank and Gaza, which derives out of a scriptural reference to land that ancient Jews were divinely granted and which is now 'settled' by modern Jews. The land is needed for both survival of the Jewish people (an extension of the idea of Israel as a haven) and the pursuit of meaning in the sense of fulfilling a divine mission. Until relatively recently, few Israelis questioned the settlement enterprise even though it was built on the land of an existing population group, the Palestinians. For various reasons, that activity has now been diminished in the name of a more important definition of 'belonging': the maintenance of the cohesion of Israel as a Jewish state. The effects of this enterprise nevertheless remain consequential: in its current plans, Israel will still keep ownership of the large settlement blocs, and compromises made to settlers who are removed may include the dangerous step of holding on to disputed core parts of Jerusalem.

State-level intervention and 'classic' diplomacy cannot fight against such embedded and misunderstood needs. The 'old school' will inevitably lose because it cannot see the 'ghost' it is battling with. As long as needs are left unattended and unidentified and are not disaggregated into modules that can be looked at individually, negotiations will not be able to resolve these problems. The old diplomat is simply blind in the face of such complexities and entanglements – it is no wonder that failure repeats itself in the attempts to find peace. The Middle East needs new organising ideas in order to shake this unholy plague of traditional forms of belonging, and new mechanisms to meet its difficult realities head on.

Forward thinking

The Old City of Jerusalem encompasses many of the complexities of the Middle East conflict – security, religious needs and symbolism, and demographic and property interests – in one square kilometre. The Old City project is attempting to find new answers to this old conflict by disaggregating needs, and presenting new concepts of governance based on meeting the needs of all parties within this small but volatile space.

The project set about identifying and explaining needs, from "sewage to symbolism". The city's history adds to its richness and its problems are many. Belonging, survival and security are interwoven in its daily fabric, in the practices of its residents, the claims of nations and the symbolic and emotive perceptions of billions around the globe. Property registries have not been kept since Ottoman times and even then in a haphazard manner; attacks on the holy sites by extremists represent a constant threat; millions of Christian, Muslim and Jewish tourists and pilgrims come every year to visit and enjoy the city's sites and spectacular location but also create congestion and competing interests, sometimes over the same locale. Above all, the question of who controls the space remains one of the thorniest political problems on the planet. Israel occupied the Old City in 1967 and has remained in control until today with many practical and political consequences for Palestinians as well as many other groups with a stake in it.

A discussion document, *The Jerusalem Old City Initiative*,[2] was prepared by the Canadian team, of which I am a member, outlining everyone's needs and defining possible structures and arrangements that could lead to needs being met.[3] These include social, property ownership, economic, political and religious, symbolic and heritage needs. Projects and research, from a comprehensive survey of housing stock and structure for the purpose of renovation and rehabilitation, to joint Palestinian–Israeli planning on improving visitor services and minimising current equities in tourism, to the development of a 'common charter' that recognises respective needs are proposed in the text.

The core suggestion, a frame of governance that would involve Israelis, Palestinians and internationals in the administration of the Old City, addresses the need for control. A tripartite governing council is proposed with an appointed administrator, agreed to by all parties and the international community. We wanted to avoid the division presented in other proposals such as the Geneva Accords. Instead, the aim is to maintain the integrity of the Old City, both from a functional point of view (the space is too small and crowded to be broken up) and from the more visionary perspective of maintaining its historical nature as one walled city and a place for future understanding and pluralism.

A single Old City police force, again composed of Israelis, Palestinians and internationals, is also suggested as the most efficacious instrument of achieving security in this most sensitive of locales. Critically, there would be, through these arrangements, freedom of access for worship for all believers as well as recognition of the historical links of all interested parties to the disputed areas. Today, many Palestinian Muslims and Christians cannot access the holy sites in Jerusalem due to Israeli security measures, restrictions on movement and the construction of the barrier around Jerusalem. In contrast, Jewish historical ties to the Temple Mount and other holy sites are often denied by Palestinians and other Arabs and Muslims, creating great distrust. The Old City initiative aims to create structures that meet such needs directly, and calm sources of friction and conflict. For example, the proposed Old City police force would permit secure access to all worshippers, and the governing council would play a role in recognising the links of all communities to their holy sites and heritage.

Through this process, the needs for belonging (participation in governance), meaning (freedom of worship) and survival (security) in the Old City are defined, and addressed practically, without large sacrifices; instead, the pie is 'enlarged' by the introduction of the international dimension, while maintaining the national interests of Palestinians and Israelis. The proposed arrangements meet these needs without using old paradigms of exclusivity.

The Old City project has been proceeding at pace for two years but it still meets many hurdles. Although the project provides some degree of meeting the needs for control, the desire for *exclusive* control, nurtured by millennia of conflation of needs as described above, still interferes with this more sensible approach, thwarting compromise. For instance:

- The level of distrust between Israelis and Palestinians remains very high due to half a century of conflict and this tends to cause rejection of any effort for accommodation, including creative ones;

- Old habits of diplomacy and politics die hard, even if they don't work;

- Many leaders are partaking in 'circles of attention' as opposed to 'circles of solution'. This makes them focus on existing plans and over-rides the drive for creative solutions that might require moving against the crowd: peer pressure keeps everyone dumbed down and lacking in daring;

- Above all, needs remain unidentified or insufficiently explained. The desire for many Jews to hold on to the Temple Mount and the counter Muslim claim on the same space is lived as unquestioned desire, rather than as a series of specific and achievable needs such as freedom of access, recognition of historical links, security, and shared authority over the site.

Our current goal is to continue to pursue the core needs, especially security, by further developing arrangements so that they are practical and meaningful to all concerned. The project is certainly against today's political climate; however, its strength remains that it is trying to address the core problems and needs and as such will ultimately be effective in conflict prevention, if implemented.

One possible road that has not been tried is to have the parties first come to an understanding of the basic needs of each side *before* starting negotiations. But, alas, the needs-based approach is almost too basic for leaders and policymakers and takes away from the much-loved complexity that drives the political world and its sister, the media.

The Old City project will proceed and, on its way, graft some new approaches on to the ongoing political dynamics but my sense is that we have barely begun. The ability to attract new people, especially decision and opinion makers, to these approaches will require proof of effect on the ground. Furthermore, it is likely that two issues will need to be addressed more directly for the Middle East to begin to leave its quandary.

1. Liberation from restraints:

New thinking is required regarding the twin pursuits of survival and meaning. The region continues to proceed, using antiquated means of achieving these needs, and is unwilling to consider a revamping of these processes. This 'unpacking' inevitably means some large reforms regarding religious understanding and relationships with those outside the faith. At a basic level, this means that people begin to consider that 'identities' of belonging are tools in the hands of people, to shape for themselves, and evolve as required at each time in history, and not permanent forms to be adapted to. This is a large step in a region where identities cut to the root of existence – but a desirable goal may, in the end, be a more flexible understanding of identity that is more inclusive.

2. Integration – a region for all:

The Old City has four distinct quarters (Muslim, Christian, Jewish, and Armenian); it has conflicting property claims over houses and shops between Jews and Arabs, disputed holy sites such as the Temple Mount and Haram Al-Sharif, and it is crowded: one square kilometre of tight alleyways, souks, Mameluke, Crusader and Ottoman buildings housing 35,000 people, and dozens of heritage sites. With such disputes, density and diversity, it is a microcosm of the region. Answers like those proposed in the Old City project are new organising principles because they are based on maintaining integrity of the space while still meeting the needs of the diversity of citizens. If implemented, these could serve as a model for the region at large. Although it is merely a vision now, a Middle East confederation (composed, for example, of Israel, Lebanon, Syria, Palestine and Jordan) could achieve greater integrity between these small states, easing mobility and recreating natural connections destroyed by war and the nation-state and facilitating economic success. A confederation, as opposed to empire or autocracy, would be a configuration that would permit interconnection, while maintaining local decentralisation. Above all, such a concept would permit the people of the region to tackle many of their problems, from refugees to water needs, on a regional basis – possibly the only way they will be resolved.

In the end, the exclusivity that Middle East identity has bred for thousands of years may simply not be as necessary as it seemed; the peoples of the region may simply be more similar to each other than their cultures would have them believe. Musk oxen gather in a circle to defend against wolves, yet, outside the circle, there may only be other oxen.

* ** ❉ ** *

John Bell is the Director of the Middle East Programme at Search for Common Ground, a global conflict resolution organisation. He is also a former Canadian and United Nations diplomat who has worked extensively in the Middle East in Cairo, Gaza, Beirut and Jerusalem on issues ranging from Islamic fundamentalism to the peace process. He has been a member of Canada's delegation to the Refugee Working Group in the peace process, political adviser to the personal representative of the Secretary-General of the United Nations for southern Lebanon, adviser to the Canadian Government during the Iraq crisis in 2002–3 and consultant to the International Crisis Group on recent developments in Jerusalem. He is a founding member of the Jerusalem Old City Initiative (Universities of Toronto and Windsor), an effort to find creative options for this contentious issue. John Bell has written extensively on Middle East issues in magazines and newspapers across the globe. He is originally from the region and a living example of its shared and mixed heritage.

Part Three

Part Three

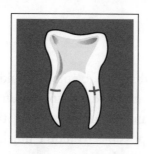

Molar memories: how an ancient mechanism can ruin lives

*When we react excessively to events, major or minor, we may be victims of a primitive survival mechanism gone awry, suggests research psychologist **Joe Griffin**. Despite often causing years of distress, it can be treated successfully – and usually remarkably quickly.*

IN TIMES gone by, whenever people displayed wildly irrational behaviour or exhibited extreme emotional responses that did damage, they were said to be possessed by an evil spirit; a demon, fiend or even 'the devil' himself. Once inhabiting the poor unfortunates, these invisible malevolent beings could transform them into the very epitome of self-ishness or self-destructiveness.

With the 'beast' in command, distressing manifestations could occur. It might induce previously peaceful individuals to become violent, producing sudden rages in the poor person or driving them to the most destructively devious activities. Others, once 'possessed', might starve themselves to the point of death, physically attack themselves or become quite hysterically fearful or mad. In some cases these demons would make people perform bizarre, lustful acts. But always supernatural forces were behind such goings on, or so it was thought for tens of thousands of years.

Today, of course, we talk differently. We speak of anger disorders, obsessions, personality disorders, depression, anorexia, self-harming, psychosis and sexual deviancy, such as cross-dressing, and so on. And yet, by changing our language we are no nearer to understanding or curing most of these conditions.

But suppose there was a hitherto unknown psychological principle at work, one that, once understood, made possible the removal of much of this suffering? One that, for example, could, in a single session of psychotherapy, cure an anorexic, or stop an unwanted perverse sexual obsession, or dissolve unreasonable and irrationally cruel outbursts of anger. If such were possible wouldn't much human misery be circumvented? In this chapter I am suggesting that such a psychological principle *does* exist and that using it may enable therapists to quickly cure at least some of these conditions.

Consider, for a moment, the following scenarios (I am sure that at least one will be familiar to you). You have a minor difference of opinion with your nearest and dearest about some entirely inconsequential domestic matter ... and yet you are left with a seething rage that persists for hours. Someone close to you pokes fun at you or teases you and you are consumed with a sense of righteous indignation and respond by getting insanely angry with them. Or you are amazed to be accused by a partner or colleague of 'winding them up' or 'pressing their buttons', after saying something you thought was completely innocuous. In other words, you sometimes (or even often) find yourself reacting emotionally in ways that are totally out of proportion to the circumstances – and no doubt you have seen countless others do the same.

Such seemingly irrational behaviour, both in myself and others, had often mystified and infuriated me over the years until, after much consideration and experimentation, I realised that 'over-the-top', 'neurotic' or otherwise inappropriate emotional reactions like these are actually the expression of a highly primitive survival mechanism: one that I have called the 'pain–pleasure *recall*' principle (to distinguish it from the 'pain–pleasure' principle beloved of psychoanalysts).

This principle, I suggest, is the key to understanding not only seemingly irrational outbursts but more serious pathological behaviour as well – habitual actions which lead to self-destructive behaviour or damage to inter-personal relationships. Most importantly, however, once understood we can change behaviour, fast. As we will see, using the pain–pleasure recall principle has already enabled me to help a woman recover her life by putting an end to 25 years of anorexia, a man in his 30s to deal with and stop his longstanding compulsion to cross-dress, and another man to stop putting his marriage at risk – each after only one session of therapy. And other experienced human givens therapists to whom I had explained this principle have since used it and reported back to me amazingly rapid progress with a range of cases previously considered difficult or intractable.

This chapter sets out the evidence to support this new finding: that it is the special way the brain has evolved to process the co-occurrence of pain and pleasure in a situation that shapes much human and animal behaviour.

I am, of course, not the first to consider the effects of pain and pleasure – countless thinkers from ancient and modern cultures around the world have speculated about the roles of pleasure and pain in motivating our behaviour. Freud famously developed the 'pleasure principle' – the demanding of immediate gratification of instinctive needs. And a wealth of evidence has been accumulated by distinguished learning theorists, such as Ivan Pavlov, B F Skinner and Edward Lee Thorndike, to show that, if an action brings us pleasure, we will choose to do it again, and that, conversely, if an action results in pain, we are reluctant to repeat it. Over the years, many laboratory experiments have shown how animals have learned to alter their behaviour in response to different amounts and types of both positive and negative reinforcements. But what has never been taken fully into account, is that, very often, an action may elicit both pleasure *and* pain.

Every animal must assess risk

All animals have needs that must be met if they are to live mentally and physically healthy lives (this is at the heart of the human givens approach). But to pursue needs without first making an assessment of the attendant risks – such as that of becoming another animal's lunch whilst in pursuit of your own – would lead, in all probability, to a greatly foreshortened lifespan. It would be surprising indeed, therefore, if evolution had left the assessment of risk to chance – the instinctive assessment of risk is key to the pain–pleasure recall principle.

We know that animals learn from painful experiences and are less likely to seek to repeat them. We also know that punishing animals, particularly human ones, for undesirable behaviour that they find rewarding is not as effective, generally, as rewarding the desirable behaviour that we would like them to perform instead. (If it were otherwise, we would have no repeat offenders in our prisons.) But, in the real world, desirable experiences almost always come at a price. Procuring access to a desirable mate may mean having to fight the alpha male, for example; hunting a substantial prey for dinner carries the risk of the predator getting injured by the prey being sought, and so on. Animals must, therefore, have evolved an instinctive method of gauging risk, using previous experience as a guide.

It was the failure of conditioning theory to predict how animals do this that has largely been responsible for the decline of pure behaviour therapy (which is based on conditioning or learning theory) as it was increasingly recognised that learning isn't just a mechanical association between things (such as the ringing of a bell when a steak appears, as in Pavlov's experiments when dogs learned to salivate on hearing the bell) but rather it comes about as a result of the perception of a meaningful relationship between different things.[1] For example, if a tone is sounded before laboratory animals receive an electric shock, they will learn to fear the tone. If, next, a light is also turned on at the same time as the tone sounds, and then a shock is received, the animals don't learn to fear the light; they continue to fear just the tone.[2] My colleague Ivan Tyrrell and I have argued elsewhere that it is just this perception of a meaningful relationship that generates consciousness.[3]

So behaviour therapy was superseded by cognitive behaviour therapy (CBT), which is based on an uneasy alliance between conditioning theory and cognitive appraisal theory – the idea that the way we think and make our judgements affects our behaviour. This alliance arose because of the demonstrable failures of conditioning theory to account for neurotic types of behaviour, especially in humans. For instance, how could conditioning theory explain why people can develop a phobia about snakes, to the point of shaking when they see a picture of a snake, when they have never actually come across a snake in their lives? However, it has become increasingly clear that the cognitive system only takes computational decisions, such as calculating which product offers the best value for money, so the alliance is becoming more and more compromised. In complex or ambiguous situations, it is the emotional brain that takes the initial decisions.[4] We see an unfamiliar manlike shape looming out of the lonely field in the dark and instantly feel fear as our bodies mobilise for fight or flight. Then our cognitive system kicks in and only at this point do we realise that we are looking at a scarecrow, and call off the red alert. Thus we can see that, for our survival's sake, it is the quicker emotional process that guides our responses in such circumstances, even if they are later informed by the cognitive system.

Much of this confusion is due to a failure to understand the pain–pleasure recall principle.

The pain–pleasure recall principle

Pain involves negative or 'avoidance' emotions – we feel bad or we avoid a situation in which we might experience pain. Pleasure involves positive 'approach' emotions – we feel good or seek out an experience that will make us feel good. (This even includes the experience of anger because when we are angry we are both motivated to do something – go forward – and get satisfaction from feeling power.) The pain–pleasure recall principle holds that, when pain and pleasure are both experienced in connection with a given stimulus, irrespective of the order in which the pain and pleasure occur, the memory of that experience will be encoded so that the recall of the pain (the negative feelings) *precedes* the recall of the pleasure (positive feelings) associated with it. I have found it useful to call these memories 'molar memories' because they have two emotional roots: the one that was painful and the other that was pleasurable. The pleasurable aspect of the experience has to stay outside of consciousness because, when a pattern match is triggered by a similar situation in the future, the negative feeling needs to be experienced first, so that risk assessment can take place. This order of events is essential, survival always being the top priority. Only if the negative feeling is defused by some response or not acted upon, mentally or physically – for instance, if we don't experience deep disgust or run away from the situation – will the positive feeling be aroused and come through to consciousness.

It is essential, I suggest, that pleasure and pain experienced in connection with the same event are coded separately like this (with the memory of the pain being accessed first, so that an informed risk assessment can be made before indulging in the pleasure again). If the negatives were not evaluated first, access to an expectation of reward might lead to a downplaying of the risks involved. This could prove fatal if, when the reward seemed sufficient, it led animals to ignore the lessons of experience.

If, however, after an automatic risk assessment, we perceive that the

The riddle of conditioned taste aversion

THE pain–pleasure recall principle also explains the well-known pheno-menon of conditioned taste aversion, which has always presented a problem for classical conditioning. In classical conditioning, Pavlov's bell and the steak need to be presented together, or at least closely together, a number of times, for the conditioning to take hold – ie for the bell to trigger salivation with or without the steak. So how can it be that, if a person or animal gets sick hours after they have eaten some improperly cooked food, they may develop an aversion to the food they had eaten?

This phenomenon has created problems even for theorists who claim that we must be genetically pre-wired to make this sort of link as a way of explaining the enigma of snake phobias, for example.[5] According to the theory, many humans are genetically pre-adapted to form fears of stimuli such as heights or snakes because both represented possible dangers in our ancestral environment, whereas motorcars, which were not around at that early time, very rarely become the object of phobias, despite the fact that they kill thousands of people every year. Con-ditioned food aversion, however, is very different from a phobia about heights or snakes because the food that becomes aversive can literally be any food or combination of foods. Most importantly, there can liter-ally be hours between the ingestion of the food and getting sick. This is no simple case of a bell ringing followed instantly by a steak appearing.

I suggest that the pain–pleasure recall principle can easily explain this phenomenon, without the need to postulate a special, questionable case of evolutionary adaptation. Since both pleasure and pain are in-volved, pleasure at ingestion and pain at disgorgement, the brain has only to make a link between the two experiences for the principle to apply. Such a link is highly probable since both experiences involve the same organs – mouth, throat, stomach, taste buds, etc – and another meal is unlikely to have been ingested in between the experience of the pleasure and the pain. The pain–pleasure recall principle predicts that the pain of vomiting will be recalled separately from the pleasure of eating, and will thus be used to evaluate the risk of eating that food when encountered in future. The feeling of discomfort from vomiting recalled without access-ing the feeling of pleasure from eating will be sufficient to discourage eating the food again. Hence a food aversion is developed. ■

negative feeling which pattern matches to our current situation is not relevant, then the positive feelings will be activated by the memory. This triggers a dopamine rush, which we experience as desire. If we act upon this desire and experience satisfaction, the pattern is reinforced. If, however, pain is experienced as a further consequence of that action, this will become coded as part of our conscious, stored negative memories, strengthening their power. (For instance, if a child sneaks a biscuit from the jar and enjoys it but is told off by her mother, the telling-off is added to other tellings-off she has received for the same transgression and, the next time, she might decide not to sneak the biscuit.)

In other words, when a behaviour is punished this strengthens the negative root memory but doesn't alter the pleasurable aspect. This is why aversion therapy for a sexual deviancy for example, is not very successful outside of laboratory conditions. When the person returns to their home environment, where there is no immediate threat of punishment, the deviant impulse can resurface because they feel safe again.

Some bizarre outcomes

This universally applied principle has immense advantages for guiding risk assessment in animals, but there are circumstances where it can have distinct disadvantages, especially for humans. For example, a pleasurable feeling experienced at the age of five, shielded from consciousness by the pain that is also connected to the same event, may be dictating inappropriate or destructive behaviour in adulthood. Thus, the pain–pleasure recall principle may predispose us to some bizarre self-destructive behaviours and, because the motivations for them are normally outside our conscious recall, we are prevented from making a rational evaluation of them. (I will give several examples of this later.) CBT, as currently practised, is not likely therefore to be effective with these types of problems. One might suppose that the negative appraisal would stop the positive aspect of the pattern running. However, positive feelings that are reinforced by reward can be highly addictive, both because of the dopamine rush and also because we assume our response has been caused by our current circumstances; we are ignorant of the hidden childish sources of our motivation. As the mechanism must have evolved to calculate immediate risk, it may be blind to long-term consequences. Fortunately, the resulting unconscious programming can be corrected quite quickly with the right therapeutic technique. I will now illustrate this, and the pain–pleasure recall principle at work, through some personal anecdotes and cases histories.

First in the queue

I fly regularly between Ireland and England and used always to become agitated about getting to the departure lounge check-in desk well before time – often before anyone else was queuing or, indeed, before the desk was even staffed. This only happened on occasions when I was flying Ryanair, however. I had no problem with Aer Lingus. The difference was that Ryanair doesn't allocate seats, so it was always a free-for-all. No matter how much I would reason with myself and do calming breathing, I had to be one of the first in the queue at the departure gates because I had to be one of the first people on the plane and be free to choose my seat. I knew this was neurotic behaviour but nothing would alter it.

On one particular day, I was at Dublin airport, anxiously looking at the time and itching to get to the head of the Ryanair queue, when my wife Liz, who had accompanied me with our granddaughter Jessica, suggested, after I'd checked in and we had enjoyed a cup of coffee, that I should take Jessica by the hand and walk her with me to the depart-ure gates. Being then only just over a year old, Jessica, of course, walked very slowly. So I said to Liz, in what I thought was a calm, reasonable manner, "You do realise there's only 35 minutes till I have to be at the departure gates!" Now Liz, who has a well-developed capacity for pick-ing up emotional nuances, responded rather negatively to me putting my preoccupation with being at the head of a non-existent queue above the pleasure of walking with my granddaughter. However, despite this, I scooped Jessica up into my arms, walked quickly to the departure gates with her, gave her a kiss and then put her back into Liz's arms.

Once I was waiting at the head of the non-existent queue, I could relax. Then I started thinking to myself, what an unfortunate way for us all to have parted company. If Liz hadn't been so unreasonable and hadn't reacted like that, everything would have been perfect! But then, al-though loath to admit it to myself, I thought, knowing Liz she must have picked up on something in the way I spoke to her to react like that. And, when I recreated the scene in my mind, I admitted to myself that maybe there *had* been a certain edge to my voice. This then led me to thinking about how absurd and ridiculous my behaviour had been – about to be away from my family for a week, wouldn't I much rather have spent more time with them instead of this pressured, neurotic need to rush to the gate resulting in our unhappy farewell?

But, as soon as I started replaying in my mind what had really happened, all the feelings of urgent desperation to get to the front of the queue resurfaced once more, along with the anger at Liz for trying to stop me. However, rather than pushing the feelings away or trying to rationalise them again, I decided to explore my odd reaction by intensifying the feeling. I then imagined how I would feel if I didn't get on a plane early, for one reason or another (perhaps because people pushed me out of the way or jumped the queue), and the frustration that came up was intense. I closed my eyes, and invited my unconscious mind to see if there was something in my past that connected with that feeling. Nothing happened for a little while. But then, slowly, a childhood memory of a time when I was sent to spend a fortnight in the summer holidays with distantly related cousins crept into the edges of my mind.

Not an idyllic summer

Now, life for me at my cousins' house that summer had been extremely disorienting. I hardly knew them and it seemed to me that they had the most bizarre and uncivilised way of going about things. For instance, there might be meals provided or there might not. In my mother's very ordered household, meals were always delivered at specific times every day, so this was extremely disturbing. The only ritual I could be sure of was that my aunt would come home from work every evening with sweets or biscuits or a bag of some kind of edible goodies, and my cousins would all start screaming and jumping on her and pulling at her, to get at the bag. At first, I stood back, aghast, but it became obvious to me, after a couple of days, that whoever screamed, jumped and behaved the worst got the lion's share of the sweets. So I soon realised that, if I wasn't to starve, I had better start jumping and screaming louder than anybody else. But, when I did so, my aunt, having thrust some sweets into my hand, instantly turned on me and exclaimed, "Joe, I'm shocked at your behaviour, a well-brought up boy like you!" I withdrew in shame – but, I had got my sweets.

The emotion I recalled, when this memory came back to me, was of the social embarrassment at being told off in front of my cousins. This puzzled me because the emotion I was experiencing at the Ryanair check-in, which had taken me to this holiday memory, was not embarrassment but aggressive determination to be at the front of the queue. So I stayed with the memory, holding on to those feelings, seeing myself jumping up for those sweets and, after a brief while, with what felt like a little rush, I reconnected with them. I was jumping up aggressively, determined to fight to get my share and so, at the Ryanair check-in, I had experienced a straightforward pattern match.

That fortnight in the country with my relations had been a free-for-all; you had to fight to get what you needed. But, in my case, the situation aroused two strong, but conflicting emotions: my need to survive (expressed as desperate greed and fighting for my due) and my desire to be a good boy. But, although I had wanted to be a good boy, what had 'worked' for me then, in survival terms, was pushing and shoving and doing anything that was needed, to get fed. So when, at the Ryanair check-in desk more than 40 years later, I again experienced a free-for-all, the instinctive reaction that was activated was, "Do what you need to do to get your place, Joe!"

We can clearly see the pain–pleasure recall principle at work here. I had pattern matched Liz's social disapproval (and, on other occasions, the potential social disapproval of other passengers if I were too forcible in pushing myself forward) combined with the pleasure of getting on the plane early and choosing my seat in comfort, to the previous experience of my aunt's social disapproval combined with the pleasure of getting the sweets. The first thing I had been aware of at the airport, however, was the pain of potential social disapproval so, in this case, I had dealt it with by lifting Jessica up and carrying her to the departure gates to speed up the whole process. I had figured that this would, to some extent, reduce Liz's disapproval. And I had also dealt with the potential social disapproval of my fellow passengers by making sure I was near the head of the queue, so that there was no need to queue-jump. Once I had a strategy in place to deal with the social disapproval (the painful or negative aspect of the memory), the positive emotion of aggression could come to the fore – getting to the front of the queue.

When I had previously brought that particular memory to mind, the only feeling I had recalled was the embarrassment at my aunt's disapproval. I had, therefore, had no conscious memory of the greed and desperation that I experienced when fighting for the sweets. But this time, when I stayed with the anger that I was experiencing as I stood in the departure lounge queue, I became conscious of my angry feelings towards her in the memory. And when, in my mind, I gave voice to those feelings ("I've got to get my share of sweets, if I'm to survive in your stupid house!"), both my desperation to get to the head of the queue, and the anger I was feeling against Liz evaporated. More importantly, the feeling of pressure to head the queue has never returned, although I have caught many more Ryanair flights since. Of course, it is always nice to be one of the first on a plane, so as to choose where to sit in comfort and have enough storage space to put cabin luggage overhead, but the crucial difference is that it is no longer an uncontrollable *compulsion*.

The technique of focusing on a current feeling that seems to be excessive given the present circumstances is known as an 'affect bridge'.[6] It is well known to psychotherapists as a powerful way to access a pattern match from the past that needs de-conditioning. I will illustrate with an example.

No time to play

All my adult life, when engaged in social conversations, I would soon get a restless feeling that I should be working. This feeling used to perplex me because it would occur even when there was nothing urgent that needed doing.

So, on one such occasion, when this compulsive feeling of needing to work came up, I stayed with it to see what memory, if any, might come to mind. Up came a childhood memory of how, every Saturday, my parents would go into town to do the shopping and my older sister would marshal us older boys to clean the house from top to bottom, while my younger brothers played outside. I could easily reconnect with the feeling of, "You can't play. You have to work!" Having accessed that feeling and relocated it back in its correct context, I have since ceased to be troubled by the compulsion to work at seemingly inappropriate times. Now I make more of a conscious choice about when I work.

This is a classic example of how the affect bridge works. In this instance it had helped me to discover a sub-threshold trauma (see box below) which was soon resolved. However, had this technique, as normally practised, been used on the childhood memory I had pattern matched to when checking in at the airport to fly Ryanair with its two associated emotions (painful and pleasurable), it would have had me focus on the first accessed emotion (the social embarrassment) and simply intensify it. But this would have been the incorrect emotion to focus upon as it was not what was driving the problem behaviour. It was only when I stayed with the memory, while acknowledging that first emotion of embarrassment, that *another* strong emotional connection, which was at first hidden, became apparent – and proved to be the troublesome one. This explains why the affect bridge doesn't work sometimes: if the initial problem has involved both pleasure *and* pain, the first emotion linked to isn't the problematic one. In the Ryanair example, the problematic emotion was the second emotion

Sub-threshold traumas

WE HAVE introduced the term 'sub-threshold trauma' here to distinguish between a memory which causes excessive negative emotional arousal (eg anxiety or sadness) when activated by pattern matching to stimuli in the present and a molar memory. It is 'sub-threshold' both in the sense that you are not consciously aware of why you are emotionally over-reacting and because the symptoms do not meet the full criteria of post-traumatic stress disorder, eg nightmares, flashbacks etc.

By contrast, a molar memory evokes excessive 'positive' emotions (eg sexual arousal or anger) when unconsciously activated by pattern matching to stimuli in the present, but negative/painful emotions when the memory of the original event is first consciously remembered. Only after focussing on the memory further will the positive/'pleasurable' emotion associated with it be evoked.

Both types of memory are capable of adversely affecting our behaviour and can be accessed via the affect bridge. ∎

related to the memory: anger.

In psychodynamic psychotherapy, anger is often regarded as a cover-up emotion. So, in a case like this, it would be common practice to encourage the patient to be in touch with the feelings of social embarrassment that are supposedly being covered up by the anger. The patient would also be encouraged to recall *other* examples of excessive anger covering up social embarrassment and to give expression to those feelings of social embarrassment along with the feeling of anger thus engendered. In this process the patient would come to recognise excessive anger in situations involving social humiliation as 'one of their issues'. But the excessive anger problem would continue to exist because its source in the angry/positive root of the molar memory would remain untreated by this method.

It is necessary, then, to *adapt* the affect bridge to resolve a pain–pleasure problem. Here is another example.

One of the boys

Throughout my adult life, I have been aware of a strong desire – stronger, I suspect, than other men might experience – to be accepted into a group of males. This has been a strong influence on my behaviour over the years – it certainly influenced me, as a young man, to drink more than I otherwise would have done because drinking 'with the boys' was an easy scenario in which I could be accepted. Indeed, I could excel – telling jokes and contributing to the 'craic', as we say in Ireland.

So, on one occasion, when I knew a party of male friends would be meeting for a few drinks and was experiencing the usual longing to meet up with them and be one of the gang, I deliberately decided not to go. Instead, I sat down quietly and focused on this longing, now thwarted, of wanting to be one of the guys. When I focused on and intensified that yearning, it brought me straight back to a ritual humiliation that I went through day after day for years during my childhood.

I was a socially inhibited child and, for socially inhibited children, team games are torture. I had no difficulty defending myself in one-to-one arguments; it was only in team sports that this inhibition manifested itself. Every day at primary school, the boys would have to play football. Two of the best players would be chosen to pick a team each, and every day I would be standing there, with a mounting sense of shame, as more and more boys' names were called, until only I and a few other boys, who were equally as unenthusiastic about the prospect of playing football, were left. But the biggest terror was that I wouldn't get picked at all, that neither captain would eventually say, "Oh, let Griffin join our side, then".

When, on the day of the proposed meeting with my male friends, I stayed with that feeling of desperation for peer-group acceptance, what came up initially was this memory of shame, as I waited to be selected for the team. Now, if I were in therapy of a certain kind, at that stage I would be encouraged to *really* experience the shame, to get right down into it and relive every gruesome second of it. But, as we have seen, it was not the right emotion. To focus on the shame would make the experience of shame many times more neurotic and entrenched. I had no trouble experiencing shame; during my childhood, I had felt that feeling every day for years. It was totally conscious, totally explicable. What was controlling my life was an unconscious excessive desire to be accepted, under any circumstances, into a group of males I saw as peers. As an adult, I recalled the shame but I had to go beyond that, to activate that original emotion of desperation, as a child, which was always satisfied when I was eventually accepted on to the team.

On this occasion, once I had become aware of that feeling of desperation to be accepted, I quietly acknowledged it and put it back into its context: "I want to join you. I can play football. I want to be a part. Let me in." And, once I had done that, my neurotic need to have a centre-stage role in male drinking camaraderie was gone.

Time to leave the marriage

Michael came to see me for psychotherapy because of concerns about his marriage to Lynette. "We had a long difficult patch but just lately we've been getting on really well again, almost like when we first met. We are best friends; we do lots together; we laugh together. But then Lynette will start haranguing me about something, and I get this extremely strong feeling that I should just walk out on the marriage. It's quite a shockingly strong feeling and it knocks me for six. I'm wondering if, underneath it all, it's a marriage that's going nowhere and I should get out of it now, before there are any kids."

In the course of our session, I asked Michael if he could recall the last time that he had had this strong feeling and he had no difficulty in doing so. Just two days previously, he and his wife had been enjoying a weekend away. They were feeling exceptionally close to each other and had just got ready to go out to dinner when Lynette received a phone call from her nephew. She had listened for a moment and then said, "Well, all right, as long as you take care." Afterwards, Michael discovered that the nephew had asked if he could borrow their car that night. When Michael expressed surprise that she hadn't asked his opinion, Lynette became quite remote and formidable. "You wouldn't have asked me. I have the right to make decisions too! You wouldn't have said no. What are you fussing about?" Not wanting to spoil the weekend, Michael said she was right and they went out for an enjoyable dinner. But, even as he laughed and joked with Lynette, inside himself he again became aware of a very strong feeling that it would make best sense to end the marriage.

On a hunch, I asked Michael to try and recapture that feeling of it being best to leave the marriage, and to intensify it and see where it took him. He shut his eyes and concentrated and at first he shook his head but then he said, "Something from my childhood that I haven't thought about in years has just popped back into my head!"

What flashed into his mind was a memory from when he was about 10 years old, living in a village in Ireland. He had a friend called Niall who sometimes used to call around to play with Michael and his brothers on the green outside their house. Whenever he came around, Michael recalled, his mother would call her boys in quickly afterwards. Michael would be told to go out and tell his friend Niall that he had better go home because they had jobs to do around the house. It happened so often that, one day, Niall said, "Why is it that, whenever I come down, your mother calls you in?" Michael had no idea so, that day, he asked his mum. She fixed him with a terrifying look and said, "Well, you've enough brothers to play with, haven't you?" Although puzzled by his mother's reasoning, Michael didn't question her authority but was painfully aware that this meant the loss of Niall's friendship. (It was only some years later that Michael learned the real reason for his mother's response: Niall's sister had become pregnant as a teenager and Michael's extremely religious mother thought Niall would be an undesirable influence on her boys.)

"What on earth would not being allowed to play with Niall have to do with my feeling ready to walk out of my marriage?" said Michael, after relating all this. I asked him to stay with the feeling and see where, if anywhere, it took him. "Just the sense that this must have been very embarrassing for me," he replied. I asked him still to remain with the feeling and suddenly, after a few moments, he said he had a strong, almost aggressive feeling of needing to disconnect from Niall. The relationship was not allowed. It was best if it was over.

Michael was surprised. He told me he had thought of his friend Niall many times but had always thought about the embarrassment he must have felt at breaking off the friendship; he had never before accessed the compelling feeling of having to break off the relationship. It had been completely hidden from him. We explored the connection. Michael's mother, a figure of authority, had, in effect, told him that he couldn't play with Niall, with whom he had been very friendly. Michael and Lynette had been very close on their weekend away and then, suddenly, Lynette had gone into authoritarian mode and started telling him off. On both occasions, a desire for closeness/connection had been threatened by an authority figure. In the incident with Lynette, however, friendship and authority were represented in the same person. As pattern matching is often by its very nature crude, this had been a close-enough fit for Michael's emotional brain.

Thus Michael was unconscious that his risk-assessment of his current situation had been based on his previous experience of pain from losing that earlier, desired relationship. As a result, in order not to bring about painful loss again, he became less confrontational with Lynette and re-established rapport with her. However, having now mitigated the potential pain of the situation, the positive side of the pain–pleasure memory was free to express itself – the seemingly inexplicable aggressive desire to end the relationship, which was a pattern match to that childish feeling all those years ago when carrying out his mother's instruction to tell Niall to go home. (As explained earlier, aggression is a positive or 'approach' emotion that makes us feel powerful and dictatorial.)

When Michael understood that, and could put the experience in context, it stopped occurring. I saw him twice more, and he had felt nothing remotely similar. Indeed, he now felt all the closer to Lynette, even though occasions had occurred when he still experienced her behaviour as over-bearing. He was able to shrug them off.

'Molar memories'

The metaphor of a molar is a useful one for this type of problematic memory. A molar (grinding) tooth, of course, has two roots and a 'molar memory' has two roots; pain and pleasure. If a molar tooth's roots become infected they have to be exposed or drilled by a dentist, in order to be treated, just as the problematic emotional memory with its two roots has to be exposed to consciousness and treated by being put into context, thereby also ceasing to cause problems. Moreover, if a dentist drills into the wrong root, he does more damage. This is analogous to a therapist who 'explores the pain' of a patient, increasing their suffering, deepening their anxiety or depression when the emotional 'abscess' is located in an unexposed pleasurable emotional root. It doesn't matter how much 'drilling' a therapist does on the *negative* root, it will have no impact on the source of the infection when it is in the *positive* root.

It might perhaps have been CBT's inability to deal with these kinds of problems that led to the foundation of cognitive analytical therapy (CAT), a fusion of CBT ideas with Freud's psychoanalytical ones. But this has had little, if any, more success, in such situations. With the identification of the pain–pleasure recall principle, however, and its resultant 'molar memories', we have a much more accessible and straight-forward explanation for unconscious emotional conflicts – one that is fully compatible with the empirically based psychological explanations from learning theory. Perhaps even more importantly, though, the in-sights it brings have the potential to change some troubled lives quickly and permanently.

An important difference

It is important to be clear how molar memories differ from traumas and phobias, which can also blight lives. Traumas and phobias *always* have excessive fear or anxiety as their core problematical symptom. Molar memories *never* have fear or anxiety as their core symptom. (Sometimes people with post-traumatic stress disorder present with anger problems,

CASE HISTORIES:

Working with 'molar memories'

SINCE first hearing about Joe Griffin's molar memories theory and how he used it to help clients, I have had numerous opportunities, through the course of my work, to apply his method of dissolving problem behaviours – with enormous success. I can confirm, as Joe explained to one reader of the *Human Givens* journal, that "Once we bring back the memory of the [inappropriate] pleasure or anger to consciousness and reframe it, symptoms however severe melt away" as this is indeed what I have found.

The first case I will describe is that of Will, an extremely aggressive 15-year-old who was always losing his temper and getting into fights. He had an ASBO, was confined in a secure unit, and deemed such a danger to others that, when he was brought to see me for 'anger management', I was told a minder had to be outside my therapy room, for my protection. After working hard to build rapport with Will over a couple of sessions (I discovered the only interest and gift he had was as a rapper), I decided to see if I could get to the root of his uncontrollable anger. It seemed that, as the anger just spilled over without any obvious rhyme or reason, it might be part of a molar memory.

So I asked Will to get the feeling of anger (extremely easy for him to do) and then to close his eyes, stay with the feeling and see where it took him. After a few moments he recalled an occasion in his bedroom at home, when he was six or seven. His father came in, drunk, beat him up, snatched the precious book in which Will wrote all of his lyrics and tore up all the pages, calling his songs "rubbish".

"What did you do?" I asked Will. "Nothing. I was frightened of him. I felt completely helpless." By getting him to stay with the feeling of anger, however, he realised that he had not just felt helpless. He had felt fury with his father too, although he had not expressed it. By this time, he was deeply in trance. I encouraged him to say to his father now what he wished he had said then. With tears pouring down his face, Will said, "How could you have done that to me? I wanted you to be proud of me and but they are acutely aware that their core problem is their untreated trauma and its associated anxiety.) For molar memories, however, the problematical emotion is always excessive anger or aggressive feelings, or inappropriate expressions of pleasure (all resulting from the 'pleasurable' aspect of the original situation). The individual beset with a molar memory is always blind to the source of these 'pleasurable'

what I was writing! I wanted you to say, 'What are you doing, son? Would you let me read it? Wow, that's really good! Why don't you sing it to me?' Instead, you just rubbished everything I'd done, everything I am."

It seemed clear to me, then, that Will had felt utterly helpless in the face of authority (his father) and reacted against helplessness in his dealings with authority now — of which there were very many — with the anger he had not acted on then. (In his unconscious 'risk assessment', he would have realised that he wasn't helpless anymore; he was a big lad and could fight back.) Thus there was continual escalation of the problem, as more and more punitive authority figures became involved in his life.

The effect of this work with Will was amazing. He became so polite and respectful that he was quickly moved out of the secure unit into foster care, with older parents and a son his own age. (At our following session, I asked him to write a rap for me there and then, "if you are so good at it", and then said, "Can I read it? Hey, that's really good! Can I hear you sing it for me?" It meant a lot to him.)

On a different occasion, I worked with another out-of-control boy whose dad made him feel bad about himself because he didn't come up to his high-flying father's own standards. Again, this manifested in anger whenever he felt helpless or put down. Through the molar memory technique, we were able to access the root of the anger — originating when he was nine — and I got him to express (as if to his dad) the anger he had had towards him then. Afterwards, he actually said to me, excitedly, "I should have said all this to him then, shouldn't I? Then none of this angry explosive stuff would ever have happened!"

Like Joe, I have also used the method to work quickly with a girl with an eating disorder. Melanie is 19 and suffers from food restriction ▶

emotions since they are screened from consciousness by the negative feelings associated with the memory, as these need to remain conscious for risk assessment purposes. If the risk assessment concludes that it is too dangerous for him or her to express the positive feelings, then these won't enter our conscious awareness at all. On the other hand, if the risk assessment concludes that it is safe to express the associated

followed by bulimia. She is underweight. When I had her focus on her compulsion to eat, what came back to her was a memory of being just three or four years old, and her mother and aunt saying that her eyes were bigger than her belly and that she must not be allowed to eat so much. "I felt disgusted with myself and disgusted with them for telling me what to do," she told me. At the age of 10, she started developing pubic hair and found that disgusting. By 12 she was bulimic, feeling angry and disgusted at her own body.

If Melanie's compulsive eating derived from a molar memory, it would make sense that, when she felt disgusted with herself and her body, she would eat (and then vomit, as she didn't want to put on weight), because as an adult there was no one there to criticise or stop her – no risk. In the course of therapy I got her to tell her mother and aunt assertively, on that occasion she had described as a young child, that she was hungry and she wanted to eat. I also did a rewind on the puberty experience and reframed the disgust: "Your body is preparing to become a beautiful, sexy, curvy woman – not like those stringy catwalk models who are unhappy with their lives but in the way of creative artists who draw the beauty of curves in a woman. [Melanie loved art.] You are an artist. If given a straight piece of wood, what would you do? Make curves!"

At the end of this work, Melanie announced, "I'd really like a ham sandwich now. I've not eaten bread for two years." Melanie started to eat normally after that. Putting the desire to eat back in context clearly took the compulsive element out of it.

I have now used this therapeutic approach on several occasions since learning it and have been amazed by how speedily unwanted behaviours have resolved. ■

Pamela Woodford

positive feelings, then that reaction is reinforced as part of the memory pattern (or template) *without* the person ever being aware of where the original motivation came from. Indeed, not knowing otherwise, we are likely to argue that our feelings have been aroused by whatever situation we currently find ourselves in. We remain oblivious to their origin in a childhood emotional conflict between clashing needs seeking their fulfilment. (As we are most likely to run into a conflict of emotions during the socialisation phase of childhood, it is during this time that molar memories will most probably be laid down.)

For an animal, molar memories laid down when young may continue to provide appropriate responses in its adulthood. (These responses are, in effect a form of 'learned instinct', a template that will be constantly used to scan the environment for appropriate pattern-matching stimuli.) But, because our lives are infinitely more complex and the circumstances we experience infinitely more varied than those experienced by early mammals, what gets filed away is not necessarily an appropriate reaction at all on many of the crudely similar occasions which, to the emotional brain, are an accurate pattern match.

Context is the key

So we are usually completely unaware of what is now maladaptive conditioning and, because we are unaware, we are condemned to repeat it endlessly. For, even though we know it isn't routine behaviour to get incensed over virtually nothing or to have an overwhelming urge to walk out on a happy marriage, we tend to justify such reactions to ourselves. "Well, she is so annoying at times that it is no surprise I sometimes feel livid with her." "Everyone wants to feel accepted." "He always knows how to press my buttons. It isn't my fault I react like this." As a result, there is nothing to tell us that there is a better way to behave. (After all, we are still surviving, so it must be 'working'.) But, when we have knowledge of the pain–pleasure recall process, we can update our molar memory conditioning.

If, as described, we stay with the feeling, when we experience an over-the-top or inexplicable reaction, we can pick up on its source. Merely recognising and acknowledging it *consciously* is enough for the hippocampus (a brain organ concerned with conscious memories) to be able to identify it as belonging to the past, with no further relevance for future action. Creating context serves to undo the maladaptive programming. For, it is when an emotion (and ensuing action) is unconscious that it is stripped of any context. It becomes a universal application working purely by association or pattern matching. But, if the inappropriate emotion can be activated and the original memory brought back, then context can be created for it. It is no longer universal and it is deactivated. The unconscious programming element of the molar memory vanishes and so ceases to influence our behaviour.

Overcoming anorexia

While I was still experimenting with this theory, I happened to receive a call from a 38-year-old woman called Catherine, who had struggled with anorexia since she was 13. I had seen her for therapy 15 years before, and we had managed to find ways to help her cope but had never cracked the anorexia itself. Her weight fell, at one point, to four and a half stones and she was still painfully thin when I met her this time around.

She had got back in touch because her obsessive-compulsive behaviours around food were worsening again. During the intervening years since I'd last seen her, she had had all different kinds of therapy, including hospitalisation, none of which had really helped. Just recently she had seen a hypnotherapist who had regressed her to a time when she was a very young girl, sitting in her room, hearing her parents arguing about the fact that she had soiled herself yet again. There had been a lot of arguing when she was young about her inability – or refusal – to control her bowels. She recalled feeling sadness that her parents were fighting again and that it was her fault. Catherine told me she had cried a lot when she relived this memory, and felt some relief. However, this was already a highly familiar memory for her, and reliving it didn't seem to help her in any way afterwards.

I wondered if she might have experienced some other emotion, more significant than the sadness, that she wasn't aware of right then. So, with her permission, I asked her to close her eyes and go back to that time when she was in the room. I asked her questions about the colour of the walls and the furniture in the room, to help her get fully back into the experience. Then I said to her, "What are you feeling now in your body?" And she said, "I feel I can't hold on any more. I have to let go." "How does that feel?" "One part of me doesn't want to let go," she said, "but the other part does and it feels great; it's a lovely warm feeling, doing this." Then, her parents had come in, and she began to feel sad about what she had done. I suggested that she stay in touch with the feeling of pleasure at emptying her bowel. I asked her to notice how the feeling changed over time. She reported that, as the stools got cold, the feeling became disgusting. Because of her parents arguing, she hadn't noticed that feeling before. Doing so reframed her memory of the pleasure of 'controlling' her bowel movement, so that the memory of it was not so pleasurable after all.

I knew that Catherine felt disgusted by her body because, when I asked how she felt about putting on weight, she had responded fervently, "My body feels disgusting when I put on weight. I know I'm not fat but I just hate the feeling of it. I feel as though I'm sticking out in all the wrong places." Her expression was one of disgust. So I asked her to focus on that feeling, too, and see what memory came up for her. She instantly went back to the time of her first period, which had occurred in class at school, and vividly recalled the dreadful embarrassment of having to rush from the room to clean herself up. But, as she relived the experience, while holding on to the feeling of disgust, the disgust she had felt at the time started to surface: "There's blood coming out all over the place and it's all sticky and it's a mess; it's all disgusting!" What made it worse to her was that it felt unnatural; her older sister had not even started her periods yet.

I then reframed the experience for her. "Yes, it must have felt disgusting when you had your period because you weren't properly prepared for it, and it felt unnatural. But it isn't unnatural now. Your body is at its most beautiful when it is putting on normal curves. It's not disgusting; it's something beautiful." I talked to her about feeding and nourishing her body and looking after it and invited her to experience her body as healthy when putting on weight. That was the end of the session.

The next day, she phoned up my house and left an excited message, telling me about the changes that had happened since the session. She had gone home and eaten a normal dinner, with dessert, for the first time in 25 years, with no voices in her head telling her not to. I have seen her since and she has reported that only occasionally, when under stress, has she felt an urge to restrict her eating. But, since it no longer felt compulsive, she could recognise it and deal with it. She is now steadily gaining weight and enjoying a range of foods she has never eaten before and her life is free from debilitating compulsive rituals.

The reframes that worked

This was an astounding outcome and what I think had happened was this. When she used to relieve herself in her pants, the desire for the pleasure of doing so immediately, under her own control, vied with the feeling that she should obey her parents' instruction that she should go to the toilet. The action she took was to soil her pants and experience the lovely warmth. Taking that control was worth the price of making her parents angry, even though that made her sad. Obsessively controlling her body in this way 'worked' for her at that time (she would later choose to no longer do it) because her risk assessment of the pain likely to be experienced concluded that the pain of her parent's displeasure was worth the feeling of pleasure she got when evacuating her bowels when she herself wanted. When her period arrived, it was out of the blue – she had been in class, enjoying her lesson and, suddenly, she had had to rush out to take care of herself. Now her body felt dangerously out of her control – not only had it let her down, it had done something unnatural, because her older sister hadn't even started her periods yet. She had already been feeling uncomfortable with her changing body shape "sticking out in all the wrong places". Her older sister's body hadn't changed like this. Now her body was even more out of her control, with this embarrassing, disgusting, sticky mess.

This was a traumatising experience for her. Her memory pattern matched back to the wonderful feeling of control she had when she controlled the emptying of the disgusting mess her bowels made. She had pattern matched to a pain–pleasure (molar) memory as the way to deal with the trauma of her unexpected and unprepared-for first period. The solution therefore was to take back control over her body shape and over her periods, just as she had kept control over her messy bowel movements and not allowed her parents to control them. And the way

"An unconscious rush of angry feelings"

JUDITH first contacted me on the recommendation of a GP who knew about the human givens approach to therapy. Judith is 44 years old, and had been married for 22 years before taking the decision, a year ago, to leave the marriage. Some of the difficulties she was experiencing were around her relationship with her husband and managing their two children while they lived apart. Judith also described having been sexually abused at the age of nine (which she said had affected her, although she was not able to state clearly in what way she considered she had been affected); she had received counselling three or four years previously to "deal with the abuse", but felt her present attitude towards relationships "had not been dealt with", and that past events were having an adverse impact on her present relationships.

In our first session, Judith described the problems she was having with her relationships. She also described how her husband used to watch her while she was in the shower, which she hated – she associated being 'watched' in this way with circumstances of previous sexual abuse (she became very upset when describing this). Having gone on to describe poor sleep (including tooth-grinding, which was so bad she needed to wear a brace at night), we discussed various strategies to improve her sleep hygiene generally. We also recorded a relaxation CD and used some guided imagery to help with her unpleasant feelings of being 'watched', including the rewind technique (see page 59) in relation to the shower and 'shower-related' incidents. We agreed to look in more detail at the impact of past events at a second session a few weeks later.

Dealing with the molar memory

At our next session, Judith reported that she had been successfully using the relaxation CD, which had helped her to feel more relaxed generally, but she was concerned about attempting, on several occasions, to walk away from situations involving her new partner which had triggered a severe stress response in her (even if the situation hadn't really warranted it), but finding this difficult to do. Judith described feeling ▶

very angry, and having an uncontrollable desire to "go on until I have *really* 'hurt' my partner" (although she also stated that she would of course never actually do so).

We looked at the triggers for the outbursts, and they appeared to occur whenever she experienced any situation that her 'limbic' (emotional) brain appeared to interpret or perceive as being 'humiliating' and/or 'abusive'; Judith described experiencing an unconscious rush of angry feelings at these times and started talking about the sexual abuse by her head teacher that she had experienced when she was nine.

While describing the abuse in detail, she appeared calm, and stated initially that she felt nothing; however, she then said she remembered feeling deeply humiliated at the time, and at that point in the session became more agitated. So I immediately invited Judith to close her eyes and focus on her breathing.

When she was in a subsequent state of deep relaxation, I asked Judith to cast her mind back to the time of the sexual abuse. Instantly, she became emotional again and tearful. When asked how she was feeling, she answered, "sad". I asked her to allow this feeling of sadness to build and build until she could let it go; at this point, she described feeling dirty and, more specifically, embarrassed, humiliated and ashamed.

Again, these primary feelings were allowed to build up and intensify until they bubbled over and disappeared – at which point, Judith immediately described another strong feeling, of anger this time, and there was a very noticeable change in muscle tension and animation around her face. I asked her to focus on this second emotion related to the memory, allowing it to build up and intensify. I then gradually, by asking her to imagine watching herself viewing a film of the memory, moved the guided imagery on to do an adapted version of the rewind technique, running backwards and forwards over past incidents of abuse, introducing ideas that unwanted images could 'fade away' with repetition, alongside the idea of 're-editing' past events; imagining how she could have taken more control had things been different.

It was apparent from her marked facial expressions of anger as we did this that the 'edited' version of events she was rewinding were involving to do this was by controlling her eating, thereby reducing her food intake, so that her body would get thin and stop sticking out in "all the wrong places". An added bonus, she was to discover later, was that her messy periods would actually stop. Of course, just as in keeping control of her bowel movements, there was a price to be paid – her parent's disapproval of her action which, in this case, was her restricted eating. Clearly, her unconscious risk assessment had concluded that this price was worth paying for the pleasure gained from controlling her bodily functions.

It is worth stressing again that this molar memory influence is *not* a conscious process. We experience the gut feeling and feel compelled to act upon it, however inappropriate we recognise it to be and to whatever degree we may manage to modify some of our reactions: Catherine knew to ingest just enough food to keep her alive. Once the original molar memory linked to her bowel training was accessed, however,

the expression of the previously unexpressed anger about what had happened that she had felt at the time. Multiple rewinds were necessary until the emotional arousal associated with the event was seen to diminish. A lengthy period of positive reframing then followed, during which Judith was helped to take a more objective view of this situation by asking her to consider how much responsibility for what had happened she personally, as an adult, would place on a child of nine years old. We also did extensive positive rehearsal of a future life that involved trusting relationships, emphasising her personal qualities and strengths.

As often happens when intensive work around reprocessing a memory like this has been done, Judith was very tired at the conclusion of this session. She also estimated that she had had her eyes closed for 10 minutes – rather than the 50 minutes that it had actually taken (a typical response to trance).

Our third session was very positive. Judith was pleased to report that she was now sleeping much better, no longer ground her teeth, had not "kicked off" with her partner once since the last session, had found that the persistent headaches she had experienced in the past had ▶

making both the pain and the pleasure conscious, and the pleasure element had been reframed to include the feeling of disgust linked to cold stools, the molar memory's power was dissolved. As this molar memory had been controlling her traumatic reaction to her first un-expected period, accessing that memory and reframing the experience as a normal and beautiful part of a young woman's development enabled that trauma to be resolved. There was no need for the anorexia any more, so she could go home and eat dinner, followed by dessert, and enjoy it.

The cross-dresser

Jake, a man in his 30s, came to see me because he was a secret cross-dresser, and had been since childhood. He was finding it more and more stressful to live his double life. He admitted that he experienced sexual arousal when cross-dressing, so, in guided imagery, I asked him to find and focus on that feeling and then to let it take him back to wherever it wanted to go. The memory that came up for him was of being caught

gone away, and had also discovered that she was no longer afraid of the dark – much to her delight.

She said she had felt "trashed" for about three days following the last session, and had cried a lot – something she had previously never done in relation to the abuse. Judith described how she used to "box off" her thoughts around the abuse in a way that she felt that she could manage it and talk about it if necessary (the case was now finally being taken to court). She described, however, how the previous session had finally enabled her to get to grips with how it had felt, in such a way that it had enabled her to move on from the experience.

Follow up

This work was consolidated in a final therapeutic session three months later; at the time of this session, Judith was able to report that she found herself remaining calm in an increasing variety of situations, that previously would have set her off, and she had experienced no further angry outbursts or feelings of rage. ■

Mike Beard

by his mother, when he was a young boy, trying on his sister's knickers in the bathroom, and seeing what it was like to pee like a girl. Jake instantly recalled the terrible guilt he felt at being caught and the horror on his mother's face. I suggested to him that he tell his mum that he wanted to try out what it felt like to wear girls' clothes. He then got a feeling of sexual excitement as his young self, as he experimented with his sister's clothing. Reliving that feeling was a shock to Jake. It was completely concealed from his consciousness – he hadn't realised that, at such a young age, he was even capable of sexual feelings.

The pain–pleasure recall principle would hold that this experience was bound to trigger a molar memory. A boy with natural childhood curiosity explores aspects of female sexual identity, experiences sexual arousal in the process, and is then humiliated by his mother's disapproval. The pain is consciously recalled but the pleasure is not. However, ever afterwards, when he encounters female underwear, his brain pattern matches back to the molar memory. He does an automatic risk assessment for potential embarrassment and, if that is not problematic, experiences the desire to wear female clothing.

If acted upon, this reinforces the pattern. Such fetishist behaviours are notoriously difficult to change in therapy. However, if we bring the underlying molar memory into conscious awareness, the inappropriate pattern match dissolves and so does the fetish. After that therapy session, during which the memory and associated pattern matches were reprogrammed by consciously putting them into context, Jake never again experienced a desire to wear female underwear.

Pain and pleasure are at the core of what motivates us in life. Pleasure is nature's currency for rewarding behaviour that gets needs met. Pain exists to warn us of danger. It is the way our ancient animal ancestors evolved to make the best use of these two systems, however, that leaves us so vulnerable to maladaptive conditioning as we grow up. I suggest that molar memories play a significant role in many neurotic, over-the-top reactions that involve both positive and negative emotions and with an understanding of this process we can significantly improve the quality of our own lives as well as that of our patients.

As well as using it with their clients, several of the psychotherapists with whom I have discussed this principle have also experimented on elements of their own behaviour too, reporting back that it brought equally rapid and effective results. Bringing molar memories into consciousness, therefore, is not only a powerful way (where applicable) to help patients, it has huge potential as a self-development tool, creating spare capacity by allowing individuals to become more objective about themselves and the way they react to life circumstances. Difficult though it can be, doing this is, of course, subject to our being ready to admit that our angry outbursts and pursuit of pleasurable experiences are not entirely due to external factors. Thus the usefulness of this technique as a self-developmental tool is entirely dependent on our willingness to investigate the sources of our own emotional responses in those very instances when we are most likely to be defensive of them because of the emotional intensity that motivates them.

The writing of this article has been a team effort and I would like to thank Denise Winn, Jane Tyrrell and Ivan Tyrrell for their contribution to helping bring clarity to my thought processes. I would also like to thank the MindFields College students who participated in the 'work in process' presentation of them at the Advanced Human Givens Course in the spring of 2006, especially those who went on to apply the insight with patients and thereby confirmed its worth.

* * ❋ * *

Joe Griffin is a research psychologist, with graduate and post-graduate degrees from the LSE. He has many years experience both in psychotherapeutic practice and in training psychotherapists and is co-founder, with Ivan Tyrrell, of the human givens approach to psychology and psychotherapy. He is Director of Studies and a tutor for MindFields College. He is also co-author, with Ivan Tyrrell, of numerous best-selling titles, including: How to lift depression ... fast; Freedom from Addiction; Dreaming Reality: How dreaming keeps us sane or can drive us mad *(the result of 12 years research by Griffin, which provides the first complete explanation of the origin, function and meaning of dreams);* How to Master Anxiety: All you need to know to overcome stress, panic attacks, phobias, trauma, obsessions and more; *and* Human Givens: A new approach to emotional health and clear thinking.

The limits of tolerance:
ethics and human nature

*At a time when we are struggling with a number of major moral dilemmas, **Ivan Tyrrell**, Principal of MindFields College, suggests that working with the human givens can help us reach ethical decisions.*

MORALITY – our character, manners and the way we conduct ourselves with others – has never produced such depths of confusion, controversy and cant as it does today.

Just some of the topics involving moral dilemmas recently, include: women's right to technologically assisted birth at 60, and beyond; human cloning; euthanasia; arms sales; the use of illegal and legal drugs; immigration policy; the rights of people to feel secure in their own land (Iraq, Israel/Palestine); restricting freedom in the name of the 'war on terror'; compulsory ID cards; the legality of waging war against countries that are not attacking us; political party funding from pornography; state welfare for single parents; cash for honours; relaxation of gambling laws; sex education in schools; penalties for antisocial behaviour; stealth taxation; wasted taxpayers money; prosecutions of people who have used violence when defending themselves from attack, and imprisoning parents for not ensuring their children attend school.

Many of these particular problems didn't exist a hundred years ago, but there has always been one constant: whenever an ethical issue has arisen throughout the ages, there have always been people prepared to take a firm stance about it.

We may think we are capable of reaching ethical decisions, yet all too often we go about it, not with an open mind prepared to review and consider the full facts, but from a 'position'. So it is that, for instance, some will view the taking of a life as wrong in any circumstances – thus ruling out abortion and euthanasia. But our biases may be considerably more subtle than that, almost invisible in fact; what we view as ethical behaviour is largely socially conditioned – our current moral philosophy merely articulates the morality of a particular social or cultural standpoint – and that makes it hard to recognise and challenge.[1]

In one culture, for example, the wishes of an individual may be considered paramount whereas, in another, the emphasis might be to give primary consideration to how an individual's behaviour impacts upon the family or the wider community. Similarly, at one time in our own recent history, it was accepted that children should be seen and not heard and physical and emotional punishments were used to keep them in line and help them develop into responsible adults. Now it is viewed as unethical to discipline a child in such ways – although we have not yet fully thought through how best to deter unruly, disruptive children who "know their rights" from running amok in schools and terrorising teachers and other students.

Institutions arise to oversee our needs for law and order, defence, medical and social care, education and commerce, and, as such, are part of the civilising process. It is institutions that evolve codes of ethics, yet, on closer inspection, they often become tyrannies because their major unacknowledged aim is to preserve an existing power structure. Such bodies commonly employ closed systems of thought and have inward-looking agendas promoting a limited, prejudiced view, in order to protect their power base. The true needs of a situation inevitably come second to this. For example, doctors have been known to close ranks to protect one of their number who, through serious medical negligence, was responsible for a personal catastrophe for a patient; politicians put their party above their duty to the people that elected them; social service departments place political correctness ahead of the needs of the individuals that they are supposed to be helping; judges can rule according to precedent, rather than in the light of the circumstances of particular cases; the police now chase targets rather than concentrating on reducing crime; and businesses may put the need to satisfy their shareholders before the needs of their customers and workers.

If we are truly to act ethically and be capable of making ethical decisions we have to operate from knowledge, not from a stance which is socially conditioned or which is prompted by unrecognised emotions such as greed and the desire to maintain power. For that we have to have a better understanding of human nature.

An interest in dealing with the dilemmas of human behaviour is as old as history. (The word ethics comes from the Greek word *ethikos,* which means 'dealing with human nature'.) Currently our knowledge of how human nature works comes from the scientific study of Nature's endowment to us all – the human givens – and also direct experience, which gives us veridical truth.

The starting point for such a study should be, therefore, that Nature endows each healthy human conception with a wonderful array of living genetic 'templates' – that infinitely rich treasure house of pre-programmed patterns for which we instinctively seek completion in the environment throughout our lives. Babies, for instance, are capable of copying some of the non-verbal behaviours of their mothers, such as facial expressions or sticking out their tongues, within just an hour of birth. They also rehearse instinctive behaviours, such as breathing and swallowing, while in the womb, in readiness for being born.

Such patterns are largely expressed as emotional needs, so that we are driven to seek their fulfilment (babies need to create a connection with their main caregivers to ensure their survival). Nature is doubly generous in that she also brings us into the world with the means to help us get our needs met. It is precisely the *way* these needs are met, through the individual circumstances of our lives, that determines our individual nature, character and mental health. Throughout life this process is in a state of continuous ebb and flow, refinement and adaptation.

As we have seen in previous chapters, only when the environment a child finds itself in healthily fulfils these innate needs can children mature into independent, fulfilled and socially integrated adults. Recent discoveries about how the mind/body system works now give us greater insight into this process. The brain is a plastic, problem-solving organ, that needs challenges in order to enable it to grow. Children therefore have to be stretched by their experiences of life if they are to develop well. Mastering any skill, whether riding a bike or learning the violin, takes time and effort – a combination of being drawn forward by the teacher and pushing oneself. There are also certain times when the brain is best equipped to learn – for instance, foreign languages are best absorbed before the age of 10. Taking advantage of such knowledge could powerfully improve the way we bring up and educate children. Indeed, we might need to question now whether it is ethical to leave language learning as largely the province of secondary school teaching, or to call 'education' the random imposition on children of ideologies, facts and procedures which do not whet their appetites for discovery and mastery. Or, as Thom Hartmann challengingly asserts in his *Complete Guide to ADHD*, is it ethical to dismiss as troublesome no-hopers, a huge number of children whose talents and behaviours are different from those of the majority, but which have significant value nevertheless?[2] Such reactions are the result of dogma rather than knowledge.

The importance of shared perceptions

Of the many obstacles which stand in the way of ethical decision making, perhaps the most important, is the illusion that we share perceptions. This serves to hide ignorance, protect territory, deceive or manipulate, and is largely the result of the language we use. And nowhere is it more easy to see than in the abstract words used to discuss ethical behaviour.

Most people assume ethics is concerned with *truth, aspirations, justice, equality, loyalty, fairness, values, principles, morals,* etc. But all these words are abstractions. They are content free. They contain no sensory information. Philosophers call such words 'reifications' but they are now more commonly known as 'nominalisations': the term used in linguistics for an abstract noun usually produced by converting a verb into a noun. For instance, when the process of enlightening somebody about something is turned into *enlightenment* it becomes an abstraction, a word that pretends to be something concrete. All such words lack specific, essential information; namely who is doing precisely what to whom.

The problem for ethics is that, because these words mean nothing in themselves, they are always going to mean different things to different people. We may think we understand the need, ethically speaking, to have *principles,* but it is dangerous to assume we hold principles in common. One person might believe, for instance, that seniority takes precedence over youth, while another holds that ability takes precedence over age.

Because nominalisations are abstractions, and therefore content free, we have to fill in the missing gaps in the information ourselves. Our brain, as a pattern-matching organ, is forced to search its memories to identify from its own experiences what it believes to be the meaning that gives reality to these words. If, for example, a politician says, "I am going to put more *resources* into *education*", everyone will tend to applaud and support him. But putting *resources* into *education* will mean something quite different to every teacher, child or parent. They will each unconsciously go on an inner search to assign a personal meaning to these abstractions. One person might think the politician means that he is going to instigate research into the best way to educate children. Others might think he is going to pay teachers more; or build better schools; or reduce class sizes; or make schools safer; or have more exams; or have fewer exams; or improve the curriculum; or train teachers better, and so on. The politician tries to win support and credit by using these abstract terms to appeal to the different individual concerns of all those listening. He is creating an illusion and not promising anything specific at all. It is impossible to 'supply', 'give' or 'input' an abstract noun like *education*. What we actually do is educate. And what people are educated about, why, how, where and by whom, are the questions that must be addressed in detail.

To deal with nominalisations, the first requirement is to learn to spot them. We can tell if a word is an abstract noun by asking ourselves, "Can I pick this up and carry it away?", or "can I touch it or feel it or see it?" or "can I buy this off the shelf?" In other words, does it have some kind of substance? If it doesn't, it is a nominalisation.

Secondly, we need to challenge them. This can be simply done by turning them back into the verbs they came from. For instance, if a boss says, "My *expectations* must be met", we are more likely to be able to achieve this if we find out exactly what it is that he or she *expects*, rather than acting on our own assumptions of what the expectations might be. If someone tells us they are full of anger, we have no real idea of their experience at all unless we ask, "What exactly is making you angry?" (People do not have *anger*. It is not a substance in them like blood. In the same way, people do not have *depression* or *fear*. They are depressed <u>by</u> something or afraid <u>of</u> something.)

Because there are no precise, commonly shared perceptions about the meaning of nominalised words, they readily confuse us and make us vulnerable to self deception and manipulation. That is why they are beloved of politicians, preachers and anyone else with something to sell or an ideology to promote.

Although it is our nature to operate through metaphor and generalisations, and this can be a great advantage to us and increase our capacity for conceptualisation, it is also a vulnerability. This is because we are social creatures and, unless we have perceptions more or less in common with those around us, it is difficult for us to cooperate, and our interactions at all levels are necessarily more crude. Then it becomes harder to ensure our real needs are met and selfish behaviour becomes more likely.

Ethical decision making within a society is only possible if its members share the majority of their perceptions. Perception is the act of understanding the world by whatever means. Our senses are the channels for information about the world and perception is what our brains do with the information. But first the information is filtered and selected. The selection process involves matching up the sensory information to what we already know by passing it through the embedded patterns of innate and learned knowledge held mainly in the limbic system and the left and right neocortex.[3,4] The brain in effect compares all new information with its instinctive templates and learned memories of past experiences, and asks, "Is this important survival information – do I need to react? Or is it just interesting, or can I ignore it?"

As the brain discriminates – excluding or accepting information through this filtering process – it is forever building and enriching its internal model of reality. But, inevitably, this model is based on heavily censored input because the discrimination process is influenced by emotion, appetites and conditioning. For instance, a young man walking down the street on a warm July day is more likely to be aware of the attractive young women in their summer clothes than of the unevenness of the cobblestones which preoccupy the unsteady old gentleman behind him.

Or, when we applaud the words of a pundit or philosopher and proceed to repeat them to others, it may not be because of the clarity of the case presented but because we happen to agree!

All living creatures, even single-celled ones, that respond to sensations such as heat and cold, light and dark, hard and soft – moving forwards or away – are in effect practising discrimination: we require 'sensitivity' in order to discriminate. The same, in a wider sense, can be said of groups or cultures. Civilisation can only exist when enough people share similar perceptions about the nature of the world and their place within it. The more refined, or subtle, the level of generally shared perceptions within a particular culture, the more highly civilised it is. In other words, a society in which there is a high level of dissent about what constitutes acceptable behaviour in people's dealings with one another, or where there is an unwillingness to establish and abide by laws, operates at a cruder level than one where there is accord about such matters.

Thus civilised (moral) behaviour can never be a static achievement; it is a process involving the refinement of shared perceptions, the discrimination of countless shades of grey. We can see that whenever this process is halted or reversed, the organisation or culture concerned 'freezes' and becomes intolerant. It then degenerates and eventually collapses, as happened in many ancient empires and more recently, in spectacular fashion, in the Soviet Union.

To increase our understanding of the friction between cultures today, and the predicaments of being human in a crowded world, we need to work at refining our perceptions as far as we possibly can. That means enlarging our perspective with the aid of the knowledge available to us from history, anthropology and psychology, to enable us better to see the bigger picture – the view beyond our own individual outlook or take on events.

Needs and wants

Looking at life from different perspectives inevitably brings about a greater understanding of others' needs and wants and how they may conflict with our own. Ethical dilemmas mainly arise when circumstances are preventing someone's physical or emotional needs from being fairly met, perhaps because they are in apparent conflict with those of another individual or organisation. The woman in her sixties who wants to bear a child, because technology now makes it possible for her to be helped to do so, may want a child because she has been unable to conceive before, or because she has lost a child, or because her children are grown up and she feels her life lacks purpose without a caretaking role. Perhaps, however, it might be considered that her need to be needed could be better met in a different way. The medical authorities may feel that she has as much right as anyone else to an assisted pregnancy; or that her needs are secondary to those of younger women; or that the pregnancy would be dangerous; or that it is inappropriate for a post-menopausal woman to bear a child when that is plainly against Nature's intent. Others might argue that the menopause, which used to signal the decline of a woman's life, now commonly occurs less than two thirds of the way through it, when women are still very healthy and active.

Yet others may be concerned that the unborn child's needs conflict with those of the mother, if it is in the best interests of a child to have a parent who is able to take an active role in their life throughout childhood or who has the ability to work to support them. Or might it be taken into account that a particular financially secure, physically and emotionally healthy 60 year old woman who has a younger husband and the support of her family could be a more competent parent than a younger woman who is alone, mentally unstable, earns no income and often uses what money she has to buy drugs?

Taking the wider view, and establishing the different competing needs and interests involved, leads us to strive to understand *each* situation in which we find ourselves, rather than relying on belief systems for resolving them. Operating out of a belief system means blindly applying rules without questioning their applicability. Although beliefs 'live on', from generation to generation, they are, in themselves, dead things, preventing the pushing outwards of mental boundaries.

Emotional arousal

Issues such as the 'right' to have a child or the 'right' to a homeland generate an enormous amount of emotion. But taking the wider perspective requires objectivity – detachment. This is impossible when we are in a state of high emotional arousal. As is now well understood, the more emotional we are, the more the rational part of the brain is overwhelmed and we are forced back onto the binary responses of the emotional brain – fight or flight. Emotional arousal locks us into one-track responses, which although they have survival value in certain circumstances, in our complex world today, are rarely helpful for dealing with difficult interpersonal problems.

When emotional, we think in black and white, all or nothing, terms. Misunderstandings occur. Feelings of being out of control develop. We tend to misuse our imagination, becoming so anxious about change or so fearful of the unknown that we cannot meet challenges or take risks. We may worry constantly about loss of power or status; develop a morbid fear of failing, illness or death; begin to doubt our abilities and competence; become anxious and depressed. Because emotional arousal makes us inflexible, we suffer disappointment when things do not work out as we expect or as we feel they should.

In effect, being governed by emotion means being driven by the instinct to get our own needs met. In such a state, we cannot solve ethical dilemmas. Nor, when our emotions are strongly bound up in an ethical problem, are we capable of recognising that someone who does not share our view is not necessarily the 'enemy' or the 'opposition'; and that if, in fact, they are standing back and taking an objective view, they are better equipped than we are to come up with a fair solution. For instance, some pressure groups might clamour for an individual's right to die when suffering from a debilitating incurable illness, and refuse to hear any dissenting voice. Yet, someone with knowledge who is unemotionally involved might usefully point out that many incurably ill people are depressed and that, if they were helped out of their depressed mood, they might no longer wish to die.

Solving difficult dilemmas that have moral or ethical aspects takes time. We have to be calm enough to allow answers to arise in us. As neuroscientist John Ratey says in his book *A User's Guide to the Brain,* "If one acts before allowing oneself time to think of the consequences, there is no willpower or self control. Values and goals are automatically ignored in the maelstrom of activity."[3]

Two and a half thousand years earlier, Aristotle and Plato also taught that moral development is achieved by educating children to modulate their emotions, saying, "The moral virtues are engendered in us neither by, nor contrary to, Nature; we are constituted by Nature to receive them, but their full development is due to habit. So it is a matter of no little importance what sort of habits we form from the earliest age – education makes a vast difference, or rather all the difference in the world."

Knowing where to go

Knowledge is not found in our conscious intellect. It is through our intellect that we refine our perceptions and come to understandings. But when we do understand something our state of knowing is unconscious. For instance, it takes conscious effort to learn a new skill, such as driving a car. Whilst learning we consciously think about every step required – the gear changes, signalling, judging distances, trying to analyse comparative speeds and so on. But there comes a moment when that conscious effort falls away. We instinctively pattern match to the required actions. Driving becomes automatic – unconscious. At that point, driving has become part of our intelligence. We know how to do it and might even be hard put consciously to describe all the elements involved. The knowledge only fully manifests itself when we get into a car and drive it.

We have probably all had experiences when, perhaps to our own surprise, we have just 'known' what to do, or recognised that something we have just heard is 'true'. One of my colleagues has a relative who was a property developer. He instinctively knew which properties in what state of disrepair to buy, and his judgement was rarely wrong. If, in an operating theatre, a sudden life-threatening situation develops and others are starting to panic, a particular surgeon may know exactly what needs to be done, and be able to stay calm and do it. Similarly, we might just suddenly know the right life course to take when faced with major conflicting options.

This kind of unconscious knowledge enables us to act objectively, unencumbered by social conditioning or inappropriate emotional responses. It is perhaps what the philosopher Alfred North Whitehead was referring to when he said, "Civilisation advances by extending the number of operations we can perform without thinking about them."[5]

It could be that consciousness evolved to help us focus more keenly on the world and question and analyse it, to help us get our needs met more efficiently and effectively. It is certainly a tool to solve problems with because it only wakes up when we realise we are ignorant about something and need an answer. If knowledge is found in the sum of the richness of the unconscious pattern-matching processes which go on in our brains, then the work of consciousness is to help the person look for more effective patterns to match to, to extend and enrich unconscious knowledge. The more successfully we do this, the more emotion serves consciousness and perception rather than controlling it.

Understanding human nature

To have our best hope of acting ethically, as individuals, as members of a community or as members of a profession, we have to begin by gaining a better understanding of ourselves. We need to understand the processes of human conditioning; how ideologies restrict understanding; how the brain/mind/body system works; how to further refine perceptions; how emotional needs can be met without trespassing on the freedoms of others; and how best to use the resources given to us by Nature to do so. Quite simply, we need to study the science of human nature, and the advances in knowledge about behaviour, biology and the brain that have accumulated in the last few decades.

In the process, we have to face the absurdities of selfish consumerism, human egoism, the blind certainties of dogmatic science and fundamentalist religious belief, including the grand unifying pessimism inherent in determinism (as expressed in the selfish gene theory), the simple 'cause and effect' ideas of some evolutionary theorists, and reliance on scientific reductionism. Post-modernism (which asserts that all opinions are of equal value, all thought is equally relevant and that there are no boundaries, no rules, no hierarchies, no objective reality, and which infects the arts, education, social policy making, and philosophy) also needs challenging.

Facing up to this may be more urgent than we realise. In the heady optimism of the mid-1960s, Idries Shah struck a sober note quite at odds with the naïve but then fashionable notion that, to resolve any conflict, 'all you need is love'. He said, "Tolerance and trying to understand others, until recently a luxury, has today become a necessity.

This is because, unless we can realise that we and others are generally behaving as we do because of inculcated biases over which we have no control, while we imagine that they are our own opinions, we might do something which will bring about the destruction of all of us."[6] His words are just as apposite now.

Developing an internal monitor

As a complex society, we will always find ourselves struggling with major ethical dilemmas, as there are multiple variables to everything. There are, however, three ethical safeguards in working from the human givens approach. First, professionalism and practice are based on the requirements of individual circumstances, rather than dogma and theory. It cannot be said too often that circumstances alter cases, and that what is appropriate in one instance may be inappropriate in another apparently similar one. Second, it focuses attention on looking largely at patterns and processes rather than content – the needs that have to be met in a situation to improve it, rather than the minute details of what maintains it. This is a mental posture which usefully helps keep us detached, vigilant, and focusing outwards, so that our own emotions do not become muddled up with those of patients/ pupils/clients/colleagues or whomever we are concerned with.

Thirdly, it is understood that uncertainties or vulnerabilities within us can easily be triggered, through pattern matching, by an event or emotional story we read or hear. When this happens, inevitably we are no longer impartial or objective in our responses. For instance, a counsellor who is fearful of breast cancer, because of a raised family risk, may find herself being overly reassuring or, conversely, unwilling to address the concerns of a client in a similar position. If people are unaware of this unconscious pattern-matching process, they may misinterpret the reason for their own reactions – perhaps assuming it is a legitimate response to the situation being considered, rather than the result of their own aroused emotions – and thus make avoidable errors of judgement.

On the Human Givens Diploma Course, run by MindFields College, we stress that first of all we are responsible for ourselves. We have to behave ethically towards ourselves if we are to behave ethically towards others, and we are behaving unethically towards ourselves if we allow any single need to dominate at the expense of the others. For example, the development of any addictive behaviour (whether workaholism, substance abuse, gambling, shopaholism, sex, or lust after money, information, gossip, power, attention or status), cannot but interfere with our personal and professional relationships. If our own needs are out of balance, or we have so many emotional demands on us that we have little spare capacity left, we cannot reliably behave ethically towards other people or be effective therapists, managers, teachers or family members.

Over the last 50 years there has been a partial breakdown in the ethical and moral systems (legal, educational and religious) that society once relied upon to maintain stability. Paradoxically, that breakdown process had to happen because reliance on rigid belief systems was making us too inflexible – and therefore too vulnerable – for survival in a more rapidly changing world. New ideas and information can only permeate a society if it does not rigidly exclude such inputs.

While many people grow and flourish today, others are not adapting well to the way the world is changing. Some appear unable to take responsibility for their actions and become fodder for the cult of passive consumerism. Consequences of this include the development of the 'victim culture', where people becoming obsessed with 'targets', 'rights' and 'blame'; and a massive increase in the numbers of people suffering mental disorders and addictions. Until we reorientate ourselves away from wants to needs, starting with a sincere examination of what Nature made us, we will continue to do more harm than good to this planet and its inhabitants.

* * * * *

Ivan Tyrrell is Principal of MindFields College, a lecturer and writer who has also worked for many years as a psychotherapist (specialising in brief therapy for depression and anxiety). He is co-founder, with Joe Griffin, of the human givens approach and together they have written numerous best-selling books, including: Freedom from Addiction; How to lift depression ... fast; How to Master Anxiety: All you need to know to overcome stress, panic attacks, phobias, trauma, obsessions and more; Dreaming Reality: How dreaming keeps us sane or can drive us mad; and Human Givens: A new approach to emotional health and clear thinking.

References

Therapy that works *(Pamela Woodford)*

1. Griffin, J and Tyrrell, I (2003). *Human Givens: a new approach to emotional health and clear thinking (Pages 234–270)*. HG Publishing, East Sussex.

2. Griffin, J and Tyrrell, I (2003). *Human Givens: a new approach to emotional health and clear thinking (Pages 382–390)*. HG Publishing Ltd, East Sussex.

3. Griffin, J and Tyrrell, I (2004). Great expectations, *Human Givens* Journal, Vol 11, No 1.

This article has been updated since it first appeared in Volume 11, No. 4 of the 'Human Givens' Journal (2004).

From self-harm to self-belief *(Emily Lindsey-Clark)*

1. Department of Health (2003). *Mainstreaming gender and women's mental health: implementation of guidelines*. Department of Health Publication, London.

2. The National Institute for Mental Health in England (2003). *Personality disorder – no longer a diagnosis of exclusion: policy implementation guidance for the development of services for people with personality disorder*. NIMHE.

3. Barker, P (2003). *Psychiatric and mental health nursing: the craft of caring*. Hodder Headline Group, London.

This article previously appeared in Volume 13, No. 2 of the 'Human Givens' Journal (2006).

Human givens in primary care *(Liz Potts)*

This article previously appeared in Volume 12, No. 3 of the 'Human Givens' Journal (2005).

Evidence of learning *(Fred Grist and Mike Beard)*

This article previously appeared in Volume 13, No. 1 of the 'Human Givens' Journal (2006).

The road to recovery *(Iain Caldwell)*

1. Bates, P (2002). *Working for Inclusion*. Sainsbury Centre for Mental Health.

2. Colombo, T, Fulford, B, Bedelow, G and Williams, S (2004). *OpenMind*, Jan/Feb, page 10.

3. Griffin, J and Tyrrell, I (2004). *Dreaming Reality: How dreaming keeps us sane, or can drive us mad*. HG Publishing, East Sussex.

This article is an updated version of the one which appeared in Volume 11, No. 1 of the 'Human Givens' Journal (2004).

It's what's right with you that fixes what's wrong *(Chris Dyas)*

1. Griffin, J and Tyrrell, I (2003). *Human Givens: a new approach to emotional health and clear thinking*. HG Publishing, East Sussex.

2. Thompson, G and Jenkins, J B (2004). *Verbal Judo: the gentle art of persuasion*. Quill/HarperCollins.

3. Ratey, J A (2001). *A User's Guide to the Brain*. Abacus Books.
4. Buzan, T (2002). *How to Mind Map*. Thorsons, London.

This article is an updated version of the one which appeared in Volume 12, No. 2 of the 'Human Givens' Journal (2005).

Good choices: autism and the human givens *(Angela Austin)*

This article previously appeared in Volume 10, No. 2 of the 'Human Givens' Journal (2003).

Just vulnerable people: working with asylum seekers and refugees *(Joanne Ashmore)*

This article previously appeared in Volume 10, No. 2 of the 'Human Givens' Journal (2003).

Why psychiatrists should be more like plumbers *(Farouk Okhai)*

This article previously appeared in Volume 10, No. 3 of the 'Human Givens' Journal (2003).

The mended fin: physiotherapy and the human givens *(Jessica Bavinton)*

This article previously appeared in Volume 11, No. 1 of the 'Human Givens' Journal (2004).

This too will pass: coping with high arousal in the classroom *(Sue Gwinnell-Smith)*

This article previously appeared in Volume 12, No. 1 of the 'Human Givens' Journal (2005).

Uncommon therapy *(Helen Card)*

This article previously appeared in Volume 12, No. 2 of the 'Human Givens' Journal (2005).

The human givens manager *(Mike Hay)*

This article previously appeared in Volume 13, No. 1 of the 'Human Givens' Journal (2006).

When time's not on our side *(James Hooton)*

1. Care Services Improvement Partnership (CSIP) and the National Institute for Mental Health in England (NIMHE) (2006). *Improving Primary Care Mental Health Services*. Department of Health, London.

This article previously appeared in Volume 14, No. 1 of the 'Human Givens' Journal (2007).

When the light bulb doesn't really want to change... *(Richard Brook)*

This article has been updated since it first appeared in Volume 12, No. 1 of the 'Human Givens' Journal (2005).

Working with stroke from the human givens approach *(Jim Tapper)*

1. Lovibond, S H and Lovibond, P F (1995). *Manual for the Depression Anxiety Stress Scales*, 2nd edition. University of New South Wales, Sydney.

2. Royal College of Physicians. (2004). *National Clinical Guidelines for Stroke*, 2nd edition. Royal College of Physicians, London.

3. Department of Health. (2001). *National Service Framework for Older People*. Department of Health, London.

4. Wolfensberger, W (1983). Social role valorisation: a proposed new term for the principle of normalisation. *Mental Retardation*, 21, 234–9.

5. Haley, J (1993). *Uncommon Therapy: the psychiatric techniques of Milton H Erickson, MD*. W W Norton, New York.

6. Forrest, D (undated). *Stroke in Merseyside*. St Helens and Knowsley Health Authority.

7. Carson, A.J. et al (2000). Depression after stroke and lesion location: a systematic review. *Lancet*, 356, 122–6.

8. Griffin, J and Tyrrell, I (2003). *Human Givens: a new approach to emotional health and clear thinking*. HG Publishing, East Sussex.

9. Griffin, J and Tyrrell, I (2004). *Dreaming Reality: how dreaming keeps us sane or can drive us mad*. HG Publishing, East Sussex.

10. Holmqvist, L W and von Koch, L (2001). Environmental factors in stroke rehabilitation. *British Medical Journal*, 322, 1501–2.

This article previously appeared in Volume 13, No. 4 of the 'Human Givens' Journal (2006).

Human givens and the NHS *(Ian Walton)*

This article previously appeared in Volume 14, No. 1 of the 'Human Givens' Journal (2007).

Common ground: diplomacy and the human givens *(John Bell)*

1. Griffin, J and Tyrrell, I (2003). *Human Givens: a new approach to emotional health and clear thinking*. HG Publishing, East Sussex.

2. Bell, M, Molloy, M J, Bell, J and Evans, M (2005). *The Jerusalem Old City Initiative – discussion document: new directions for deliberation and dialogue*. University of Toronto, Munk Centre for International Studies.

3. This document also served as the basis for discussion on Jerusalem by Israeli, Palestinian and international experts at a workshop in Istanbul in December, 2005.

This article previously appeared in Volume 13, No. 2 of the 'Human Givens' Journal (2006).

Molar memories: how an ancient survival mechanism can ruin lives *(Joe Griffin)*

1. Mackintosh, N J (1983). *Conditioning and Associative Learning*. Oxford University Press, New York.

2. Rescorla, R A (1980). Pavlovian conditioning: it's not what you think it is. *American Psychologist*, 43, 151–60.

3. Griffin, J and Tyrrell, I. (2003). *Human Givens: A new approach to emotional health and clear thinking*. HG Publishing, East Sussex.

4. Damasio, A (1994). *Descartes' Error: emotion, reason and the human brain*. Avon Books, New York.

5. Seligman, M (1971). Phobias and preparedness. *Behaviour Therapy*, 2, 307–20.

6. Watkins, J G (1971). The affect bridge: a hypnoanalytic technique. *International Journal of Clinical and Experimental Hypnosis*, 19, 1, 21–7.

This is an amended and expanded version of the article which first appeared in Volume 13, No. 3 of the 'Human Givens' Journal (2006).

The limits of tolerance: ethics and human nature *(Ivan Tyrrell)*

This article previously appeared in the Human Givens Journal Vol 9, No.2, 2002

1. Smith, D M (2000). *Moral Geographies: ethics in a world of difference*. Edinburgh University Press.

2. Hartmann, T (2002). *Complete guide to ADHD: help for your family at home, school and work*. Underwood Books.

3. Ratey, J (2001). *A User's Guide to the Brain*. Little, Brown.

4. Robertson, I (1999). *Mind Sculpture: unleashing your brain's potential*. Bantam Books

5. Cialdini, R B (2001). *Influence: science and practice (4th edition)*. Allyn and Bacon.

6. Shah, I (1968). *Reflections*. Octagon Press.

This is an amended version of the article which first appeared in Volume 9, No. 2 of the 'Human Givens' Journal (2002).

* * * * *

For further articles which show the practical application of the human givens organising idea, see Appendices III–VII of *Human Givens: A new approach to emotional health and clear thinking**:

- Human givens and social work (by Jan Little)
- Human givens and disability (by Mike Hay)
- Human givens and physical pain (by Grahame Brown)
- Human givens and trauma treatment (by Keith Guy & Nicola Guy)
- Human Givens and education (by Andy Vass)

* Griffin, J and Tyrrell, I. HG Publishing (2003).

Index

Further Information

If you have found the information in this book of interest, you might also like to know about the following:

- ### The Human Givens Institute (HGI)

  The HGI is a membership organisation and resource open to anyone interested in the human givens approach. It is also the professional body for human givens psychotherapists, and its website has a wealth of information available to the general public. For more details, call 01323 811662 or visit: **www.hgi.org.uk**

- ### Register of human givens therapists

  For details of all fully qualified human givens therapists currently working in private practice, and information about how human givens psychotherapists and counsellors can help, call 01323 811662 or visit: **www.hgi.org.uk/register**

- ### Training in effective psychotherapeutic skills

  MindFields College, the only specialist psychology college in the UK, is the foremost institution teaching the human givens approach. Due to a growing demand and interest in the application, the College's educational programme is continually developing. For full details, including information about the Human Givens Diploma Course, please visit: **www.mindfields.org.uk** or call the College on 01323 811440 for a copy of their latest prospectus.

- ### The Human Givens Foundation

  The Human Givens Foundation (HGF) is a registered charity whose objectives are to promote research and public education into the 'givens' of human nature and their application into the treatment and care of those suffering from mental illness. It fosters initiatives by those endeavouring to use up-to-date knowledge about the human givens in practical ways, particularly in fields where the development of life skills is vital. For more details, see: **www.hgfoundation.com**

- ### Publications

  For information about the *Human Givens* journal, and a wide range of other publications from HG Publishing, visit: **www.humangivens.com**

Human Givens:
A new approach to emotional health and clear thinking

by Joe Griffin & Ivan Tyrrell

"*Human Givens* is the most practical and intuitive book I've read in years."
Charles Hayes, Autodidactic Press, USA

"Harnessed between these pages are scientific insights and practical techniques of sufficient power to completely revolutionise our approach to parenting, teaching and the caring professions."
Nick Baylis, Lecturer in Positive Psychology, University of Cambridge

"An entirely attainable and reasonable road map for good mental health." *Irish Examiner*

"In *Human Givens* Griffin and Tyrrell offer innovative perspectives on promoting effective living. They have synthesized brain and social research in such a way that they provide new templates for understanding how to unlock the best in human nature." *Jeffrey K. Zeig, Director of the Milton H. Erickson Foundation*

"A wonderfully fresh and stimulating view of dreaming, evolution, and human functioning. *Human Givens* also provides both an encompassing model and practical, specific applications to enhance the effectiveness of psychotherapy. It will deepen and widen every reader's perspective."
Arthur J. Deikman MD, Clinical Professor of Psychiatry, University of California

"An inspiring book which I believe is a wake up call to all working in talking therapies." *Journal of Primary Care Mental Health*

"Real breakthroughs in the behavioural sciences are rare ... But not all scientific progress is incremental. Sometimes, as in the germ theory of disease, it's exponential. Griffin and Tyrrell's contribution advances psychology as much as the introduction of the Arabic numeric system, with its zero digit, advanced mathematics." *Washington Times*

"This book is a must read for anyone interested or working in the field of mental health." *Reviewer, Amazon*

"While books are never a cure for what ails us in life, they are often a catalyst, a trigger that fires off those rare and profound 'aha!' moments that lead to deeper insights and understanding. *Human Givens* is such a catalyst." *Jack Davies*

Published in paperback by HG Publishing (2004)
ISBN: 1-899398-31-7   ISBN-13: 978-1-899398-31-7

Dreaming Reality:
How dreaming keeps us sane, or can drive us mad

by Joe Griffin & Ivan Tyrrell

"The conclusions arrived at in *Dreaming Reality* are breathtaking, and given the freedom that the reader has to apply them to his or herself, they prove to be astonishing. This book gives such rational explanations that the cumulative effect is like turning on a light in a room full of shadows. Read it for yourself, without prejudice, and try it out – just feel those dark shadows withdraw." *Mental Health Practice*

"*Dreaming Reality* exquisitely scythes through the Gordian knot created by past dream theories. Even better, like all the very best explanations, its central theme is as far-reaching as it is intuitive. Through a fascinating combination of dream examples and scientific findings, it provides lucid and compelling evidence for how our night and daydreams not only mould our personalities but also lie at the very heart of being human." *Clive Bromhall, author of 'The Eternal Child'*

"A remarkable book that makes compelling reading. Griffin and Tyrrell's adroitly written text challenges traditional views on our knowledge and understanding of the mystifying covert world of dreams." *Tony Charlton, Professor of Behavioural Studies, University of Gloucestershire*

"This book is revolutionary in more than one way. Past and sometimes overlooked research is re-evaluated, and a persuasive theory emerges... long overdue to my mind." *Doris Lessing*

"For anyone who has speculated on the meaning and purpose of dreaming, Griffin and Tyrrell's astounding insights light up the dark corners of the mind. Not since 1964 when Carl Jung's book *Man and his Symbols* was published has anyone set out to write so conclusively on dreaming for a wide audience. Griffin and Tyrrell [propose] that dreaming functions to cleanse the undischarged emotional arousals of the day and they explain how this happens through metaphorical pattern matching. From this one sets off on the journey to understanding the true causes of (and routes to healing) depression. This book is revolutionary in thought, revelatory in content and will be established as the most important twenty-first century milestone on the road to accessible mental health treatment for all. It's a must for all who live with mental illness or work for its relief." *Ian Hunter OBE*

Published in paperback by HG Publishing (2006)
ISBN: 1-899398-91-0   ISBN-13: 978-1-899398-91-1

How to lift depression... *fast*

by Joe Griffin & Ivan Tyrrell

"An empowering book... immediately useful... Read, use, enjoy and reap the benefits for yourself and others." *Ruth Morozzo, 'Footnotes' Journal*

"As a GP I see many people suffering from depression, and have searched for many years for a good book to recommend to them. At last I have found one. This book draws together the most effective methods from many different approaches to treatment, yet is written in a style which makes the ideas easy to understand and put into practice. The 'human givens' approach detailed in this book is a major step forward in helping people suffering from depression and other mental health problems." *Gina Johnson, GP*

"Everyone involved in administering personal therapy should read this book." *Nursing Standard*

"At last some concrete practical advice. This book offers some real solutions and insight into depression. I can't recommend it enough. If you are suffering from depression or you are caring or treating anyone with this condition, this book will be indispensable. I have spent a lot of money and time researching depression and can say this is without doubt the best book I have read on the subject – I urge you to buy it." *Amazon Review*

"I recommend the book *How to lift depression ...fast*. Rather than spending months and years exploring all the things that have gone wrong in your life, human givens therapists provide you with the tools, insights and support to turn your mood, focus and life around quickly." *Dr Mark Atkinson*

"Fantastic tips and explanations – the best self-help." Amazon Review

"This book is the first I have come across on depression that is easy to read and understand for both professionals and lay people. It will prove an invaluable resource... The title cover carries the phrase 'Change is much easier than you think' and that theme flows throughout the book. [It] offers readers much practical help and advice ... a book for every library and one that should not sit on the shelf and gather dust." *Professional Social Work Magazine*

Published in paperback by HG Publishing (2004)
ISBN: 1-899398-41-4   ISBN-13: 978-1-899398-41-6

Freedom from Addiction:
The secret behind successful addiction busting

by Joe Griffin & Ivan Tyrrell

"Following *How to Lift Depression...fast* this second title is highly recommended. It sidesteps jargon, avoids the medicalisation of addictive behaviour, explodes the lies that maintain addiction and offers realistic, practical solutions." *Peter Barraclough, Nursing Standard*

"So many books promise so much, and then fail to deliver. This book is of an entirely different quality. If you have an addiction/compulsive behaviour, do yourself a big favour, buy it – it gives answers ... a big thank you to the authors." *Richard J. Prasad*

"An easy-to-read, empowering self-help guide for those considering themselves 'addicted' to anything... It breaks down simply the self-assessment needed for discerning problem areas and their development, adding relevant research in a jargon-free manner; with a fascinating explanation for how neurophysiology and 'pattern-matching' underpin symptoms like craving." *Neia Glynn, The Psychologist*

"Full of insights, this book is truly superb, not just in the area of under-standing and managing addictions but also in providing a broader, clear, coherent and wholly convincing insight into human thought processes and behaviours. " *Amazon Review*

"Here is another excellent book from that groundbreaking team, Joe Griffin and Ivan Tyrrell. This time the focus is on addiction, how it comes about, and a highly effective way of dealing with it – whether it be a life threatening addiction (and many are) or an annoying habit which one would like to be rid of... There are techniques and ways of looking at problems which we can assimilate and pass on to our clients. *Freedom from Addiction* is easy to read, gives clear guidance and is an ideal book to have to hand to enable you to help yourself, your family, your friends and your clients." *Ruth Morozzo, 'Footnotes' Journal*

"I purchased this book to help me stop smoking. After [applying] the principles in it, I haven't had a cigarette for three weeks. *Freedom from Addiction* is amazing – it takes you through the chemical process behind addiction and reveals the tricks the mind plays to trap one into perform-ing addictive behaviours. The advice contained in it for defusing the addictive process and handling cravings is first class." *Amazon Review*

Published in paperback by HG Publishing (2005)
ISBN: 1-899398-46-5   ISBN-13: 978-1-899398-46-1